Advance Praise for *The Cost of Courage in Aztec Society*

"Inga Clendinnen's books and essays are among the finest historical writings of our time, and some of her best essays are collected
here for the first time. Each one is a gem – a brilliant, beautifully
written entry into the subject at hand, and also a model of precise
historical inquiry and an unflinching engagement with puzzling,
morally troubling acts of casual or calculated violence.

"In Clendinnen's explorations of 'the more interior experience
of conquest and colonization' in Mexico and Australia, all the
parties involved are 'fit subjects for wonder and analysis.' She
finds that experience in her remarkable readings of their words
and recorded actions. Above all, her subject is what James Joyce
called 'the mystery of the conscious' – what people did as they
understood it. She is always alert to the opacity of the historical
record, 'the mysteriousness of human consciousness,' our capacity for self-delusion, and the daunting task at hand. Historians,
she writes, are 'Ahabs pursuing our great white whale, dimly
aware that the whole business is, if coolly considered, rather less
than reasonable.' But she does not shrink from the hard, delicate
work of discerning and reckoning with actual experience and
consequences. Here is history as 'exact imagining' at its best."

– William B. Taylor, University of California, Berkeley

The Cost of Courage in Aztec Society

Essays on Mesoamerican Society and Culture

How can men be brought to look steadily on the face of battle? Tenochtitlán, the great city of the Aztecs, was the creation of war, and war was its dynamic. In the title work of this compelling collection of essays, Inga Clendinnen reconstructs the sequence of experiences through which young Aztec warriors were brought to embrace their duty to their people, to their city, and to the forces that moved the world and the heavens. Subsequent essays explore the survival of Yucatec Maya culture in the face of Spanish conquest and colonisation, the insidious corruption of an austere ideology translated into dangerously novel circumstances, and the multiple paths to the sacred constructed by 'defeated' populations in sixteenth-century Mexico. The collection ends with Clendinnen's transition to the colonial history of her own country: a close and loving reading of the 1841 expedition journal of George Augustus Robinson, appointed 'Protector of Aborigines' in the Port Philip District of Australia.

Inga Clendinnen is Emeritus Scholar in History at La Trobe University, Melbourne. Her publications include *Aztecs* (Cambridge, 1991), *Reading the Holocaust* (Cambridge, 1999), and *Ambivalent Conquests: Maya and Spaniard in Yucatan, 1517–1579* (second edition, Cambridge, 2003). Her memoir, *Tiger's Eye,* was published in 2001; her Boyer Lectures, *True Stories,* in 1999; and a collection of her literary essays, *Agamemnon's Kiss,* in 2006. Her book on the meeting between the First Fleet and Aboriginal Australians, *Dancing with Strangers* (Cambridge, 2003), won several awards, including the Pacific Rim Kiriyama Prize.

The Cost of Courage in Aztec Society

Essays on Mesoamerican Society and Culture

INGA CLENDINNEN

CAMBRIDGE
UNIVERSITY PRESS

CAMBRIDGE UNIVERSITY PRESS
Cambridge, New York, Melbourne, Madrid, Cape Town, Singapore,
São Paulo, Delhi, Dubai, Tokyo

Cambridge University Press
32 Avenue of the Americas, New York, NY 10013-2473, USA

www.cambridge.org
Information on this title: www.cambridge.org/9780521732079

© Inga Clendinnen 2010

First published 2010

Printed in the United States of America

A catalog record for this publication is available from the British Library.

Library of Congress Cataloging in Publication data

Clendinnen, Inga.
The cost of courage in Aztec society : essays on Mesoamerican society and culture /
Inga Clendinnen.
p.   cm.
Includes bibliographical references and index.
Summary: "A collection of pathbreaking essays on Aztec and Maya culture
in the sixteenth century" – Provided by publisher.
ISBN 978-0-521-51811-6 (hardback)
1. Aztecs – Rites and ceremonies.   2. Aztecs – Warfare – Social aspects.   3. Aztecs –
Religion.   4. Violence – Mexico – History – 16th century.   5. Mayas – Rites and
ceremonies.   6. Mexico – History – Conquest, 1519–1540.   I. Title.
F1219.76.R57C55   2010
972'.02–dc22   2009043215

ISBN 978-0-521-51811-6 Hardback
ISBN 978-0-521-73207-9 Paperback

Contents

Introduction   *page* 1

1. The Cost of Courage in Aztec Society
   Originally published in: *Past and Present*, No. 107   6

2. "Fierce and Unnatural Cruelty": Cortés and the Conquest
   of Mexico
   Originally published in: *Representations*, Vol. 33   49

3. Disciplining the Indians: Franciscan Ideology and
   Missionary Violence in Sixteenth-Century Yucatán
   Originally published in: *Past and Present*, No. 94   91

4. Ways to the Sacred: Reconstructing "Religion" in
   Sixteenth-Century Mexico
   Originally published in: *History and Anthropology*, Vol. 5   116

5. Landscape and World View: The Survival of Yucatec
   Maya Culture Under Spanish Conquest
   Originally published in: *Comparative Studies in Society
   and History*, Vol. 22, No. 3   156

6. Breaking the Mirror: From the Aztec Spring Festival to
   Organ Transplantation
   Originally published in: *The Australasian Journal of
   Psychotherapy*, Vol. 21, No. 2   179

7. Reading Mr. Robinson
   Originally published in: *The Australian Book Review*,
   No. 170   191

Index   209

Introduction

The first time I crossed from North America into Mexico, and once past the fun-house mirrors of the border town, I felt I was entering a place where a multi-layered past was still urgently present in the dress, manners, practices and aesthetics of the people rather than in monuments and museums. That impression of an exposed and visible temporal archaeology makes Mexico seductive to historians. These essays are the fruits of my love-affair with the place.

Working on early Mexico was the happiest time of my academic life. The literary sources were sumptuously equivocal: sixteenth-century Spaniards watching Indians, or glimpsing them from the corner of an eye; Indians acting, reacting, memorialising their experience in ways quite unfamiliar to the outsider. Mexico was also my introduction to non-literary sources: to figurines and pots, to ceremonial dress and dramas, to customary practices sacred and mundane, to local landscapes drenched with transcendent meanings – a baptism by full immersion as a cultural anthropologist, and about as disorientating as full-immersion baptism must be. The challenge of learning to use unfamiliar sources, unfamiliar theories and unfamiliar disciplines, and the hunt to find the words to express those new-hatched understandings, constitute the dynamic of the essays collected here.

In time I began to understand some of the rules structuring the myriad ways Indians had inscribed their understandings on the world: to feel I was in (intermittent, always fragile) communication with these people remote from me in time, place and thought. Now that I see the essays together I realise that they pivot around 'religion', 'culture', and the difficulties of uncovering and translating between different systems of meaning, which

I

is swiftly said but is painfully slow in the doing. As for individual essays: I am fond of 'Landscape and World View', in part because it was my first essay to be published in an international journal, more because in the course of its writing I began to see how variously religion works on the ground: how apparently commonplace objects and places and apparently innocuous actions can be exalted to the sacred by covertly shared imaginings. I am fond of 'The Cost of Courage' because it taught me how violence can be formalised into acceptability. To be honest, I am fond of them all, because they represent an intellectually enthralling time of my life.

I have not attempted to bring the essays up to date, in part because 'updating' only leads to confusion; because they have the flaws and enthusiasms of their time; more because the problems are ongoing, especially for those of us who inquire into what happens when people of different cultures struggle to achieve a tolerable accommodation with each other. As for the present 'state of the field' – the best historians require an improbable combination of curiosity, tenacity, precision, and an athletic but always disciplined imagination. I am happy to report that I find these qualities displayed in the work of more than a few of the new generation of Mexican scholars. Over the years there has been a notable deepening from Charles Gibson's majestic study of the material conditions of Indian life in the Valley of Mexico to, for example, William Taylor's fine-textured investigations into the intimate politics of post-contact religion as practised in metropolis, town and village. I once dismissed 'religion' as an unholy mix of élite metaphysics and popular credulity. Mexico taught me to understand that the exploration of how religion works in a particular locality offers the most alluring methodological problems, demands the most delicate theorising and analysis, and promises to generate more understanding than any other historical enterprise I know. A woman's pink swami slip, a glistening object from some remote elsewhere, swathes the loins of an agonised Christ in a village church. The garment glows; it seems to gather the light. What local textures of piety and pride, what aesthetic understanding, what vision of 'male' and 'female' suffuse its presence? Nowadays I can hope that someone is preparing to tell me. The state of Mexican Colonial Studies in this twenty-first century is almost enough to make me believe in progress.

It is now rather more than a decade ago since I fell ill, received a liver transplant, and was forbidden to go back to Mexico because I am now immuno-suppressed and Mexican pathogens are famously vicious.

I left unsatisfied. I would have liked to better understand the sequence of strategies by which, for example, Tlaxcalans struggled to maintain their favoured status, and how they accommodated to, explained and overcame its loss. I would have liked to inquire more deeply into what Spaniards lumped together as 'indian superstitions' in the years immediately after the military conquest. I would have liked to have spent more hours with Motolinía; I would have liked to retrieve the story Cortés was telling himself during his disastrous Honduran expedition and to see how it differed from the story he had told himself during the Mexican Conquest. Now some of those things are being done. I had also planned to shift south from Yucatan to discover how the Highland Maya of Chiapas and Guatemala responded to the great fact of Spanish invasion and domination. At the time leaving Mexican studies seemed an expulsion from Eden, especially as I also had to give up teaching, one of the joys of academic life, and the society of my colleagues, which is another. But then I re-engaged, first with the cognitively and morally complicated business of putting memories on paper, then straining to identify the differences between autobiography, biography and history, later trying to trace the frontier between history and fiction. Now I am preoccupied with the opaque encounter-history of my own country. The transition to that history was eased by serendipity: getting to know George Augustus Robinson (essay no. 7). Through Mr. Robinson I discovered that the brief Australian colonial past contains its own irresistible mysteries, and that, whatever the locus, the study remains the same: to understand why different groups of humans do as they do, with what degree of self-knowledge, at what cost to themselves and to others.

As Clifford Geertz once said: 'You can study different things in different places, and some things – for example, what colonial domination does to established frames of moral expectation – you can best study in confined locations.' I like my locations confined. But how 'confined' is a bunch of hunter-gatherers? What systems of thought locate them in those shifting landscapes? How to arrive at the 'frames of moral expectation' of these chronically elusive people? It might seem that the Mexican experience would be of little use in coming to understand the inner history of indigenous Australians, given that Mexicans were (largely) village-dwelling agriculturalists, while Aboriginal Australians travelled light in small family bands through their traditional territories, cropping seasonal products. They clustered their camps only for as long as some brief local abundance (eels by a lakeside, natural yam-fields) lasted to trade goods, songs, dances and to confirm or re-negotiate alliances frayed by distance and exigency. Post-contact their enigmatic footprints have to be tracked through infuriatingly intermittent written sources: the journals of explorers and other transients, the occasional eruption of some crisis into legal or administrative records reliably skewed by alien assumptions. The non-written sources are richer but dauntingly recalcitrant. What am I to make of dance forms which after the lush elaborations of Mexican choreography seem wilfully laconic, or where the representations of 'land-scapes' and histories of ownership can be reduced to subtle variations in panels of cross-hatching? Then I remember the exhausting, exhilarating effort to decipher Mexican writing-by-symbols: the slow business of re-constructing the meaning, as the scribe had once constructed it, by the precise locating of signs, with qualifications or expansions intimated by the addition or omission of a conventional detail or an unexpected juxtaposition of colours.

That language, apt for both theological reflection and innovation, was cast in a declamatory mode as bold and gestural as the athletic semaphoring of Aztec public ritual. Priests and other players climbed into their minutely-prescribed regalias to perform the actions which would elevate a selected human body into an instantiation of a god, their ritualised movements marking out shapes and spaces to build a sacred moment in sacred time here, now, in this transfigured world. What patternings, what expectations sustained Aboriginal dance? What story of the world and of humans' place within it were they telling? There are eerie resemblances. Both Mesoamerican agriculturalists and Aboriginal hunter-gatherers took pleasure in cryptic knowledge, in its deciphering, storing, reciphering and communicating, and its relishing by a strenuously-selected male élite. As this anxious speleologist lowers herself deeper, the resonances seem to multiply. But are they real, or simply a ringing in my ears?

After 'Mr. Robinson' I first went backwards in time to the early years of the encounter between the British of the First Fleet and the beach nomads they met around the body of water we call 'Sydney Harbour.' I wrote a book about those early encounters titled *Dancing with Strangers*. It was, in my account of it, a sunny beginning. Our entwined histories since (they cannot be called 'shared') have demonstrated a widening gulf in understanding and a compounding mutual mistrust. With the Mesomerican experience still vivid in my mind, I will try to write another book, this one titled *After the Dancing*, to unravel the reasons for that alienation.

Why? Because I believe the sustained effort to comprehend a different way of surviving in the world makes us better able to live intelligently in the present, and to prepare intelligently for the future. In that conviction I offer these essays to you.

Inga Clendinnen

I

The Cost of Courage in Aztec Society*

Proud of itself
is the city of Mexico-Tenochtitlán.
Here no one fears to die in war.
This is our glory...

Who could conquer Tenochtitlán?
Who could shake the foundation of heaven?[1]

Today we are tempted to read this fragment of an Aztec[2] song-poem as a familiar piece of bombast: the aggressive military empire which insists on its invincibility, its warriors strangers to fear. In what follows I want to indicate how the business of war was understood in the great city of Tenochtitlán, and then, in more but still inadequate detail, to enquire into how warrior action was sustained and explained, in the hope of drawing closer to an Aztec reading of this small text.

* My thanks are due to members of the Shelby Cullom Davis Seminar on War and Society at Princeton University, who responded to an initial draft of this article with lively interest, subtle and acute criticism, and generous encouragement. The Plates are reproduced by permission of the Bibliothèque de l'Assemblée Nationale, Paris, and Akademische Druck- und Verlagsanstalt, Graz (Plate 8), the Bibliothèque Nationale, Paris (Plate 2), the Bodleian Library, Oxford (Plates 1, 3, 4), the British Library, London (Plates 6, 7), the Instituto Nacional de Antropología e Historia, Mexico (Plate 9), and the Museum für Volkerkunde, Basle (Plate 5).

[1] "Cantares mexicanos", fos. 19ᵛ–20ʳ, trans. Miguel Leon-Portilla in his *Pre-Columbian Literatures of Mexico* (Norman, Okla., 1969), p. 87.
[2] The people who had come to dominate central Mexico at the time of European conquest, ruling their tribute empire from the island city of Tenochtitlán, called themselves the "Mexica" or the "Tenocha", but common usage has established them as the "Aztecs".

Article originally published as "The Cost of Courage in Aztec Society," in *Past and Present*, No. 107 (May 1985): 44–89. © 1985 The Past and Present Society. Reprinted with permission.

I

That Tenochtitlán was the creation of war and the courage and stamina of its young fighting men was indisputable. The splendid city which Cortes and his men saw shimmering above its lake waters in the autumn of 1519 had been founded as a miserable collection of mud huts less than two hundred years before. Some time late in the twelfth century the final abandonment of the once-great imperial city of Tula to the north had begun a restless movement of peoples southwards, to the gentler lands of the valley of Mexico. By the close of the thirteenth century more than fifty "miniscule polities" jostled in the valley, bound together by trade and increasingly, as population and ambition grew, by the determination to exact tribute from each other.³ The Aztecs, latecomers in the migration, lived miserably and marginally on the narrow tolerance of their longer-settled neighbours until the lord of Azcapotzalco allowed them to settle the swampy lands in the south-west of Lake Texcoco. He had been impressed by their ingenious exploitation of previously despised lake resources; by their energetic reclamation of productive land through the dredging and piling system of *chinampa* agriculture long practised in the valley; and most of all by the unusual ferocity of their young fighting men.

The Aztecs were to live essentially as mercenaries for the next difficult years, as their city and neat patchwork of *chinampas* slowly grew. Their tribal deity Huitzilopochtli, who spoke through the mouths of his four god-bearer priests, had led them through the years of the migration, and with settlement internal affairs were ordered by the leaders of each *calpulli* or lineage group, who distributed land and labour and gathered the young men for war.⁴ With time came the need for more formal and unified representation for negotiations with other valley peoples, so the *calpulli* leaders approached a prince of Culhuacan who could claim descent from the Toltecs of Tula to become their *tlatoani*, or "Speaker". The outsider was integrated into the group and created an instant aristocracy by the

³ Edward A. Calnek, "Patterns of Empire Formation in the Valley of Mexico, Late Post-classic Period, 1200–1521", in George A. Collier, Renato I. Rosaldo and John D. Wirth (eds.), *The Inca and Aztecs States, 1400–1800: Anthropology and History* (New York, 1982), p. 44. Calnek elegantly reviews recent developments in this complex area.
⁴ Gordon Brotherston, enquiring into Huitzilopochtli's "indelibly secular streak", suggests that a one-time leader was transformed into the god by the creators of the empire, as a vivifying figure of unbounded energy and terror. Gordon Brotherston, "Huitzilopochtli and What Was Made of Him", in Norman Hammond (ed.), *Meso-american Archeology: New Approaches* (London, 1974), pp. 155–65.

neat device of marrying twenty Aztec wives, one from each *calpulli*, or so
the story goes.[5]

That first *tlatoani* probably had little influence on the administration
of Aztec affairs, but in the late 1420s, a hundred years after the establishment of Tenochtitlán, there was a significant shift in the locus of authority.
Itzcoatl, son of the borrowed prince, in alliance with two other client
cities, led his warriors against those of the overlord city, and won. The
spoils of victory – plunder, land and the labour to work it, even the chance
of securing the tribute due to Azcapotzalco from its subject cities – lay
in his hand. He chose not to distribute that wealth directly to the *calpullis*,
but rather to his warriors and especially to his royal kin through the
creation of an elaborate system of military offices and titles, each carrying
with it rights to tribute and the produce of tribute fields. It has been
persuasively argued that with Itzcoatl and his victory began the recruitment of *calpulli* leaders into service and identification with the nascent
state, and the development of an increasingly sharp distinction between
a privileged hereditary aristocracy and a tributary commoner class.[6]
The *calpulli* was not extinguished: it remained the key local unit for the
distribution of *calpulli* land and for the organization of labour for public
works, war and collective ritual until the sixteenth century and the Spanish attack. But with Itzcoatl and those who followed him, both power
and authority moved decisively from the locally based lineage groups to
the palace of the ruler and the great temple complex adjacent to it.

Under Itzcoatl's successor Moctezuma the Elder the armies of the
Triple Alliance of Tenochtitlán, Texcoco and Tlacopan spilled beyond the
valley to carve out the broad shape of their magnificent if unstable tribute
empire. That expansion was paralleled by the increasing magnificence of
Tenochtitlán. In 1519, the last year of its grandeur, it contained perhaps
200,000 to 250,000 people, with many more densely settled around the
lake margin. (Seville, the port of departure for most of the conquista-
dores, numbered in the same year not more than 60,000 persons.)[7] The

[5] More correctly, one of the stories: *Códice Ramirez: relación del orígen de los Indios que habitan esta Nueva España, según sus historias* (Mexico, 1944), p. 42. The few and sketchy accounts conflict for this early period.

[6] J. Rounds, "Lineage, Class and Power in the Aztec State", *Amer. Ethnologist*, vi (1979), pp. 73–86. For a different emphasis, see Elizabeth M. Brumfiel, "Aztec State Making: Ecology, Structure and the Origins of the State", *Amer. Anthropologist*, lxxxv (1983), pp. 261–84.

[7] For a review of recent discussion on population figures, see William T. Sanders, Jeffrey R. Parsons and Robert S. Santley, *The Basin of Mexico: Ecological Processes in the Evolution of a Civilization* (New York, 1979). For Seville, see J. H. Elliott, *Imperial Spain, 1469–1716* (New York, 1964), p. 117.

city lived more by trade than tribute, but that trade had been stimulated and focused by war, just as its war-fed splendour attracted the most skilled artisans and most gifted singers to embellish its glory further.[8] The one-class society of the early days of hardship had given way to an elaborately differentiated hierarchy. But that hierarchy had been created through the distribution of the spoils of war, and success in combat remained its dynamic. Performance on the field of battle was as central for the confirmation of an elevated position as for escape from a lowly one, and concern regarding that performance gripped young males of all social ranks.

It also concerned those who directed the city. From the age of ten or eleven all commoner youths save those few dedicated to the priesthood came under the control of the "House of Youth", the warrior house in their own *calpulli*. These were not exclusively military schools: each lad was expected to master a range of masculine skills, most particularly the trade of his father. The great mass of Aztec warriors were essentially part-time, returning from campaigns to the mundane pursuits of farming, hunting or fishing, pulque brewing and selling, or the dozen other trades the city supported. Few commoners were so successful in battle as to emancipate themselves entirely from such labour. Nonetheless it was war and the prospect of war which fired imagination and ambition.[9] At fifteen the lads began intensive training in weapon-handling, gathering

---

[8] For trade and tribute into Tenochtitlán, and the development of hierarchy, see Calnek, "Patterns of Empire Formation in the Valley of Mexico"; Edward Calnek, "The Internal Structure of Tenochtitlán", in Eric R. Wolf (ed.), *The Valley of Mexico* (Albuquerque, N. M., 1976), pp. 287–302; Johanna Broda *et al.*, *Estratificación social en la Mesoamérica prehispánica* (Mexico, 1976); Pedro Carrasco and Johanna Broda (eds.), *Economía política e ideología en el México prehispánico* (Mexico, 1978); Frances Berdan, "Trade, Tribute and Market in the Aztec Empire" (Univ. of Texas at Austin Ph.D. thesis, 1975).

[9] Bernardino de Sahagún, *Florentine Codex: General History of the Things of New Spain*, trans. Arthur J. O. Anderson and Charles E. Dibble, 13 pts. (Santa Fe, 1950–82), bk. 8, ch. 20, pp. 71–2. Other information on warrior schools and the conduct of war is to be found in bk. 3, app., chs. 4–6; bk. 6, chs. 3, 21–31; bk. 8, chs. 12, 14, 17–18, 20–21, apps. B, C. See also, for the regalias and the training and disciplinary procedures, *Codex Mendoza*, ed. James Cooper Clark, 3 vols. (London, 1983); Thelma D. Sullivan, "Arms and Insignia of the Mexica", *Estudios de cultura náhuatl*, x (1972), pp. 155–93 (translation of the relevant sections of the Códice Matritense de la Academia de la Historia); Johanna Broda, "El tributo de trajes de guerreros y la estructuración del sistema tributario", in Carrasco and Broda (eds.), *Economía, política e ideología en el México prehispánico*, pp. 113–72. For garrisons, see C. Nigel Davies, "The Military Organization of the Aztec State", *Atti del XL congreso internazionale delli Americanisti*, xl pt. 4 (1972), pp. 213–21. Descriptions of campaigns are most abundant in Diego Durán, *Historia de las Indias de Nueva-España y islas de Tierra Firme*, ed. Jose F. Ramirez, 2 vols. (Mexico, 1867–80).

every evening in the warrior house with the mature warriors – local heroes – to learn the chants and dances which celebrated warriors past and the eternal excitements of war. Assigned labours became a chance to test strength, as boys wrestled logs from the distant forest to feed the never-dying fires in their local temple or to meet their ward's obligations at the central temple precinct. But war provided the crucial and indeed the sole consequential test. Performance in that test was measured in a quite straightforward, arithmetical kind of way. Movement through the ranks of the warrior grades depended on taking alive on the field of battle a specified number of captives of specified quality. (See Plate 1.) Each promotion was marked by the award of designated insignia and by a distinctive cutting and arranging of the hair, although the "warrior lock", at the centre and slightly to the back of the head, was always kept intact. (Some of the most elevated warriors, the "shaven-headed Otomi", kept only that lock, bound with bright cord close to the scalp so that it floated banner-like above the shaven pate.) It was possible for the commoner who distinguished himself over several campaigns to graduate into the lower ranks of the royal administration, or even to enjoy the perquisites of lordship, at least for his lifetime. Rewards were not only individual: if success in battle brought increasingly gorgeous insignia and increasing opportunities for their public and ceremonial display, it also increased access to the goods of the tribute warehouse, which could then be dispersed to kin and friends: a nice example of vertical integration. The connection between the honours heaped on the triumphant warrior and the general benefits enjoyed by civilians associated with him by blood or friendship were well understood. Long after the conquest men recalled what happened when "the man dexterous in arms" was successful:

such honour he won that no one anywhere might be adorned [like him]; no one in his [own] house might assume all his finery. For in truth [because] of his dart and his shield there was eating and drinking, and one was arrayed in cape and breech-clout. For verily in Mexico were we, and thus persisted the reign of Mexico...[10]

The conditions of warrior training for the sons of the lords are less clear. Some appear to have been associated with local warrior houses, taking their specialized training there, while others, dedicated

---

[10] *Florentine Codex*, bk. 8, app. C, p. 89.

PLATE 1. Warrior-priests in various regalias awarded for taking between one and six captives. Codex Mendoza (c. 1541–2), fol. 65r. Courtesy of the Bodleian Library, University of Oxford, Shelfmark: MS. Arch. Selden. AS.1, fol. 65r.

early to a particular order of warriors, trained within its exclusive house.[11]

While the lords certainly wore the hair cuts designating levels of prowess, their ladder of promotion may not have coincided precisely with that climbed by commoners. It was probably significantly more rigorous. For a noble in the later years of empire the cost of cowardice was high. Access to office and the perquisites of office – its tribute fields, its dependent labourers – depended on adequate performance in battle, and the higher the office the more spectacular the required performance. The ruler

[11] For the warrior training of the sons of lords, see *Florentine Codex*, bk. 8, ch. 20. For training within the house of the knightly order, see Durán, *Historia*, ii, ch. 88. For the complex business of access of commoners to high military office, see Virve Piho, "Tlacatecutli, Tlacochtecutli, Tlacateccatl y Tlacochcálcatl", *Estudios de cultura náhuatl*, x (1972), pp. 315–28. My own suspicion is that a rhetoric of access and an actuality of restriction was tempered by the occasional exception – a not unfamiliar situation – but that the positions of *tlacateccatl* and *tlacochcálcatl* of Tenochtitlán were reserved to members of the ruling dynasty. See J. Rounds's absorbing discussion in his "Dynastic Succession and the Centralization of Power in Tenochtitlán", in Collier, Rosaldo and Wirth (eds.), *Inca and Aztec States, 1400–1800*, pp. 63–89.

PLATE 2. A Warrior-king, Ixtlilxochitl of Texcoco. Codex Ixtlilxochitl (1582?), pt. 2, Mexicain 65–71, fol. 106. Courtesy of the Bibliothèque nationale de France.

himself was not exempt. His inner Council of Four, drawn from the royal kin, included the two highest military commanders, and the ruler himself had usually held one of those two positions. After his "election" by that same council, and the obligatory period of seclusion and fasting, his first public duty was to lead his fighting men to war, the splendour of his later installation being a direct measure of the success of his campaign.[12] (See Plate 2.)

---

[12] *Florentine Codex*, bk. 8, ch. 18, *passim*.

A dramatic toughening in required warrior performance for the nobility had come in the middle years of the rule of Moctezuma the Elder, just before the Aztec expansion beyond the valley. Tlacaelel, a young general under Itzcoatl, adviser to Moctezuma and to three rulers after him and chief architect and strategist of empire, made the new rules clear. The most coveted jewels, the richest cloaks and shields could no longer be bought in the market-place. They could be purchased only with valorous deeds. Any male who failed to go to war, even if he were the king's son, would be deprived of all signs of rank and would live as a despised commoner, while great warriors would eat from the king's dish. This was a sufficiently crucial matter to breach the hardening divisions of class: should a legitimate son prove cowardly, and the son of a slave or servant excel him in battle, the bastard would replace the coward as legitimate heir.[13] Furthermore Tlacaelel proclaimed the initiation of a particular kind of warfare against five precariously independent provinces across the mountains – provinces noted, as were the Aztecs, for the toughness of their fighting men. In these so-called "Flowery Wars" the sole end would be the mutual taking of warrior captives for ritual killing. At the same time Tlacaelel was preparing the great campaigns of subjugation which would bring hundreds, even thousands, of prisoners to Tenochtitlán. The building of the Great Temple was already in train. In the next years the Aztecs were to become notorious among their neighbours for their mass ceremonial killings, and for the extravagant theatricalism in which those killings were framed.

It is tempting to see this intensification in military and religious ardour as a response to the events of the year One Rabbit, 1454 in our reckoning. Three seasons of wildly unstable weather, of snows and frosts and drought, had culminated that year in a great famine so severe as to threaten the life of the young city. Men sold themselves or their children into slavery for maize, and Moctezuma formally released his subjects from their duty, to seek their lives elsewhere. The next year had seen recovery with good rains and full harvest. Still, the sequence is seductive: the famine, and then the double drive to appease angry gods and to demonstrate, in face of the famine's bleak lesson as to the limits of coercion, the central role of the warrior in securing prosperity. So it has been conventionally understood, and so, perhaps, it happened. But two key sources note the famine as occurring after the initiation of the Flowery Wars and

---

[13] Durán, *Historia*, i, pp. 240–2.

the renewed emphasis on warrior virtues.[14] Further, the conventional
explanation derives its plausibility from concepts of causation and of
the continuity and uniformity of the temporal process which are familiar
to us, but alien to Aztecs. In their cyclic system each year, indeed each
day, had its own particular and discrete characteristics. The glimpses we
have of their understanding of the famine show them identifying or, more
correctly, recognizing the year One Rabbit as characterized by dearth, and
so planning to prepare for the recurrence of the dangerous year by the
anxious storing of ordinarily despised foods. The famine's consequences
were understood as short-term not so much because of opportune rains,
but because of this "sufficient unto the year-sign are the evils thereof"
kind of view. The year of the rains also saw the end of a fifty-two-year
cycle, the completion of a "Bundle of Years". We are told that in the
cleansing and renewal of the New Fire Ceremony of 1455 there was
special happiness and rejoicing, "for thus it is ended; thus sickness and
famine have left us".[15]

It is possible that the New Fire Ceremony, marking as it did the opening of a new epoch, had more to do with Aztec expansionism and a
new vehemence in war and ritual action than the famine which preceded
it. Clifford Geertz has warned of the insensitivity of modern Europeans
to the possible complexities in the connections between what, following
Bagehot, he calls the "efficient" and the "dignified" parts of government. He presents an example of the complexity by unravelling for our
instruction the "politics of competitive spectacle" practised in the theatre
state of nineteenth-century Bali.[16] In late fifteenth- and sixteenth-century
Mexico the politics of competitive spectacle were equally if differently
crucial. Of course there was what is for us a reassuringly pragmatic edge
to the Mexican activities. For those within the city, some of them "Aztec"

---

[14] Hernando Alvarado Tezozómoc, *Crónica mexicana*, ed. M. Mariscal (Mexico, 1944),
pp. 163–4; Durán, *Historia*, i, ch. 30. Regarding the effect on human population of the
ritual killings, the most systematic estimate of the population of the valley of Mexico
on the eve of conquest puts the number at 800,000 to 1,200,000: Sanders, Parsons and
Santley, *Basin of Mexico*. Rapid intensification of agricultural techniques indicates the
population pressed close to the valley's limits. However, the great mass of victims were
drawn from beyond the valley, and even there the killing of relatively few young men
(consensus hovers around 20,000 per year for all of central Mexico) could have had little
impact on general population levels, although it would, presumably, debilitate potential
military resistance.

[15] *Florentine Codex*, bk. 7, ch. 12, p. 31.

[16] Clifford Geertz, *Negara: The Theatre State in Nineteenth-Century Bali* (Princeton, 1980),
"Conclusion: Bali and Political Theory", pp. 121–36.

only by adoption, others made restless by the intrusive demands of the state, those great ceremonial performances with their mass killings were a vivid reminder that there were clear advantages in being inside rather than outside the Aztec polity. Rulers of other territories, whether allies or enemies, were coerced into observing how Aztecs dealt with those who resisted them. But the significance of the performances went well beyond a conventional politics of terror. Their spectacular victories had persuaded the Aztecs that their own tribal deity Huitzilopochtli was in reality the Sun destined to rule through this current epoch. In the first days of empire Itzcoatl had taken the precautionary measure of destroying tribal records, to allow the construction of a past more compatible with the Aztec present and what he had come to recognize as the glory of their predestined future. But the other peoples of the valley had inconveniently long memories: they knew the Aztecs' miserable beginnings, and they too had tribal deities who hinted at glory and the destiny to dominate. The problem was to persuade not only Aztecs but other tribes that Aztec domination was no mere freak of fortune, an incident in the affairs of men, but part of the design of the cosmos. When actually or potentially recalcitrant tributaries were "invited" to Tenochtitlán's massive ritual displays, the gift exchanges in which they were obliged to participate were games of dominance and submission that the Aztec ruler, drawing on the resources of empire, routinely won. But the ceremonial performances they were then required to attend were not only statements about dominance. They were intended as the most efficacious of political acts; the most direct demonstration of the high legitimacy of Aztec supremacy.

The city itself, so recently constructed, imaged in its massiveness the massive presence of Tula, and before Tula of Teotihuacán. Its quadripartite divisions and its central temple precinct replicated the shape of the cosmos, while the great temple pyramid which dominated the precinct was a "cosmogram in stone",[17] asserting that here was the centre and creative core of the world, resting indeed upon "the foundation of heaven", and rising up as the Mountain of Sustenance, the Earth Mother from

[17] This is the phrase which Eduardo Matos Moctezuma, archaeologist in charge of the recently completed excavations of the Templo Mayor in Mexico City, used in a paper delivered to Dumbarton Oaks Conference on the Aztec Templo Mayor, 8–9 Oct. 1983. Relevant commentaries can be found in H. B. Nicholson with Eloise Quiñones Keber, *Art of Aztec Mexico: Treasures of Tenochtitlán* (National Gallery of Art, Washington, D.C., 1983); Esther Pasztory, *Aztec Art* (New York, 1983). For a magnificent analysis of this and other complex matters, see Richard Townshend, *State and Cosmos in the Art of Tenochtitlán* (Washington, D.C., 1979).

whose womb the Sun leaped, as he does at every dawning, to strike down his murderous sister Moon and to scatter the Uncounted Stars. Only the recently completed excavations of the Great Temple have revealed the full complexity of that stone tableau of the endless moment of the birth of the Sun, whose name, the Aztecs insisted, was Huitzilopochtli. Their best proof of that identification they presented in their sumptuously mounted, magnificently choreographed ritual performances, played out within those central sacred places. The heaped-up wealth, and above all the war captives massed for killing before Huitzilopochtli's shrine, declared that there was nothing fortuitous or merely human about Aztec success in war, and that resistance, or even resentment, was futile.

The declarations made in that theatre of dominance were understood by the Aztecs' neighbours, although few found them permanently compelling, as Cortes was to discover to his advantage. But in the Aztec politics of spectacle the great ceremonies which consumed so great a part of the fruits of war constituted the final, necessary and consummatory act of war; they transformed human victory into sacred destiny.

II

All of that great enterprise rested on the warriors: men who were, if we are to believe the chant, strangers to fear. It is now some years since two remarkable books, appearing in the confused and bitter aftermath of the war in Vietnam, swung the study of men in combat from its traditionally peripheral position very much closer to the centre of human studies. John Keegan's concern was to discover how men could be brought to fight on cue: indeed, how they could be brought to stand to fight at all, when confronted by the terrifying face of battle. How does a distant society contrive to reach into that "wildly unstable physical and emotional environment" to counter fear of wounds, death, abandonment? How, and how well, are men prepared for the actual experience of battle? And (a problem for historians) how are we, sitting pensive at our typewriters, to reconstruct any part of that experience? For Keegan the emphasis lay with how soldiers are made. Paul Fussell sought to trace how combatants in our own Great War struggled to make civilian experience relate to the experience of battle, and then how the experience of battle, and the men whose burden it had become, could be reintegrated into a society returned to peace.[18]

---

[18] John Keegan, *The Face of Battle* (New York, 1977), p. 487; Paul Fussell, *The Great War and Modern Memory* (Oxford, 1975).

Aztecs were not soldiers, at least not in the modern European sense. While Agincourt would have been more intelligible to them than any battle which followed it, it would have seemed, with its archers and crossbowmen, its cavalry and infantry, an over-regimented and over-specialized affair. They had no organized "army", nor officers either. But the Aztec warrior, like the European soldier, was a social product: it should be possible to discover how he was made. He faced, again and again, the threat of injury or death deliberately inflicted: it should be possible to discover something of how that threat appeared to him. And, a man trained to violence, he moved constantly in and out of civilian society: it should be possible to discover how he made that passage. The benefits of warrior action and warrior status were manifest, and not all material. What concerns me now is to count the costs of Aztec courage.

There was, of course, the obvious and familiar cost of war: the grief attending the death of a loved father, son, husband, brother, friend. Women were allowed to weep for that, even in prospect. In the great festival which initiated the season of war the warriors received their insignia and danced in their glory to the high lament of the women who dreaded to see them go. A prayer to the warrior god acknowledges the anguish of the warrior's kin, "the old men, the old women... one's aunt, one's uncle... the mother who gave him strength, by whose side he was laid to sleep", who do not know how or where their young warrior will meet his death.[19]

The kin had been well disciplined for the relinquishment. Childbed was conventionally designated a battlefield, where a woman could "take a captive" by capturing a baby. The midwife greeted the birth of a male child with warcries and a formal exhortation, addressed to the child, but directed, of course, to the panting, newly delivered mother, who was emphatically not given the baby to hold:

My precious son, my youngest one... heed, hearken: thy home is not here, for thou art an eagle, a jaguar... here is only the place of thy nest... out there thou has been consecrated... War is thy desert, thy task. Thou shalt give drink, nourishment, food to the sun, lord of the earth... perhaps thou wilt receive the gift, perhaps thou wilt merit death by the obsidian knife... The flowered death by the obsidian knife [that is, death on the killing stone].

A sufficiently explicit intervention by society in a zone we might consider private. It was the parents who then formally dedicated the infant to war,

[19] *Florentine Codex*, bk. 3, ch. 3, pp. 11–15.

presenting him to the "Rulers of Youth" at the local warrior house, where he would live from puberty to marriage:

Our lord has given a jewel, a precious feather; a child has arrived . . . he is your property, your child, he is your son. In your laps, in the cradle of your arms, we place him. For there are your sons; you instruct them, you make Eagle warriors, you make Jaguar warriors . . .[20]

A sufficiently decisive relinquishment. Nonetheless such disciplining neither did nor was expected to obliterate sentiment.

If success had its negative aspects, and as will be seen they were several, failure could be a lifetime bitterness. One strength of the Aztec system was that it was not necessary to succeed to survive: it was possible to live by one's own labour, saved from want by periodic handouts from the tribute warehouse or from a successful neighbour or kinsman. But failure was public, and publicly marked, at an age when such marks burn deep. From about ten each lad grew a long lock of hair at the nape of the neck, which remained uncut until he had participated in the taking of a captive on the field of war. If after two or three campaigns he still had not forced himself to enter the fray – and it was always possible to hang back – he was thrown out of the warrior house, his head shaven in a tonsure to dramatize the loss of the warrior lock and to prepare him for the carrying pad of humble labour: forever a peripheral man.

Long-distance campaigns, increasingly frequent as the empire grew and its edges so frequently unravelled, had their special hardships for all warrior grades. While the ruler took official responsibility for provisioning his warriors, a sensible man carried what he could of dried maize cakes, bean flour and crushed seeds, a dour but surprisingly nutritious diet. As long as the route lay through "friendly" territories he could presumably hope for some supplementary supplies, as any defect in hospitality could be defined as a lack of proper friendliness.[21] In unequivocally hostile zones there was the chance of plundering local food supplies. But always the living was hard. Aztec armies took few carriers and cooks with them. Food was the dried rations mixed with water and swallowed down, and sleep a matter of wrapping close in a cloak and stretching out on the ground. These hardships probably troubled Aztecs little: they were used to cold, having in their nightly dancing gone nearly naked, at over 7,000 feet elevation a chilly business, while the frequency of ritual engagement

---

[20] *Ibid.*, bk. 3, ch. 4, p. 51.
[21] For example, Durán, *Historia*, i, p. 172.

through fasting and vigil had taught them to survive on poor food and little sleep over long periods.

However informal their provisioning, the warriors marched in reasonably orderly sequence, grouped according to their localities, and in joint enterprises, their cities. While spies scouted ahead, and there was hopeful talk of devious ways to penetrate the target town, they usually found the defending warriors massed to meet them close by their city. Victory came when so many individual warriors had been brought to flee as to make for a general rout. Here the pure fury of the Aztec warrior was at its most impressive. Such a warrior "hurled himself against the foe . . . he shook others off scornfully, drove them into corners, broke into enemy ranks, took after those who fled, threw himself upon them . . . He aroused complete terror. . . ."[22] The attackers then pursued the fleeing defenders into the city, assaulted the main temple and put its shrine to the torch. When the temple burst into flame, resistance ceased. (In the painted Mexican books the conventional sign for conquest is a pyramid temple with a burning brand thrust into it.) The victors settled to pillage at leisure, until their leaders could be brought to listen to the increasingly desperate pleas and offers of the defeated. Then tribute terms were set (see Plate 3), Huitzilopochtli's image installed in the refurbished temple, and an image of the local tribal deity carried back at the head of a long train of captives to a jubilant Tenochtitlán. Only in the case of chronically restless tributaries or to secure a specially useful trade route was a governor or a garrison imposed.

If we find the wars on the edges of empire reassuringly instrumental affairs, yielding so many bunches of feathers, so many loads of cacao, there are indications that for Aztec fighting men they were less satisfactory, with either too much or too little resistance. (Of the 24,000 Aztec and allied wariors who went out against the Tarascans only 4,000 limped back to their cities.) "Barbarians" fought by different rules or, as it seemed to the men of Tenochtitlán, by no rules at all. And distance could preclude the bringing back of captives, so they had to be killed on the spot. More rewarding emotionally and morally were wars fought closer to home, against opponents of like mind.

Just how those more serious wars were experienced – how the "face of battle" appeared to the Aztec warrior – has to be pieced together from very disparate kinds of sources, and troubling blurs and blanks remain. Some of the most poignant texts are those relating to the last great

[22] *Florentine Codex*, bk. 4, ch. 10, pp. 38–9.

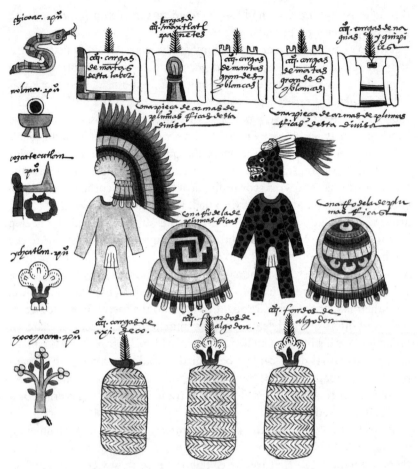

PLATE 3. An Aztec tribute list. The five towns on the left paid four hundred mantles in each specified design, dried chillies, cotton and feathered warrior suits, head-dresses and shields. Codex Mendoza (c. 1541–2), fol. 54r. Courtesy of the Bodleian Library, University of Oxford, Shelfmark: MS. Arch. Selden. AS.1, fol. 54r.

battles fought for Tenochtitlán between Aztec warriors and the Spanish and native forces led by Cortes, for there we have accounts from both sides.[23] But for the reconstruction of Aztec battle their use is limited: what they demonstrate most powerfully is that warfare is as much a cultural

---

[23] The major Nahuatl accounts are in the *Florentine Codex*, bk. 12. For a modernized and reorganized translation, see Bernadino de Sahagún, *The War of Conquest: How It Was Waged Here in Mexico*, trans. Arthur J. O. Anderson and Charles E. Dibble (Salt Lake City, 1978). See also "Historia de Tlatelolco desde los trempos mas remotos" (1528), in *Unos annales históricos de la nación mexicana*, ed. Heinrich Berlin (Mexico, 1948).

expression as worship, and that when such unlike enemies, sharing no language for communication, engage, they can only end, like Konrad Lorenz's turkey and peacock, with the one pecking the other to death.

What is clear is that Aztec combat was highly individualistic, and depended utterly on the courage of the individual. For his first venture into war the fledgeling warrior went only as an observer, to "carry the shield" of an experienced warrior whose technique he was to study. On his second time out he was expected to participate in a group capture: up to six novices could combine to drag a warrior down. The body of the victim of the joint assault was later exquisitely portioned out: torso and right thigh to the major captor, left thigh to the second; right upper arm to the third; left upper arm to the fourth; right forearm to the fifth; and left forearm to the sixth.[24] With that initial capture, co-operation was at an end: from that time on the youth was in direct competition with his peers, as he searched through the dust-haze and the mind-stunning shrieking and whistling to identify and engage with an enemy warrior of equal, or preferably just higher, status. The nice portioning out of the first captive suggests that even there, in-group ranking was more important than any notion of team spirit.

The lads of each warrior house had lived and trained together, and we could expect some camaraderie to have developed. Discipline within the houses was maintained by a kind of extreme prefect system, with peers set to watch peers and to punish delinquents with savage beatings, or with the searing from the head of the treasured warrior lock. Would male bonding have survived all that – or, perhaps, thrived on it? Certainly sentiment towards one's companions on the field of battle was firmly and officially discouraged. To go to the aid of a threatened comrade would probably provoke a charge of having tried to steal his captive, and not only the false claiming of a captive, but the giving of one's captive to another, was punishable by death.

The task of the men we would be tempted to call officers was to order the initial disposition of the warriors, to develop the element of surprise as much as their impatience would allow, and to form up the lines for the attack, dealing out rough discipline as the men jostled for advantage. Once the conchshell trumpets had blasted they had no further role save to

---

For the major Spanish accounts, see Bernal Diaz del Castillo, *The True History of the Conquest of New Spain*, ed. and trans. A. P. Maudslay, 5 vols. (Hakluyt Soc., 2nd ser., xxiii–xxv, xxx, xl, London, 1908–16); Hernan Cortes, *Letters from Mexico*, ed. and trans. A. R. Pagden (New York, 1971). Patricia Fuentes, *The Conquistadors* (London, 1963), conveniently offers English translations of other Spanish participants' accounts.
[24] *Florentine Codex*, bk. 8, ch. 21, p. 175.

adjudicate conflicts over captives among their own men. It was the great warriors who leapt forward, lending courage and inciting emulation by their own superb example.

Analysis of the Aztec armoury intensifies the impression that serious combat was very much a one-to-one, hand-to-hand affair. While they had spears and bows and arrows, these projectile weapons were probably discharged early, and largely for irritating effect. The best evidence of their lack of penetrating power was the Spaniards' early adoption of the native quilted cotton armour, which they found adequate to deflect all but the luckiest shot. The slingshot was probably more valued, giving hope of the opportune stunning of a potential captive. (Spaniards clung to their metal helmets.) The preferred weapon for combat was the *macana*, the heavy flat oak club, each edge studded with flint or obsidian blades. The small shield offered sturdy and mobile protection for all the delicacy of its feather-work and gilding, being solidly built from bamboo or fire-hardened wood with hide reinforcing, while the close-fitting warrior suit with its bird or animal "head" was almost as light and flexible as the feathers from which it was made. The standards which rose up so imposingly were constructed on a fine wicker frame which strapped neatly to the back and offered no impediment to action. (See Plate 4.)

Given that the preferred form of combat was the duel with a matched opponent, locating an appropriate antagonist in an ordinary battle could be a vexing affair, especially for the more elevated ranks, which suggests the utility of the banners and head-dresses floating above the swirl of the battle. The great warrior's best protection against being molested by trivial and over-ambitious opponents was the terror inspired by the ferocity of his glance, the grandeur of his reputation, and the fact that every warrior bore his war record inscribed in his regalia. But it was a limited protection. A novice warrior could flinch and edge away if suddenly confronted by the looming figure of an Eagle or Jaguar knight, or even take to his heels, with no more penalty than private shame, but more established warriors strove to proclaim boundless courage in every gesture, so it could be a difficult thing to disengage from a mutually unwanted encounter. The élite corps in the Aztec system took special vows, some never to turn their backs in battle, and others, even more superb, not to take a backward step. This latter group perhaps mitigated the magnificent arrogance of the vow by habitually fighting in pairs, which meant some protection on the flank. They were kept to their vows: should one fall, and his disoriented partner turn to flee, he was deprived of all his honours and expelled from the company of warriors.[25] But unacceptably lowly challengers or the swarms of eager juveniles eager to test their collective strength must have marred the experience for the authentic connoisseur. For those warriors who had gazed longest and most steadily upon the face of battle there was a special kind of war: the "Flowery Wars" initiated by the first Moctezuma.

Modern commentators rendered uneasy by their difficulty in penetrating "beneath the religious cloak to the underlying material causes and issues",[26] as one of them puts it, have emphasized the importance of the Flowery Wars for the training of neophyte Aztec warriors, who would presumably then go and fight more intelligibly materialistic wars somewhere else. But it was only the best of established Aztec warriors who marched out on those scheduled occasions to meet the leading warriors of the transmontane provinces: indeed after attaining a certain eminence status could only be enhanced by taking a captive from one of those states which participated wholly, if perhaps not wholly voluntarily, in the Aztec ethos. Here there was no purpose and no outcome save the mutual taking of captives for ritual killing. It is also worth noting that while in other kinds of wars the odds normally heavily favoured the Aztecs (the Tarascan disaster being unique), in these combats the odds were always even.

It was on that field of battle that the Aztec aesthetic of war could be most perfectly displayed and most profoundly experienced; and here "aesthetic" must be understood to comprehend moral and emotional sensibilities. Glimpses in both the painted and written sources suggest that combat was initiated by a formal rhetoric of gesture, with a "presentation stance" of the club arm dropped and the body in a half-crouch. Since each warrior had an interest in not damaging his opponent too severely, there being no honour to be won by killing in the field, and a maimed man being useless for the most engrossing rituals, it is likely there was an initial preference for using the flat side of the club to stun, resorting to the cutting edges only when faced with a singularly difficult antagonist.

The action, when it came, was very fast: the clubs, although heavy, were handy. Even against the quite unfamiliar bulk and speed of a Spanish horseman native warriors could calculate their blows for maximum effectiveness through a remarkable combination of speed, strength, balance

---

[25] *Ibid.*, bk. 8, app. C, p. 88.
[26] Frederic Hicks, "'Flowery War' in Aztec History", *Amer. Ethnologist*, vi (1979), p. 87.

PLATE 4. Four war leaders in battledress. Codex Mendoza (c. 1541–2), fol. 67r. Courtesy of the Bodleian Library, University of Oxford, Shelfmark: MS. Arch. Selden. AS.1, fol. 67r.

and timing.[27] The aim was to stun or sufficiently disable one's opponent so that he could be grappled to the ground and subdued. It is possible that the seizing of the warrior lock (see Plate 1), the formal sign of dominance in the pictographic codices, was accepted as deciding the matter, or so the elaborately bound and defiantly graspable warrior lock of the "shaven-headed Otomi" would suggest.

The dramatic shape of the combat, its "style", was poised stillness exploding into violent action. Aztecs described the two creatures most closely associated with warriors in the following terms: "the eagle is fearless ... it can gaze into, it can face, the sun ... it is brave, daring, a wing-beater, a screamer ... ".[28] The lordly jaguar, "cautious, wise, proud ... reserved", if troubled by a hunter first seats itself, casually deflecting the flying arrows, and then "stretches, stirs ... and then it springs". And so dies the hunter.[29]

---

[27] For example, Bernal Diaz's awed recollections in his *True History of the Conquest of New Spain*, i, pp. 229–32. There are useful pictorial representations in the *Florentine Codex*, but perhaps those of the Lienzo de Tlaxcala are most graphic, being cartoons of actual encounters, although typically encounters between natives and Spaniards: *El Lienzo de Tlaxcala*, ed. Alfredo Chavez (Mexico, 1979).

[28] *Florentine Codex*, bk. 11, ch. 2, p. 40.

[29] *Ibid.*, bk. 11, ch. 1, pp. 2–3.

A vignette from a major warrior festival called the Feast of the Flaying of Men points in the same direction. Very briefly, those warriors who offered a captive at the pyramid killings on the first day of the festival were decked in the flayed skins of the victims and displayed at appointed places within the city, where they became challenges to the audacity of relatively untested youths. There sat the great warriors, impassive in their skins. The youths had to bring themselves to advance, in a thrilling game of critical distances, to "snatch at their navels" and so "bring out their rage, their anger". That is, they had to make a full-frontal approach to a terrifying figure, just as was required on the field of battle – a figure who might explode into action at any moment (and did, for warriors would suddenly take off after the boys and give any they caught a thorough drubbing).[30]

Explosions of anger, paralysing eruptions of rage, transformations from the stillness of perfect control to furious violence – great Aztec warriors would seem to be uncomfortable people to be with. And lesser warriors had less control. Young men kept at a pitch for war and trained to a style of touchy arrogance were hard to maintain peaceably in a city. To an outsider there was a startling incidence of violence tolerated within Aztec society, much of it generated from the young men in the warrior houses. So-called "ritual combats", which had little pretence about them, raged through the streets, as priests and warriors fought out their antagonisms, or as warriors harassed the surrogate "captives" whom merchants were authorized to offer at what warriors claimed as a warrior ceremony. On those occasions, ordinary people had to do their best to keep out of the way. On other occasions – playful occasions, but Aztecs had very rough notions of play – the townsfolk were themselves the victims, likely to be despoiled of their cloaks, or intimidated into offering "tribute" to a squad of young men. This casual tribute could become institutionalized: the ruler found it necessary to pronounce the death penalty against those men of the warrior houses who dared to levy "tribute on the town, of *chocolatl*, of food, of whatsoever they wished . . . ".[31] The lavish gifts regularly exacted from the merchants by the great warriors were transparently a levy, an insurance against pillage.

So, it would seem, society strove to contain and limit the undesired costs of courage by a determined effort to impose order on the unruly men of war. Penal codes were savage, with swift and violent retribution

[30] *Ibid.*, bk. 2, ch. 21, p. 50.
[31] *Ibid.*, bk. 8, ch. 14, p. 43.

laid down for all socially disruptive acts, from drinking and adultery
to theft and extortion, and the higher the rank the more strenuous the
punishment.[32] Public rhetoric insisted on the virtues of humility, modesty,
frugality, self-control. In the formal homilies delivered at all moments
of social transition, in which the wisdom of the elders was distilled,
youth was constantly urged to a self-effacing submissiveness, to go "with
thy head bowed, thy arms folded, thy head lowered ... with weeping,
with sighing, with meekness".[33] These recommendations were made in
a society which rewarded its warriors with the opportunity to bask in
public adulation, and in the very public display of magnificent costumes,
plumes and jewels. On the one hand we have high and gaudy rewards for
aggression: on the other, formal denunciations of aggressive behaviour
and of personal vanity. Is this simply a "contradiction", the manifestation
of the strain imposed on a society avid for the material rewards of empire
but unprepared for its social costs, and so developing a rhetoric of control
to net a violent reality of its own making?

So to see it is to miss the opportunity to explore Aztec understandings
of violence, and the deeper bonds between warrior and society. The most
extreme forms of violence were, after all, officially imported into the city,
in the great killing rituals which marked most collective occasions. Nor
were these killings remote top-of-the-pyramid affairs. The victims, living
and dead, were endlessly moved about the neighbourhoods; in one festival the lieutenant of Huitzilopochtli ran through the streets slaughtering
slaves staked out like goats along his way; in the Feast of the Flaying
of Men, as we have seen, men in newly flayed human skins skirmished
through the streets – and then went on to penetrate individual houses:

> ... They pursued one. Many appeared. All went wearing the skin, dripping grease,
> dripping blood, thus terrifying those they followed ... and then the young men
> garbed like Xipe Totec, wearing human skins ... went everywhere from house
> to house. They were placed upon seats of sapote leaves; they provided them
> with necklaces formed of maize ears; they placed garlands of flowers upon their
> shoulders; they placed crowns of flowers upon their heads ...[34]

A simple notion of the unforeseen and undesired consequences of military
expansion will not penetrate far into this. Only through the glass of ritual

[32] In his first address to the people after his installation, the ruler dwelt at length on
the horrors, and the dangers, of jimson weed, pulque and all other restraint-reducing
substances. Drinking at least was probably very much more widespread – and covertly
tolerated – than the formal homilies admit. *Ibid.*, bk. 8, ch. 14.

[33] *Ibid.*, bk. 6, ch. 20, p. 111.

[34] *Ibid.*, bk. 1, ch. 18, pp. 39–40.

action, smoky and obscure as that glass is, do we have much chance of discerning how violence, on the field of battle and off it, was understood, and how warrior and civilian society cohered.

III

Analysis of ritual has come to have rather a bad name among historians, for good and bad reasons. No general brief can be developed for its universal utility: rituals relate variously to the societies which produce them. They may also be analysed from different perspectives. Let it be granted at the outset that Aztec rituals dramatized social hierarchy, and so – probably – reinforced it; that they provided the occasion for the redistribution of goods and for reciprocal exchanges; that the bloodier rituals were consciously used to terrify recalcitrant tributaries. I want to set these narrowly instrumental notions aside, to seek through the analysis of one small sequence of ritual action what Victor Turner has called the "root paradigms" of a culture: those "irreducible life stances" displayed not in theological systems or explicitly stated moralities but "in the stress of vital action [where] firm definitional outlines become blurred by the encounter of emotionally charged wills".[35] That pursuit involves two major claims: that Aztec rituals were areas of vital action, and that we are, at this distance, able adequately to reconstruct them.

Ritual constantly structured Aztec experience, from the cloud of customs ordering response to the events of the individual life to the high dramas of public ceremonial. The Aztecs in effect concocted much of that public ceremonial cycle after their arrival in the valley, building on the eighteen-month seasonal calendar of its settled agriculturalists, and integrating into that calendar rituals they found compelling from other zones, or dramatizing their own mythic past, or celebrating their own already mythic victories. Tensely involved in change, they struggled through ritual at once to dramatize coherence and continuity, and to explore those strains, like the deep ambivalence veining the merchants' position, or the irritable competitiveness between trainee priests and warriors, contingent on that change. Aztec rituals were living maps of current and dynamic meanings, more street theatre than museum piece. The great, intricately woven skein of ceremonial action which bound time and seasons and men together is best understood as an intensified discourse: a discourse

---

[35] Victor Turner, "Religious Paradigms and Political Action", in his *Dramas, Fields and Metaphors: Symbolic Actions in Human Society* (Ithaca, N.Y., and London, 1974), p. 64.

framed in declaratory statements but also permitting, through a developed vocabulary of feathers and fire and human bodies living and dead, a tense, continuous investigation into the nature of things.

Few material traces of Aztec rituals survived the conquest. There are the magnificent remains of the temple precinct recently excavated in Mexico City, and the rest of the archaeological material exhumed over the years. There is the scatter of objects retrieved from the store-rooms of Europe. None of the surviving pre-conquest pictographic codices is certainly from the valley of Mexico. The Codex Borbonicus (see Plate 8) is Aztec, and if not pre-conquest a very early copy, and contains a section on the rituals of the solar calendar, but it (like the other codices) resists confident interpretation.[36] To compensate for this sparsity there is a mass of Spanish writing on Aztec ritual and religion, most particularly from men professionally interested in such matters, the missionary friars, and they provide engrossing and indispensable sources. But if "professional interest" focuses attention, it can also blinker it. The writings of the Dominican Diego Durán exemplify some of the weaknesses of the genre. They contain vivid and apparently richly detailed descriptions of ritual action. But those descriptions are very much constructs, welding together fragments of information from different regions – it is "Indian religion" he is after – and readily incorporating dubious detail, and even more dubious psychology.[37] For Durán there is nothing, finally, problematical about what the Indians were up to. He knew he was looking at the work of the Devil.

Only one source to my knowledge gives us accounts from the native point of view. The Franciscan Bernardino de Sahagún collected accounts of pre-conquest life from native informants at three separate locations, having them questioned by mission-trained native scribes, who then wrote down their Nahuatl speech in European script. The Nahuatl compilation produced by this process has been named by scholars the Florentine

---

[36] For the objects and the excavations, see Nicholson and Quiñones Keber, *Art of Aztec Mexico;* Pasztory, *Aztec Art.* Recent attempts to discover the syntax of the codices are discussed in Edward B. Sisson, "Recent Work on the Borgia Group Codices", *Current Anthropology,* xxiv (1983), pp. 653–6.

[37] For example, Durán gave a vivid and moving account of the death of a warrior going as a messenger to the Sun on the Cuauhxicalli, or Stone of Tizoc; he described the warrior's throat as being slit, and the blood conducted along a groove in the stone: Durán, *Historia,* ii, ch. 88. The groove was cut into the stone some time after the conquest. Tlacaelel is presented as the "devilish inventor of cruel and terrifying sacrifices", and as concocting the Feast of the Flaying of Men, for example, out of his own evil imagination to celebrate the victory of the Aztecs over the Huasteca: Durán, *Historia,* i, ch. 20.

Codex. It bears the marks of its colonial context in the initial structuring of the questions, as in Sahagún's editings and selections. There are obscurities within it, as there are conflicts with Sahagún's own Spanish gloss. But the codex derives narrowly from Tenochtitlán and its sister city Tlatelolco,[38] and preserves the accounts of participants in those sacred performances of long ago. It is therefore the incomparable source for my purposes, as those narratives, obscure and difficult as they are, are the products of the minds I seek to penetrate.

To return, then, to the Feast of the Flaying of Men. With the first gathering of the agricultural harvest and the onset of the frosts the Aztec season of war began. Eighty days after that harvest, the first crop of warrior captives was killed, and eighty days after that, as the first signs of spring indicated the beginning of the planting season, came the Feast of the Flaying of Men. It was an important festival in that its first two days and all the evenings of the twenty days to follow required the attendance of those in authority in Tenochtitlán. It starred the warriors, especially the great warriors, and it honoured Xipe Totec, the Flayer or the Flayed One,[39] who was associated with the east, a zone of plenty, and with the early spring, and who was represented by a priest wearing a flayed human skin, and a mask of a flayed human face. (See Plate 5).

The first day of the festival saw the killing of the less important war captives. The victims, decked in elaborate regalias, were brought from the local warrior houses in which they had been kept, tended and displayed since their capture and delivered by their captors to the priests waiting at

---

[38] The conditions of Sahagún's enterprise are most conveniently laid out in Charles Dibble, "Sahagún's Historia", in *Florentine Codex*, pt. 1, pp. 9–23. See also Alfredo López Austin, "The Research Method of Fray Bernardino de Sahagún: The Questionnaires", in Munro S. Edmonson (ed.), *Sixteenth-Century Mexico: The Work of Sahagún* (Albuquerque, N. M., 1974), pp. 111–49. The translation of particular passages remains in dispute, usually because of obscurities in the initial transcription. For the focus on Tenochtitlán and Tlatelolco, see H. B. Nicholson, "Tepepolco, the Locale of the First Stage of Fr. Bernardino de Sahagún's Great Ethnographic Project: Historical and Cultural Notes", in Hammond (ed.), *Mesoamerican Archeology*, pp. 145–54.

[39] For a different translation of "Xipe Totec", see Alfredo López Austin, *Hombrédios: religión y política en el mundo náhuatl* (Mexico, 1973). For a different reconstruction of some of the action of Tlacaxipeualiztli, see Johanna Broda de Casas, "Tlacaxipeualiztli: A Reconstruction of an Aztec Calendar Festival from 16th Century Sources", *Revista española de antropología americana*, v (1970), pp. 197–274. Broda has attempted to piece together a composite account from diverse sources. It is a gallant and impressively scholarly attempt, but in my view rests on the mistaken epistemological assumption that our notions of plausibility are an adequate guide for the reconstruction of the actions and meanings of alien peoples. On that issue, see Paul Rock, "Some Problems in Interpretative Historiography", *Brit. Jl. Sociology*, xxvii (1976), pp. 353–86.

the foot of Xipe's pyramid in the main temple precinct. Ideally they were meant to go leaping up the steps of the pyramid, shouting the chants of their city as they went, and some did: others had to be dragged up by the priests. At the top, before the shrine, they were flipped on their backs over a small upright stone, a priest securing each limb, while a fifth priest struck open the chest with a flint knife, took out the heart, and raised it towards the sun. (See Plate 6.) The body was sent hurtling and tumbling down the stairs to be collected at the bottom by old men from the appropriate ward temple, where they carried it to be flayed and dismembered, probably by the captor. One thigh was reserved to Moctezuma, the other and most of the rest of the body going to the captor, who summoned his kin to a feast at his house. There, amid weeping and lamentations, the kinsmen of the captor each ate a small piece of flesh served with a dish of "dried" (unsoftened?) maize kernels. The captor himself, whose splendid captor's regalia had been replaced by the white chalk and feathers which marked the victim destined for the killing stone, did not participate in the feast.

The killings at the pyramid went on for much of the day. It is difficult to establish the numbers usually killed – presumably that varied according to the fortunes of war – but perhaps sixty or so died. It was those captors who on the following day were displayed in the city in their victims' skins, and who were teased into skirmishings by the foolhardy lads of the town in the episode already described. But it is what happened later on that second day which seems to have been the most compelling sequence in the whole complex affair. It also involved a mode of killing specially identified with the Aztecs, revived in Tenochtitlán to mark the victory of Moctezuma the Elder over the Huastecs.

For this ritual only the greatest captives were selected, their captors being accordingly the more honoured. The victims were chosen to die on what the Spaniards later dubbed the gladiatorial stone, at the base of Xipe's pyramid. They had been rehearsed for the occasion. Their captors had presented them to the people in a sequence of different regalias over the preceding four days, at the place where they were to die. There they were forced to engage in mock combats, and then to submit to a mock heart excision, the "hearts" being made of unsoftened maize kernels. The night before their deaths they spent in vigil with their captors, their warrior lock being cut and taken at midnight. Then early in the afternoon of that second day of Xipe's festival they were marshalled close to the stone, their captors still beside them, before assembled dignitaries and as many other people as could fit into the temple precinct, as four of the greatest Aztec warriors, two from the order of Jaguar warriors, two from

PLATE 5. Aztec stone carving of Xipe Totec seated and wearing the flayed skin of a warrior victim (note the dangling hands and the separate "face" mask). © Museum der Kulturen Basel, Switzerland. Photograph: Peter Horner.

the order of Eagles, presented their weapons in dedication to the sun. Then down from Xipe's pyramid came in procession the high priest of Xipe Totec in the regalia of his lord, followed by the other high priests as representatives of their deities, to take their seats around the gladiatorial stone. This was a performance worthy of the contemplation of the gods.

The stone was about waist high and a metre and half wide, but set on an elevated platform about the height of a man.[40] The first victim, now stripped of his regalia and clad only in a loincloth, was given a draught of "obsidian wine" – pulque, the Aztec alcoholic drink, probably spiked with a drug from their ample pharmacopoeia – and tethered by the waist to a rope fastened at the centre of the stone. He was presented with weapons; four pine cudgels for throwing, and a war club. The club was studded not with flint or obsidian blades, but with feathers. Then the first Jaguar warrior, equipped with a real club, advanced and engaged him in combat. (See Plate 7.)

There must have been a system of timing of rounds or of counting passes or exchanges, although it is not recorded, because exceptionally

[40] Durán, *Historia*, i, ch. 20, p. 175.

fine fighters were sometimes able to survive the assaults of all four warriors. In those cases a fifth warrior, a left-hander, was brought into play to bring him down. When he was down, the lord Xipe advanced, struck open the breast and cut out the heart, which was raised "as a gift" to the sun, and then placed in the eagle vessel in which it would be later burned. The priest then submerged a hollow cane in the blood welling in the chest cavity, and raised the cane, so, as it was said, "giving the sun to drink". The captor was given the cane and a bowl of the blood which he carried throughout the city, daubing the blood on the mouths of the stone idols in all the temples. The circuit completed, he went to Moctezuma's palace to return the magnificent regalia of he who offers a victim at the gladiatorial stone, and from there went back to his local temple to flay and dismember his captive's body. And then, later in the day, he watched his lamenting kin eat the maize stew and the flesh of his captive, while they wept for their own young warrior. He did not participate, saying "Shall I perchance eat my very self?".[41] Meanwhile at the foot of Xipe's pyramid other victims had been tethered to the stone, and had fought and died. At the end of the day, when the last of the victims had been dispatched, the priests performed a dance with their severed heads, which were then skewered on the skull rack beside the stone.

It is obvious even from this sketchy account that a great many things were going on, but I want to focus on what was understood to be happening on the actual stone. There are a thousand ways of killing a man, but why tether him to a stone, restricting his movements but giving him the advantage of height? Why arm him with a club, a formidable weapon in its weight and reach, but with its effectiveness reduced by the replacement of its cutting blades with feathers? And why, given this finely calculated inequality, did the victim co-operate? It was clearly imperative that he fight, and fight as well as he was able: for this ritual only warriors from tribes fully participant in Aztec understandings of war were chosen. He could not fight for his life, for that was forfeit. Why then?

He, like his Aztec counterparts, had been long prepared. From his earliest days those who spoke for society had made his mission plain: to give the sun the hearts of enemies, and to feed the insatiable earth with their bodies. Every lad training in the warrior houses knew that access to the warrior paradise in the House of the Sun was restricted to those who died

[41] *Florentine Codex*, bk. 2, ch. 21, p. 54.

PLATE 6. Painted skin screenfold portraying death on the killing stone. Codex Zouche-Nuttall (West Oaxaca, pre-conquest), fol. 3, Add. MSS 39671. © Trustees of the British Museum.

in either of two ways: on the field of battle, where death was rare, given that the end of combat was the taking of captives, or on the killing stone. That death he had to strive to desire, or at least to embrace. Just as only ritual action made "victory" from the outcome of battles, so for the individual warrior action on the field of battle was consummated only later, and ritually. Behind the desperate excitements of battle lay the shadow of the killing stone, and a lonely death among strangers. This is why the captor, in the midst of the adulation accorded him for having taken a victim for the sun, wore at the cannibal feast of his kin the chalk and down of the victim; why the kin lamented; why he could not eat of what was indeed his "own flesh", for he too, ideally, would die on the stone,

PLATE 7. The gladiatorial combat. Codex Zouche-Nuttall (West Oaxaca, pre-conquest), fol. 83, Add. MSS 39671. © Trustees of the British Museum.

and his flesh be eaten in another city. In the rhetoric of Aztec ideology the battlefield was as much a sacred space as the temple precinct – or as much as human confusion and the terrible contingency of war permitted. But it was only on the stone that the meaning of the death could be made manifest.

To be overcome in battle was not fortuitous: it was the sign that the warrior was a warrior no longer, and had begun the transition to victim. From the moment of the seizing of the warrior lock his separation from the ordinary world began. The "rehearsals", as we might cynically call them – the garments changed again and again, the mock combats at the stone, the mock heart excisions – all marked his passage to increased sacredness. Then, with the taking of his warrior lock of hair, "the eagle man was taken upwards" – that is, the warrior made his flight to the sun: before his physical death the individual was extinguished, the transition completed. It was as victim that he watched other men from his city, men he had known when they were alive, fight and die on the stone, until it was his turn for a last display of maximum valour, the exemplary passionate acceptance of his fate. And if he died well his praises would be sung in the warrior houses of his home place.

The attacking Eagle and Jaguar warriors did not aim to disable quickly: a single blow behind knee or ankle would have done that. The aim was rather to exhaust, and to weaken slowly, until the victim "faltered, he fainted... he threw himself down as if dead, as if he wished that breath might end, that he might endure it, that he might perish...".[42] The performance of the four warriors was a display of high art, of Aztec mastery in weapon handling: an exhibition bout for the gods, for their own warriors, and for the onlookers, who included at Moctezuma's invitation secret watchers from recalcitrant tribes. They sought to demonstrate the superb control of the great warrior, who in the heat of combat, under threat of wounds or capture, or in this case of most painful and public humiliation, and opposed by a warrior at last freed from inhibition, can still inhibit his own stroke to avoid the killing or the crippling blow. And there was the deeper fascination that combat was the most comprehensive metaphor for Aztec understanding of how human society, the world and the cosmos worked. The endless repetitious struggles between the natural elements were endlessly replicated in the ritual ball game, in the mock combats which studded the ritual cycle, and in this most solemn contest on the gladiatorial stone.

The victims were called "the striped ones", and the action on the stone "the striping". What the assailants strove to do was not to club or to stun, but to wound delicately; to slit the skin with an obsidian blade so that blood would spring forth. Xipe, who himself wore a human skin, represented the early spring, when the husk of the seed must be pierced if the sprouting life within is to break through, and when the winter-hardened skin of the earth is pierced by the new growth. Certainly the offerings bestowed on the skin-wearers – the garlands of flowers and the necklaces of maize ears – make the agricultural connection plain. But the most important aspect and the dominant meaning of "the striping" for those who performed and for those who watched was the effusion of warrior blood.

This leads into what are as yet only sketchily chartered waters, but there is a need for speculation if the connections between Aztec warriors and Aztec society are to be searched out. Analysts, especially those working from a class model of society, have proceeded on the assumption that warrior cults were and must have been divorced from those practised by

---

[42] *Ibid.*, bk. 2, ch. 21, p. 53.

the commoners.[43] (As is clear, I see the warrior as very firmly integrated into the general society, however headily exclusive the highest orders might have been.) Others assume the division on historical grounds: that the warrior cult was imported from the nomadic north, and so came to be practised in parallel with the indigenous rites of the valley farmers.[44] Spaniards and the Europeans who came after them have presented an urban-imperial image of Tenochtitlán, with its splendid hierarchies of priests and warriors and its whole sections of artisans and mechants. But it was a city green with growing things, banked with the *chinampas*, the ingenious system of shallow-water agriculture which had brought the Aztecs their first prosperity. The bulk of the population were not agriculturalists, but those specialist artisans and priests and warriors lived in a vegetable-growers' world, and the centrality of agriculture to their lives could not have been in doubt.

The *chinampas* required men's exquisite manipulations of earth, seeds, sun and water in an alchemy of vegetable abundance. It was highly precise cultivation, its small stages laid out from when each seed in its individual block of earth, covered against frost, watered by hand, was raised until it was brought to sprout, and then transferred to the only slightly less intensive cultivation of the *chinampa*. The *chinampa* itself was formed by the piling of thick mats of water weed, which provided a fibrous, permeable, and slowly composting base for the rich silt dredged up from the lake bottom. More water could be scooped up at need. Today the few surviving *chinamperos* protect their plants from frost or excessive rain and sun by blankets of straw, or light structures of sticks and mats, and in the sixteenth century the materials, needs and skills were there to do the same.[45]

The Aztec seasonal ritual calendar was geared to the most precisely observed and minutely differentiated stages of vegetable growth. Those stages must have been derived from observation of the "greenhouse" *chinampas*, as they were well in advance of the natural season of the lakeside

[43] For example, Broda and Carrasco and their associates in the cited works; Johanna Broda de Casas, "Estratificación social y ritual en México", in *Religion in Mesoamerica: XII Round Table* (Mexico, 1972), pp. 179–92.
[44] For example, Warwick Bray, "Civilizing the Aztecs", in J. Friedman and M. J. Rowlands (eds.), *The Evolution of Social Systems* (Pittsburgh, 1978), pp. 373–98.
[45] For *chinampa* agriculture, see Michael D. Coe, "The Chinampas of Mexico", in *New World Archeology: Readings from the Scientific American* (San Francisco, 1974), pp. 231–9; Jeffrey Parsons, "The Role of Chinampa Agriculture in the Food Supply of Aztec Tenochtitlán", in Charles E. Cleland (ed.), *Cultural Change and Continuity* (New York, 1976), pp. 233–57.

fields. I would further argue that the *chinampas* not only made Tenochtitlán experientially an agricultural city, and that the plants so raised provided essential ritual equipment – models of what was to come – for ceremonies designed to influence growth in the open fields, but that those highly visible *chinampa* manipulations provided the model for men's part in the natural order, and for their role in aiding the growth of essential foods. In the Feast of the Flaying of Men, when the *chinampa* city turned from the business of war to the growing of things, those manipulations of earth, water, sun and seed through which men found their sustenance were explored through the symbolic medium of the human body, and the interdependence between agriculturalist and warrior set out.

Aztecs called human blood, most particularly human blood deliberately shed, "most precious water".[46] They understood it to be a non-renewable resource, so its value was enhanced. It was thought to have extraordinary fertilizing power. The creation myths, confused and contradictory as they might be on the role of particular "deities", pivot on the creative efficacy of shed blood, as when the great darkness which preceded this Fifth Sun was dispersed only when a little pustular god threw himself into the fire, to be transformed into the Sun. But the Sun only came to move – that is to be alive – when the other gods had spilled their blood, some voluntarily, others unwillingly. A singularly terrifying creation story, and the one most often assumed in Nahuatl texts, tells of the gods Quetzalcoatl and Tezcatlipoca gazing down on the great earth monster swimming in the primeval waters. They went down and seized her by her giant limbs, and wrenched her body in half, one part forming the sky, the other the earth. Then the other gods descended, and from her hair they created trees, flowers and herbs; from her skin, grass and flowers; from her eyes, wells, springs and small caverns; from her mouth, rivers and large caves; from her nose mountain valleys; from her shoulders, mountains. This terrible creature cried out in the night and refused to bring forth fruit until she was soaked in human blood and fed with human hearts. When satisfied, she brought forth the plants which provide man's sustenance. It is she who is obsessively represented on the underside of the ritual vessels designed to receive human blood and hearts. Whatever icons they bear on their upper surfaces, whatever great forces they invoke,

---

[46] It is moot whether one should say "deliberately" or "voluntarily" here. Even tribute slaves who went to their deaths as representations of aspects of the deities were in a sense thought of as "volunteers", in that they had submitted to ritual preparation. The warrior's death on the stone or in battle, however little the result of a particular act of choice, was implicit in the vocation of warrior.

underneath she is there, her insatiable maw wide open, great claws at elbows and knees, in the squatting position Aztec women adopted to give birth.[47]

So much, for the moment, for blood. Consider now the experience which participation in the gladiatorial ritual brought the captor. The conventional rewards for the warrior were public adulation, the presentation of insignia by the ruler, gifts of capes, flowers, tobacco pipes, which could then be proudly displayed. For many evenings after Xipe's festival young warriors gathered to adorn themselves and to dance before Moctezuma's palace. Sometimes Moctezuma himself, flanked by the other two rulers of the Triple Alliance, came dancing slowly out through the gates to join them: the might of the Aztec empire on display. Later came more exuberant dancing with the women of the city.

From all that festivity the captor was excluded. For all those days he and his kin were in a state of penance, eating meagrely, prohibited from washing, living secluded from the ordinary pleasures. For those days he was engaged in a different zone. The young man he had captured had been close to him in age, aspirations, prowess. He had tended him through the days before the ceremony, through his unmaking as the warrior, his making as the victim. And he had watched his captive's performance in an agony of identification: it was his own prowess being tested there on the stone. Then came a different intimacy, as he flayed the young body he had known in life and saw youths who sought to participate in his glory clamber into the dank skin. In a society which passionately valued cleanliness and treasured sweet scents, he and his kin had to live in a stench of corruption for the full twenty days. Then, at the end of the period of penance, he struggled for the last time into the crumbling, stinking shroud, to experience its transformation, its slow turning into matter, until, like the pierced casing of the maize seed, it was cast off and sealed away in a cave at the base of Xipe's pyramid, and so returned to the earth.

The explosion of relief which followed the casting off of the skins – the great cleansing and washing, initially with cornmeal to get off the grease, and then a sequence of progressively more playful and rowdy re-enactments of the festival – suggests the strain for those warriors

---

[47] "Histoire du Mechique", ed. Eduard de Jonghe, *Journal de la Société des américanistes*, new ser., ii (1905), pp. 1–42, esp. pp. 28–9; *Codex Chimalpopoca: anales de Cuauhtitlán y leyenda de los soles*, trans. Primo Feliciano Velázquez (Mexico, 1945); *Florentine Codex*, bk. 3, ch. 1; bk. 7, app.

"privileged" to be taken through the ritual glass to confront what lies on the other side of the adulation, the tobacco pipes, the plumes, the grand display. Just as the captive was rehearsed at the stone, so his captor rehearsed through those days his own death and decay; for the transformation of his own flesh into vegetable matter. The Nahuatl word *tonacayotl* means "things of the sun's warmth", that is, the fruits of the earth. It is also used metaphorically to mean "our flesh".[48] When the kin took into their mouths the morsel of human flesh and the stew of dried maize kernels – maize in its least modified form – the lesson they were being taught was that the two substances, perceptually so different, were of the same stuff, although at different points in the cycle. While we transmute bread and wine into flesh and blood, reflecting the centrality of man in our cosmology, they saw human flesh and human blood as transmuted into sacred maize and sacred water. Our "man is dust and will be dust again" focuses on the pathos of the brief reign of the flesh: for them man's flesh has been, is and will be again part of the vegetable cycle. (Maize was the only deity always represented in the terms of a natural human biography.) The Flayed Lord Xipe Totec sang of the identity of the tender maize and the warrior flesh it would become:

> I am the tender corn
> Of jade my heart is made
> The gold of rain I'll see
> My heart will be refreshed
> The fledgling man grow firm
> The man of war be born.[49]

The "man of war" was Cinteotl, Young Lord Maize Cob, who would at his harvesting at the end of the agricultural season lead his warriors out to war. (See Plate 8.)

The body of the warrior captive was disassembled with extraordinary care, and allocated very deliberately: the warrior lock to the captor; the heart, the "precious Eagle Cactus fruit", offered to the Sun; the blood to give drink to the Sun and all the stone images, the skin to be worn through all the days of the festival, and then laid away; the flesh to the captor's kin and to Moctezuma; the head skewered on the skull rack. Further, the thighbone, scraped or boiled clean of flesh, was draped with

[48] The most convenient Nahuatl dictionary remains Remi Simeón, *Dictionnaire de la langue nahuatl ou mexicaine* (Graz, 1963). See also Alonso de Molina, *Vocabulario en lengua castellana y mexicana, 1571* (Madrid, 1944 edn.).

[49] *Florentine Codex*, bk. 2, app., p. 240.

PLATE 8. Facsimile copy of codex Borbonicus (early 16th century), fol. 13. Detail depicting Tlazolteotl, aspect of Tlaltecuhtli, wearing a flayed skin and bringing forth the Maize God (vellum). Private Collection/ Jean-Pierre Courau/ The Bridgeman Art Library. Original located in Bibliothèque de l'Assemblée Nationale, Paris.

the captive's warrior jacket and victim's heron plume and set up as a sacred object in the courtyard of the captor. Only small parts of that so careful disassembling had to do with the human and social world: the taking of the warrior lock, which spoke of valour and the right to tribute goods, and the setting up of the thighbone as the sacred possession of the captor. It is possible that the bone, along with that other piece of bone the skull, was further associated with the dead warrior's lineage, and more widely with seed in general. Distinguishing bone from flesh mattered to the Aztecs: it was a preoccupation in many ceremonies, and after natural death the bones were separated from the flesh by burning, and then carefully "interred". It is only our predilection which identifies skulls swiftly and exclusively with death: in Mexican painted and carved representations they are insistently associated with fertility beings. The great temple skull racks which so oppressed the Spaniards probably spoke of more than the desire to count coup, while the interred bones of the Aztec dead were offered collective commemoration as the forefathers in the domestic ritual of Izcalli, and as paradigm hunters in the festival of Quecholli.[50]

The earliest Nahuatl account we have of the parts of the body is from the Florentine Codex, and is one of the sections of that compilation most heavily marked by European influence and categories. Nonetheless, the descriptions are suggestive. Blood is described as "Our blood, our redness, our liquid, our freshness, our growth, our life blood . . . it wets the flesh, it moistens it like clay, it refreshes it, it reaches the surface . . . it strengthens one . . . one is greatly strengthened. . . . " Blood vessels are likened to reeds. The analogies between the movement of blood through the flesh and that of water through the earth are vivid. The description of the heart relates it closely to the sun: it is "round, hot, that by which there is existence. It makes one live. . . . "[51] Unhappily for my case there is no general account given of bone, and in the specific references to particular bones

---

[50] Jill Furst, in her penetrating commentary on a Mixtec codex, notes the skull/fertility connection, and explores the possibility that bone was understood as seed. Jill Leslie Furst, *Codex Vindobonensis Mexicanus, i: A Commentary* (The Vienna Codex) (Albany, N.Y., 1978). For the maize-flesh transformation, see Willard Gingerich, "Tlaloc, His Song", *Latin American Indian Literatures*, i no. 2 (1977), pp. 79–88. To pursue these connections fully would involve the reconstruction of Aztec understandings of the processes of human and vegetable reproduction. Alfredo López Austin, *Cuerpo humano e ideología: las concepciones de los antiguos náhuas*, 2 vols. (Mexico, 1980), provides relevant information and superb scholarly exposition, focusing on Aztec understandings of the mind-body problem. For the Izcalli offerings, see *Florentine Codex*, bk. 2, p. 167; for Quecholli, see *ibid.*, pp. 135–6.

[51] *Florentine Codex*, bk. 10, ch. 27, pp. 128, 130–2. For an analysis of the material relating to the body and disease collected by Sahagún, see Alfredo López Austin, "Sahagún's

no association with seed. However, myth lends some support to the identification. After this Fifth World had been made, Quetzalcoatl went down into the underworld to beg the bones of the men of an earlier creation from the lord of Mictlán. Initially the ruler agreed, but as Quetzalcoatl gathered them up the Death Lord changed his mind and sent orders that Quetzalcoatl be stopped. In his hurry to get away Quetzalcoatl dropped the bones, but he snatched up the broken fragments and made his escape. Cihuacoatl, an aspect of Earth Mother, ground the bones like maize kernels on her grinding stone. The gods then moistened them with blood drawn from their penises, and from the soft dough so formed man and woman emerged.

What we have in that careful analysis of the human body, an analysis at once physical and conceptual, is the setting out in terms of its components of those elements the Aztecs saw as being manipulated in *chinampa* agriculture, and which they identified as those which made up the world: human flesh being equated with maize, vegetable foods and the earth itself; human blood with rain and flowing water; the human heart with the sun's heat; and (this less confidently) human bone with seed. Note that this analysis was performed upon the body of a great warrior. While the same essential understanding must have informed all accounts of the relationship between the human and the natural order, the Aztecs, specialists in warfare, chose to render it most explicit when dramatizing the unobvious but crucial connection between the feats of warriors and the food of men.

Notions of an afterlife have their place here. Aztecs understood that men who died by water-related accident or disease returned to a springtime world with Tlaloc, He who Makes Things Sprout, and who manifests himself in rain and the mountains. (Tlaloc's chosen ones were, atypically, buried without preliminary burning.) Babies who died so young that they had not been committed to this world were buried by the grain bins, and thought to have returned, still unblemished, from whence they came. Those who died in battle (including women dead in childbirth) and those who died on the killing stone went to a warrior paradise. And all others, regardless of rank, travelled for four bitter and bleak years through the increasingly chill nine layers of the underworld until they arrived at the lowest level, presented their gifts to the Death Lord, and dissolved into Nothingness – or, rather, into Everything, for "there is our common home, there is our common place of perishing; there, there is an enlarging

Work and the Medicine of the Ancient Nahuas: Possibilities for Study", in Edmonson (ed.), *Sixteenth-Century Mexico*, pp. 205–24.

of the earth where forever it [the individual life] hath ended. . . . "[52] After that four-year journey, the "person" had quite gone. For all of the four years kin made offerings of garments and equipment to ease the pains of the journey: the journey completed and the four years passed, the ceremonies ceased.[53]

It is often said that those who died a warrior's death, in battle or on the stone, escaped this general annihilation of self. It is true that in the course of a moving prayer addressed to the dangerous god Tezcatlipoca, warriors are said to "attain the Sun . . . the turquoise prince", and there to live "forever": there always, "forever, perpetually, time without end, they rejoice, they live in abundance, where they suck the different flowers. . . . "[54] That emphasis on the permanence of their tenure in the warrior paradise is unusual: much more frequently we are told that the warrior reward was to spend the four years of transition in attendance on the Sun, shouting, singing, displaying – the joys of the warrior house – as they escorted him from his dawning to the zenith, and basked in his warmth. (From the zenith to the west his escort was provided by the Women Warriors, a very much more sinister group.) Then, after four years, "they changed into precious birds; hummingbirds, orioles, yellow birds . . . chalky butterflies, featherdown butterflies; they sucked the honey from the flowers there where they dwelt. And here upon earth they came to suck honey from the various flowers. . . . "[55] There is no suggestion in either case that their awareness was continuous with that of this world; rather, "they lived drunk . . . not knowing, no longer remembering, the affairs of the day, the affairs of the night". Generalized warriors had become generalized birds and butterflies, dancing endlessly, anonymously, without memory in the sun. They enjoyed no dispensation from that final dissolution of self.

There was nothing "personal" in the relationship between men and those powers which, for want of a better term, we call by the altogether misleading word "gods". The first Spanish friars unsurprisingly thought in terms of pantheons when faced with the astonishing array of names and images which were paid reverence by the natives. Generations of iconographers and historians of religion spent years in the construction of ingenious theologies to bring order to what seemed a shimmering mist of the sacred. But now there is a growing consensus that what Aztecs meant by all these names and images was the invocation of different aspects of

---

[52] *Florentine Codex*, bk. 3, app., ch. 1, p. 41.
[53] *Ibid.*, p. 44.
[54] *Ibid.*, bk. 6, ch. 3, p. 13.
[55] *Ibid.*, bk. 3, app., ch. 1, p. 49.

relatively few great natural forces or principles, and a commentary on the relationships between them – as when Earth was addressed as Our Grandmother, Mother of the Sacred Ones, She who Eats our Filth, Heart of the Earth, Mother of our Sustenance, and so on. Aztec sculpture (like the Aztec language and like the construction of ritual objects) exhibits the same compiling mode whereby icons, most of them sturdily naturalistic representations of hearts, flowers, skulls, serpents, are compiled into remarkably abstract commentaries on the nature of things: a kind of metaphysical poetry in stone.

The great forces thus invoked and reflected upon had no engagement with man, with one exception. The exception was Tezcatlipoca, invoked as the Night Wind, the Enemy on Both Sides, the Youth, the Lord of the Close Vicinity. He was arbitrary, the personification of capricious power, coming among men from time to time to wreak casual havoc and dispense casual rewards. He was associated with sorcerers, who injure men wantonly and by stealth, and with the jaguar, with its superb annihilating power. He was also the deity associated with human rulership. Neither with him, nor with the more abstract natural elements, was there any hint of a contract. There was instead a key word in Nahuatl, *tequitl*, which can be roughly translated as "debt", "levy" or "tribute", but carrying with it a strong implication of what we might call "vocation", being applied to the whole-hearted performance of one's obligatory occupation in the world. It was used most insistently, however, to describe the offerings made of one's own blood, in the routine daily offerings, or on the battlefield or the killing stone. Only in those two places did the individual wholly and completely pay his or her "debt". But all forms of the payment were penitential, and some grievously so. In a great warrior festival midway through the season of war, a representation of Huitzilopochtli was moulded out of a rich dough of maize and seeds (its "bones", by the way, being separately constructed). It was killed by a blow to its vegetable heart in the presence of all the military chiefs, and the heart presented to the ruler. Each year the body was divided in rotation between the paired warrior houses in Tenochtitlán and the sister but subordinate city of Tlatelolco. All the members of the two warrior houses ate a fragment of the dough. The ingestion initiated a year of such strenuous penance and obligation that men were driven to pawn their land or their labour, or even to seek a once-for-all settlement of their "debt" through death in battle rather than endure it to the end.[56]

[56] *Ibid.*, pp. 6–9.

To eat the flesh of Huitzilopochtli was a heavy thing. Thus the young warriors began to learn the lesson – a lesson only to be learnt in the ritual zone, not on the field of battle – of what it was to be a warrior. The lesson took time to learn, and had been learnt best by those who had risen to eminence and so, for example, had had the dark experience of offering a captive at the gladiatorial stone. The rough exuberance of the warrior youth gave way to sedate melancholy for those who knew how fleeting were the pleasures of this life, its riches, its public acclaim, and how heavy the burden of humanity.

The tempo and dramatic structuring of the ritual at the gladiatorial stone, as of many other Aztec rituals, reiterated the same understanding. We are used to thinking of ritual as fully scripted, so releasing men from distracting nervousness. Victor Turner has borrowed the notion of "flow" from the psychologist Mihali Cjikszentimhalyi to bring this quality into focus. Cjikszentimhalyi identifies flow as "the holistic sensation present when we act with total involvement"; "the state in which action follows action according to an internal logic which seems to need no conscious intervention on our part", as when a game's rules exclude from the skilled players' awareness as irrelevant most of the "noises" which make up our daily reality. The rules simplify and focus, and above all facilitate the experience of intense but harmonious and fluent action. Turner sees an equivalent "flow" experience as being achieved in ritual where, with self-consciousness reduced through drugs, vigil, chants or fasting, action and awareness fuse as attention centres on a limited stimulus field, so that only the "now" matters.[57] This is interesting in that it is an accurate description of the situation of a number of the protagonists in this ritual, above all of the victim who is scripted to the end. But for others – the attacking warriors, the anxious captor – insecurity is scripted in; the risk that the flow will be interrupted, and the airy structures of the "really real" collapse. The Aztecs characterized their universe as composed of heavens above and underworlds below this seen world, those heavens and underworlds being stable and enduring. This layer, Tlalticpactli, "on earth", the layer manifest to the senses, they characterized as chronically unstable, and called it "that which changes". That understanding of the fragility of the perceived world, and of human arrangements within it, could be dramatized by making human statuses uncertain: the triumphant warrior does not display his status as his captive fights there on the

---

[57] Victor Turner, "Variations on a Theme of Liminality", in Sally F. Moore and Barbara G. Myerhoff (eds.), *Secular Ritual* (Amsterdam, 1977), pp. 36–52.

PLATE 9. Aztec stone relief of Tlaltecuhtli, the Earth Lord, found in the Templo Mayor precinct of Mexico-Tenochtitlán (note the fanged jaws at knees and elbows, and the sacrificial knife "tongue"). Instituto Nacional de Antropología e Historia, Mexico.

stone; he strives to achieve it afresh. That constant challenge and testing structured all the hierarchies.

The deliberate insertion into ritual of the problematical and the unpredictable, like the capriciousness attributed to the sole interventionist god Tezcatlipoca, spoke of the uncertainty of the things of this world. Ephemerality made those things the more treasured. Aztec "lyric poetry" strikes an easy and mistaken response from the European reader, with its pretty imagery of falling flowers and misty patios (in Aztec reality, images of death on the stone). But the elegiac "where have all the flowers gone?" note is correctly recognized. Only briefly were men warmed by the sun in this world, between the dark and the dark. The particular beauties which most profoundly moved them – the shimmer of feathers, the shaped sounds of a chanted poem, the scent of a flower, the translucence of fragile jade – were moving precisely because they were as ephemeral as the lives of men.[58]

"Courage", in such a context, becomes a complex notion. There seem to have been two kinds of bravery recognized in the Aztec fighting man which, although touched by the connotations of class, were far from exhausted by them. One was the attribute of those warriors like the "shorn ones" or the "shaven-headed Otomi" who hurled themselves heedlessly into the fray. Such men were richly rewarded and highly valued.[59] But they were not accorded positions of authority, nor unqualified social approval. In one of the great homilies in which a father instructs his son in correct and controlled social demeanour, the "so-called furious in war" who goes "foolishly" encountering his death is classified along with the clown and buffoon as one who understands nothing and lives for vanities and acclaim.[60] He knows no fear because he has no knowledge. Admiration is reserved for the warrior who is morally informed; who understands his obligation. He will go humbly and quietly in this world, watchful, prudent; but when the Earth Lord Tlaltecuhtli stirs, "openeth his mouth, parteth his lips", when the flame of war is kindled, he will be ready. (See Plate 9.) The same great prayer to Tezcatlipoca which acknowledges the anguish of the bereaved kinsfolk also acknowledges the anguish of the true warriors, "those who suffer pain, who suffer torment in their hearts" and ask that they be given their only release, their only ease – the final encounter with Tezcatlipoca:

Show him the marvel. May his heart not falter in fear. May he desire, may he long for the flowery death by the obsidian knife. May he savor the scent, savor the freshness, savor the sweetness of the darkness . . . Take his part. Be his friend.[61]

---

[58] For the songs, see *Poesía náhuatl*, ed. Angél Maria Garibay K[intana], 3 vols. (Mexico, 1964–8). Excellent translations of some of the songs are to be found in Miguel Leon-Portilla (ed.), *Native Mesoamerican Spirituality* (New York and Toronto, 1980). The sacred songs are in *Florentine Codex*, bk. 2, app.; the "Prayers to Tezcatlipoca" and the great song to Tlaloc are in bk. 6, chs. 1–9.

[59] *Florentine Codex*, bk. 10, ch. 6, pp. 23–4.

[60] Ibid., bk. 6, ch. 22, p. 123.

[61] Ibid., bk. 6, ch. 3, pp. 11–14.

And this to the "Enemy on Both Sides".

When we hear an official rhetoric of acute self-control, and watch scenes of extraordinary public violence, we are not confronting some unresolved social dilemma of how to enjoy the profits of military expansion without having to bear with socially disruptive warriors. Aztec rhetoric and Aztec ritual were unified in the endeavour to sustain a social order sufficiently in harmony with the natural order to survive within it. To describe as "violence" the deliberate sequence of bloody acts which we see brought into the frame and focus of ritual action is to assume that their point lay in their destructiveness. But the crucial understandings which grounded those killings and slow dismemberings were that human flesh and maize – "maize" as metonym for all vegetable sustenance – were the same matter in different transformations; that the transformations were cyclic, and the cycles constantly in jeopardy; and that men's actions played a part recognized as small but, given the delicacy of the balance, always potentially decisive in maintaining the sequence of those transformations, and so men's slight purchase on existence.

They were bleak understandings, reducing man to object, and declaring human society to be peripheral, important only to itself. It took courage enough, and long years of training, to accept them.

2

"Fierce and Unnatural Cruelty"

Cortés and the Conquest of Mexico

I

THE CONQUEST OF MEXICO matters to us because it poses a painful question: How was it that a motley bunch of Spanish adventurers, never numbering much more than four hundred or so, was able to defeat an Amerindian military power on its home ground in the space of two years? What was it about Spaniards, or about Indians, that made so awesomely implausible a victory possible? The question has not lost its potency through time, and as the consequences of the victory continue to unfold has gained in poignancy.

Answers to that question came easily to the men of the sixteenth century. The conquest mattered to Spaniards and to other Europeans because it provided their first great paradigm for European encounters with an organized native state;[1] a paradigm that quickly took on the potency and the accommodating flexibility of myth. In the early 1540s, a mere twenty years after the fall of Mexico-Tenochtitlán before the forces led by Hernando Cortés, Juan Ginés Sepúlveda, chaplain and chronicler to the Spanish emperor Charles V, wrote a work that has been described as

---

[1] Anthony Padgen notes several editions of Hernando Cortés's letters to his emperor in five languages between 1522 and 1525; *The Fall of Natural Man* (Cambridge, 1982), 58.

An earlier version of this paper, "Cortés, Signs and the Conquest of Mexico," has been published in Anthony Grafton, ed., *Culture and Communication in Early Modern Europe* (Philadelphia, 1990). It was first presented before the Shelby Cullom Davis Center for Historical Research, Princeton University.

Article originally published as "'Fierce and Unnatural Cruelty': Cortés and the Conquest of Mexico," in Representations, Vol. 33 (Winter 1991): 65–100. © 1991 The Regents of the University of California. Reprinted with permission.

"the most virulent and uncompromising argument for the inferiority of the American Indian ever written." Sepúlveda had his spokesman recite "thc history of Mexico, contrasting a noble, valiant Cortés with a timorous, cowardly Moctezuma, whose people by their iniquitous desertion of their natural leader demonstrated their indifference to the good of the commonwealth."[2] By 1585 the Franciscan Fray Bernardino de Sahagún had revised an earlier account of the Conquest, written very much from the native point of view and out of the recollections of native Mexicans, to produce a version in which the role of Cortés was elevated, Spanish actions justified, and the whole conquest presented as providential.[3]

The Mexican Conquest as model for European-native relations was reanimated for the English-speaking world through the marvelously dramatic *History of the Conquest of Mexico* written by W. H. Prescott in the early 1840s, a bestseller in those glorious days when History still taught lessons.[4] The lesson that great history taught was that Europeans will triumph over natives, however formidable the apparent odds, because of cultural superiority, manifesting itself visibly in equipment but residing much more powerfully in mental and moral qualities. Prescott presented Spanish victory as flowing directly out of the contrast and the relationship between the two leaders: the Mexican ruler Moctezuma, despotic, effete, and rendered fatally indecisive by the "withering taint" of an irrational religion, and his infinitely resourceful adversary Cortés. Prescott found in the person of the Spanish commander the model of European man: ruthless, pragmatic, single-minded, and (the unfortunate excesses of Spanish Catholicism aside) superbly rational in his manipulative intelligence, strategic flexibility, and capacity to decide a course of action and to persist in it.[5]

[2] Ibid., 117, referring to Juan Ginés de Sepúlveda's "Democrates secundus sive de justis causis belli apud Indos."

[3] S. L. Cline, "Revisionist Conquest History: Sahagún's Revised Book XII," in J. Jorge Klor de Alva, H. B. Nicholson, and Eloise Quiñones Keber, eds., *The Work of Bernardino de Sahagún, Pioneer Ethnographer of Sixteenth-Century Aztec Mexico* (Albany, N.Y., 1988). The claim as to the providential, indeed miraculous character of the Spanish achievement was not novel, having been made earlier by Fray Toribio de Motolinía in his *History of the Indians of New Spain* (1541), trans. Elizabeth Andros Foster (New York, 1950). It infuses Franciscan attitudes as described by John Leddy Phelan, *The Millennial Kingdom of the Franciscans in the New World*, 2nd ed. (Berkeley, 1970).

[4] W. H. Prescott, *History of the Conquest of Mexico and the History of the Conquest of Peru* (New York, n.d.).

[5] For Prescott see the fine study by David Levin, *History as Romantic Art* (Harbinger, N.Y., 1963); and more succinctly in his "History as Romantic Art: Structure, Characterization, and Style in *The Conquest of Mexico*," *Hispanic American Historical Review* 39, no. 1 (February 1959): 20–45.

The general contours of the Prescottian fable are still clearly discernible in the most recent and certainly the most intellectually sophisticated account of the Conquest, Tzvetan Todorov's *The Conquest of America: The Question of the Other*. Confronted by the European challenge, Todorov's Mexicans are "other" in ways that doom them. Dominated by a cyclical understanding of time, omen-haunted, they are incapable of improvization in face of the unprecedented Spanish challenge. Although "masters in the art of ritual discourse," they cannot produce "appropriate and effective messages"; Moctezuma, for example, pathetically sends gold "to convince his visitors to leave the country." Todorov is undecided as to Moctezuma's own view of the Spaniards, acknowledging the mistiness of the sources; he nonetheless presents the "paralyzing belief that the Spaniards were gods" as a fatal error. "The Indians' mistake did not last long...just long enough for the battle to be definitely lost and America subject to Europe," which would seem to be quite long enough.[6]

By contrast Todorov's Cortés moves freely and effectively, "not only constantly practicing the art of adaptation and improvisation, but also being aware of it and claiming it as the very principle of his conduct." A "specialist in human communication," he ensures his control over the Mexican empire (in a conquest Todorov characterizes as "easy") through "his mastery of signs." Note that this is not an idiosyncratic individual talent, but a European cultural capacity grounded in "literacy," where writing is considered "not as a tool, but as an index of the evolution of mental structures": it is that evolution which liberates the intelligence, strategic flexibility, and semiotic sophistication through which Cortés and his men triumph.

In what follows I want to review the grounds for these kinds of claims about the nature of the contrast between European and Indian modes of thinking during the Conquest encounter, and to suggest a rather different account of what was going on between the two peoples. First, an overview of the major events. Analysts and participants alike agree that the Conquest falls into two phases. The first began with the Spanish landfall in April of 1519, and Cortés's assumption of independent command in defiance of the governor of Cuba, patron of Cortés and of the expedition; the Spaniards' march inland, in the company of coastal Indians recently conquered by the Mexicans, marked first by bloody battles and then by alliance with the independent province of Tlaxcala; their

[6] Tzvetan Todorov, *The Conquest of America: The Question of the Other*, trans. Richard Howard (New York, 1984), part 2, passim but esp. 63–67, 80–81, 86–89. For Todorov's rather metaphysical notion of the defeat enclosed within the Spanish victory, see p. 97.

uncontested entry into the Mexican imperial city of Tenochtitlan-Tlatelolco, a magnificent lake-borne city of 200,000 or more inhabitants linked to the land by three great causeways; the Spaniards' seizing of the Mexican ruler Moctezuma, and their uneasy rule through him for six months; the arrival on the coast of another and much larger Spanish force from Cuba under the command of Panfilo Narváez charged with the arrest of Cortés, its defeat and incorporation into Cortés's own force; a native "uprising" in Tenochtitlan, triggered in Cortés's absence by the Spaniards' massacre of unarmed warriors dancing in a temple festival; the expulsion of the Spanish forces, with great losses, at the end of June 1520 on the so-called "Noche Triste," and Moctezuma's death, probably at Spanish hands, immediately before that expulsion. End of the first phase. The second phase is much briefer in the telling, although about the same span in the living: a little over a year. The Spaniards retreated to friendly Tlaxcala to recover health and morale. They then renewed the attack, reducing the lesser lakeside cities, recruiting allies, not all of them voluntary, and placing Tenochtitlan under siege in May of 1521. The city fell to the combined forces of Cortés and an assortment of Indian "allies" in mid August 1521. End of the second phase.

Analysts of the conquest have concentrated on the first phase, drawn by the promising whiff of exoticism in Moctezuma's responses – allowing the Spaniards into his city, his docility in captivity – and by the sense that final outcomes were somehow immanent in that response, despite Moctezuma's removal from the stage in the midst of a Spanish rout a good year before the fall of the city, and despite the Spaniards' miserable situation in the darkest days before that fall, trapped out on the causeways, bereft of shelter and support, with the unreduced Mexicans before and their "allies" potential wolves behind. This dispiriting consensus as to Spanish invincibility and Indian vulnerability springs from the too eager acceptance of key documents, primarily Spanish but also Indian, as directly and adequately descriptive of actuality, rather than as the mythic constructs they largely are. Both the letters of Cortés and the main Indian account of the defeat of their city owe as much to the ordering impulse of imagination as to the devoted inscription of events as they occurred. Conscious manipulation, while it might well be present, is not the most interesting issue here, but rather the subtle, powerful, insidious human desire to craft a dramatically satisfying and coherent story out of fragmentary and ambiguous experience, or (the historian's temptation) out of the fragmentary and ambiguous "evidence" we happen to have to work with.

Against the consensus I place Paul Veyne's bracingly simple test: "Historical criticism has only one function: to answer the question asked of it by the historian: 'I believe that this document teaches me this: may I trust it to do that?'"[7] The document may tell us most readily about story-making proclivities, and so take us into the cultural world of the story maker. It may also tell us about actions, so holding the promise of establishing the patterns of conduct and from them inferring the conventional assumptions of the people whose interactions we are seeking to understand. It may tell us about sequences of actions that shed light on impulses and motivations less than acknowledged by the writer, or (when he is recording the actions of others) perhaps not even known to him. The following pages will yield examples of all of these. The challenge is to be at once responsive to the possibilities and yet respectful of the limitations of the material we happen to have.

The story-making predilection is powerfully present in the major Spanish sources. The messy series of events that began with the landfall on the eastern coast has been shaped into an unforgettable success story largely out of the narratives of Cortés and Bernal Díaz, who were part of the action; the superb irresistible forward movement that so captivated Prescott, a selection and sequence imposed by men practiced in the European narrative tradition, and writing, for all their artfully concealed knowledge of outcomes, when outcomes were known. The foot soldier Díaz, completing his "True History" of the Conquest in old age, can make our palms sweat with his account of yet another Indian attack, but at eighty-four he knew he was bequeathing to his grandchildren a "true and remarkable story" about the triumph of the brave.[8] The commander Cortés, writing his reports to the Spanish king in the thick of the events, had repudiated the authority of his patron and superior the governor of Cuba, and so was formally in rebellion against the royal authority. He was therefore desperate to establish his credentials. His letters are splendid fictions, marked by politic elisions, omissions,

---

[7] Veyne continues: "Other than the techniques of handling and checking documents, there is no more a method of history than one of ethnography or of the art of travelling," which might just possibly be true if the notion of "checking" is sufficiently expanded; Paul Veyne, *Writing History: Essay on Epistemology* (Middletown, Conn., 1984), 12.

[8] Bernal Díaz del Castillo, *Historia verdadera de la Conquista de la Nueva España*, introduction and notes by Joaquín Ramírez Cabañas (Mexico City, 1966), 40, 45. For information on Spanish and native Conquest-related materials, see Robert Wauchope, ed., *Handbook of Middle American Indians*, (Austin, Tex., 1964–76), vols. 12–15, *Guide to Ethnohistorical Sources*, ed. Howard F. Cline.

inventions, and a transparent desire to impress Charles of Spain with his own indispensability. One of the multiple delights in their reading is to watch the creation of something of a Horatio figure, an exemplary soldier and simple-hearted loyalist unreflectively obedient to his king and the letter of the law: all attributes implicitly denied by the beautiful control and calculation of the literary construction itself.[9]

The elegance of Cortés's literary craft is nicely indicated by his handling of a daunting problem of presentation. In his "Second Letter," written in late October 1520 on the eve of the second thrust against Tenochtitlan, he had somehow to inform the king of the Spaniards' first astonishment at the splendor of the imperial city, the early coups, the period of perilous authority, the inflow of gold, the accumulation of magnificent riches – and the spectacular debacle of the expulsion, with the flounderings in the water, the panic, the loss of gold, horses, artillery, reputation, and altogether too many Spanish lives. Cortés's solution was a most devoted commitment to a strict narrative unfolding of events, so the city is wondered at; Moctezuma speaks, frowns; the marketplace throbs and hums; laden canoes glide through the canals; and so on to the dark denouement. And throughout he continues the construction of his persona as leader: endlessly flexible, yet unthinkingly loyal; endlessly resourceful, yet fastidious in legal niceties; magnificently daring in strategy and performance, yet imbued with a fine caution in calculating costs.

J. H. Elliott and Anthony Pagden have traced the filaments of Cortés's web of fictions back to particular strands of Spanish political culture, and to his particular and acute predicament within it, explaining the theme of "legitimate inheritors returning" by demonstrating its functional necessity in Cortés's legalistic strategy, which in turn pivoted on Moctezuma's voluntary cession of his empire and his authority to Charles of Spain – a splendidly implausible notion, save that so many have believed it. Given the necessity to demonstrate his own indispensability, it is unsurprising that along the way Cortés should claim "the art of adaptation and improvisation" as "the very principle of his conduct," and that we, like his royal audience, should be impressed by his command of men and events: dominating and duping Moctezuma; neutralizing Spanish disaffection by appeals to duty, law, and faith; managing Indians with kind words, stern

---

[9] *Hernán Cortés: Letters from Mexico*, trans, and ed. Anthony Pagden, with an introduction by J.H. Elliott (New Haven, 1986), "Second Letter," 88. See also J.H. Elliott, "The Mental World of Hernán Cortés," *Transactions of the Royal Historical Society*, 5th ser., 17 (1967): 41–58.

justice, and displays of the superiority of Spanish arms and the priority of the Spanish god.

The "returning god-ruler" theory was powerfully reinforced by Sahagún's *Florentine Codex*, an encyclopedic account of native life before contact compiled from the recollections of surviving native informants. Book 12 deals with the Conquest. It introduces a Moctezuma paralyzed by terror, first by omens and then by the conviction that Cortés was the god Quetzalcoatl, Precious-Feather Serpent, returned.[10] We are given vivid descriptions of Moctezuma's vacillations, tremulous decisions, collapses of will, as he awaits the Spaniards' coming, and then of his supine acquiescence in their depredations, while his lords abandon him in disgust. Sahagún's was a very late-dawning story, making its first appearance thirty and more years after the Conquest, and by the Veyne test it conspicuously fails. In the closed politics of traditional Tenochtitlan, where age and rank gave status, few men would have had access to Moctezuma's person, much less his thoughts, and Sahagún's informants, young and inconsequential men in 1520, would not have been among those few. In the first phase they can report on certain events (the entry of the Spaniards into the city, the massacre of the warrior dancers) that were public knowledge, and to which they were perhaps witness, although their reporting, it is worth remembering, will be framed in accordance with Mexican notions of significance. They speak with authority and precision on the fighting, especially of the second phase, in which some at least seem to have been involved. But the dramatic description of the disintegration of Moctezuma, compatible as it is with "official" Spanish accounts, bears the hallmarks of a post-Conquest scapegoating of a leader who had indeed admitted the Spaniards to his city in life, and so was made to bear the weight of the unforeseeable consequences in death. What the informants offer for most of the first phase is unabashed mythic history, a telling of what "ought" to have happened (along with a little of what did) in a satisfying mix of collapsed time, elided episodes,

---

[10] Fray Bernardino de Sahagún, *Florentine Codex: General History of the Things of New Spain*, trans. Charles E. Dibble and Arthur J.O. Anderson (Salt Lake City, Utah, 1950–82); hereafter cited as *Florentine Codex*, with book, chapter, and page. Quetzalcoatl-Topiltzin, ruler of the mythic "Tollan," or Tula, the previous great imperial power in the valley, before he withdrew to the east in some shadowy former time, was ambiguously associated with Quetzalcoatl-Ehecatl, the Wind God. For the confusions clustering around the stories to do with the self-exiled Quetzalcoatl-Topiltzin, legendary ruler of Tollan, see H.B. Nicholson, "Topiltzin Quetzalcoatl of Tollan: A Problem in Mesoamerican Ethnohistory" (Ph.D. diss., Harvard University, 1957).

and dramatized encounters as they came to be understood in the bitter years after the Conquest. With the fine economy of myth Moctezuma is represented as being made the Spaniards' prisoner at their initial meeting, thenceforth to be their helpless toy, leading them to his treasures, "each holding him, each grasping him," as they looted and pillaged at will.[11] In the Dominican Diego Durán's account, completed sixty years after the Conquest, and built in part from painted native chronicles unknown to us, in part from conquistador recollections, this process of distillation to essential "truth" is carried even further, with Moctezuma pictured in a native account as being carried by his lords from his first meeting with Cortés already a prisoner, his feet shackled.[12] It is likely that Durán made a literal interpretation of a symbolic representation: in retrospective native understanding Moctezuma was indeed captive to the Spaniards, a shackled icon, from the first moments.

Throughout the first phase of the Conquest we confidently "read" Cortés's intentions, assuming his perspective and so assuming his effectiveness. The Spanish commander briskly promises his king "to take [Moctezuma] alive in chains or make him subject to Your Majesty's Royal Crown." He continues: "With that purpose I set out from the town of Cempoalla, which I renamed Sevilla, on the sixteenth of August with fifteen horsemen and three hundred foot soldiers, as well equipped for war as the conditions permitted me to make them."[13] There we have it: warlike intentions clear, native cities renamed as possessions in a new polity, an army on the move. Inured to the duplicitous language of diplomacy, we take Cortés's persistent swearing of friendship and the innocence of his intentions to Moctezuma's emissaries as transparent deceptions, and blame Moctezuma for not so recognizing them or, recognizing them, for failing to act.[14] But Cortés declared he came as an ambassador, and as an ambassador he appears to have been received. Even had Moctezuma

---

[11] *Florentine Codex*, 12.16.17–18, 45, 48–49.

[12] "This I saw in a painting that belonged to an ancient chieftain from the province of Texcoco. Moctezuma was depicted in irons, wrapped in a mantle and carried on the shoulders of his chieftains"; Fray Diego Durán, *Historia de las indias de Nueva España y islas de Tierra Firma*, ed. José F. Ramirez, 2 vols. plus atlas (Mexico City, 1967), chap. 74, pp. 541–42.

[13] Cortés, "Second Letter," 50.

[14] Cortés's own confusion deepens our confidence in our reading, as he aggressively seeks to collect what he called "vassals" along the way, with no demur from Moctezuma. For example, the lord "Pánuco" sent gifts, and freely offered to supply certain Spaniards in his region whom he took to be members of Cortés's party with food; "Second Letter," 54. See also the reception offered by "Sienchimalen," ibid. These were almost certainly not gestures of political subordination but the normal courtesies – the provision of supplies, and if necessary fuel and shelter – extended to official travelers within the more effectively

somehow divined the Spaniards' hostile intent, to attack without formal warning was not an option for a ruler of his magnificence.[15] We read Moctezuma's conduct confidently, but here our confidence (like Cortés's) derives from ignorance. Cortés interpreted Moctezuma's first "gifts" as gestures of submission or naive attempts at bribery. But Moctezuma, like other Amerindian leaders, communicated at least as much by the splendor and status of his emissaries, their gestures and above all their gifts, as by the nuances of their most conventionalized speech. None of those nonverbal messages could Cortés read, nor is it clear that his chief Nahuatl interpreter, Doña Marina, a woman and a slave, would or could inform him of the protocols in which they were framed: these were the high and public affairs of men. Moctezuma's gifts were statements of dominance, superb gestures of wealth and liberality made the more glorious by the arrogant humility of their giving: statements to which the Spaniards lacked both the wit and the means to reply. (To the next flourish of gifts, carried by more than a hundred porters and including the famous "cartwheels" of gold and silver, Cortés's riposte was a cup of Florentine glass and three holland shirts.)[16] The verbal exchanges for all of the first phase were not much less scrambled. And despite those reassuring inverted commas of direct reportage, all of those so-fluent speeches passed through a daisy chain of interpreters, with each step an abduction into a different meaning system, a struggle for some approximation of unfamiliar concepts. We cannot know at what point the shift from the Indian notion of "he who pays tribute," usually under duress so carrying no sense of obligation, to the Spanish one of "vassal," with its connotations of loyalty, was made, but we know the shift to be momentous. The identifiable confusions, which must be only a fraction of the whole, unsurprisingly ran both ways. For example, Cortés, intent on conveying

---

subdued Mexican territories. Where Cortés made the condition of "vassal" more explicit by requesting not food or carriers but gold, the request was denied.

[15] The lodging of the Spaniards in a royal palace is not especially remarkable, visiting rulers and ranking ambassadors being routinely luxuriously housed and feted, in the not unfamiliar determination to impress potentially troublesome visitors while keeping an eye on them. Durán, *Historia*, chap. 43; *Florentine Codex*, 12.15.41. Despite the intense traditional hostility between Tlaxcala and the Mexicans, a Mexican embassy numbering more than two hundred people sought out Cortés during his first stay in Tlaxcala, its members being permitted to come and go without hindrance. "Second Letter," 69. The phrasing of the *Florentine Codex* on the Spanish assault on the warrior dancers affords a dizzying perspective on Spanish-Mexican relations, the Spaniards being described as "friends" to that point, and then as having "risen up against us [the Mexicans]" to become "enemies"; 12.29.81.

[16] Díaz, *Historia*, chap. 39.

innocent curiosity, honesty, and flattery, repeatedly informed the Mexican ambassadors that he wished to come to Tenochtitlan "to look upon Moctezuma's face." That determination addressed to a man whose mana was such that none could look upon his face save selected blood kin must have seemed marvelously mysterious, and very possibly sinister.

So the examples of miscommunication multiply. In this tangle of missed cues and mistaken messages, "control of communications" seems to have evaded both sides equally. There is also another casualty. Our most earnest interrogations of the surviving documents cannot make them satisfy our curiosity as to the meaning of Moctezuma's conduct. Historians are the camp followers of the imperialists: as always in this European-and-native kind of history, part of our problem is the disruption of "normal" practice effected by the breach through which we have entered. For Cortés, the acute deference shown Moctezuma's person established him as the supreme authority of city and empire, and he shaped his strategy accordingly. In fact we know neither the nature and extent of Moctezuma's authority within and beyond Tenochtitlan, nor even (given the exuberant discrepancies between the Cortés and Díaz accounts) the actual degree of coercion and physical control imposed on him during his captivity. From the fugitive glimpses we have of the attitudes of some of the other valley rulers, and of his own advisers, we can infer something of the complicated politics of the metropolis and the surrounding city-states, but we see too little to be able to decode the range of Moctezuma's normal authority, much less its particular fluctuations under the stress of foreign intrusion. Against this uncertain ground we cannot hope to catch the flickering indicators of possible individual idiosyncrasy. We may guess, as we watch the pragmatic responses of other Indian groups to the Spanish presence, that as *tlatoani* or "Great Speaker" of the dominant power in Mexico, Moctezuma bore a special responsibility for classifying and countering the newcomers. From the time of his captivity we think we glimpse the disaffection of lesser and allied lords, and infer that disaffection sprang from his docility. We see him deposed while he still lived, and denigrated in death: as Cortés probed into Tenochtitlan in his campaign to reduce the city, the defenders would ironically pretend to open a way for him, "saying, 'Come in, come in and enjoy yourselves!' or, at other times, 'Do you think there is now another Moctezuma to do what you wish?'"[17] But I think we must resign ourselves to a heroic act of renunciation, acknowledging that much of Moctezuma's conduct must remain enigmatic. We cannot know how he categorized the newcomers,

---

[17] Cortés, "Third Letter," 188.

or what he intended by his apparently determined and certainly unpopular cooperation with his captors: whether to save his empire, his city, his position, or merely his own skin.[18] It might be possible, with patience and time, to clear some of the drifting veils of myth and mistake that envelop the encounters of the first phase, or at least to chart our areas of ignorance more narrowly.[19] But the conventional story of returning gods and unmanned autocrats, of an exotic world paralyzed by its encounter with Europe, for all its coherence and its just-so inevitabilities, is in view of the evidence like Eliza's progression across the ice floes: a matter of momentary sinking balances linked by desperate forward leaps.

Of Cortés we know much more. He was unremarkable as a combat leader: personally brave, an indispensable quality in one who would lead Spaniards, he lacked the panache of his captain Alvarado and the solidity and coolness of Sandoval. He preferred talk to force with Spaniards or Indians, a preference no doubt designed to preserve numbers, but also indicative of a personal style. He knew whom to pay in flattery, whom in gold, and the men he bought usually stayed bought. He knew how to stage a theatrical event for maximum effect, as in the plays concocted to terrify Moctezuma's envoys – a stallion, snorting and plunging as he scented a mare in estrus; a cannon fired to blast a tree. When he did use force he had a flair for doing so theatrically, amplifying the effect: cutting off the hands of fifty or more Tlaxcalan emissaries freely admitted into the Spanish camp, then mutilated as "spies"; a mass killing at Cholula; the shackling of Moctezuma while "rebellious" chiefs were burned before his palace in Tenochtitlan. He was careful to count every Spanish life, yet capable of conceiving heroic strategies – to lay siege to a lake-girt city requiring the prefabrication of thirteen brigantines on the far side of the mountains, eight thousand carriers to transport the pieces, their reassembly in Texcoco, the digging of a canal and the deepening of the lake for their successful launching. And he was capable not only of the grand design but of the construction and maintenance of the precarious alliances, intimidations, and promised rewards necessary to implement

[18] Unsurprisingly few commentators are prepared to be so austere. For an attractive display of indulgence, see R. C. Padden, *The Hummingbird and the Hawk* (Columbus, Ohio), 1967.

[19] Possible, but difficult: e.g., for art historians' divisions on the meanings of a pleasantly substantial and certainly pre-contact artifact, the "Hamburg Box," a superb lidded greenstone box carved on both inner and outer surfaces, compare Esther Pasztory, *Aztec Art* (New York, 1983), 255–56; and her "El arte Mexica y la Conquista Española," *Estudios de cultura Nahuatl* 17 (1983): 101–24; with H.B. Nicholson and Eloise Quiñones Keber, *The Art of Ancient Mexico: Treasures of Tenochtitlán* (Washington, D.C., 1983), 64–66.

it. In that extraordinary capacity to sustain a complex vision through the constant scanning and assessment of unstable factors, as in his passion and talent for control of self and others, Cortés was incomparable. (That concern for control might explain his inadequacies in combat: in the radically uncontrolled environment of battle, he had a tendency to lose his head.)

He was also distinguished by a peculiar recklessness in his faith. We know the Spaniards took trouble to maintain the signs of their faith even in the wilderness of Mexico; that bells marked the days with the obligatory prayers as they did in the villages of Spain; that the small supplies of wine and wafers for the Mass were cherished; that through the long nights in times of battle men stood patiently, waiting for the priests to hear their confessions, while the unofficial healer "Juan Catalan" moved softly about, signing the cross and muttering his prayers over stiffening wounds. We know their faith identified the idols and the dismembered bodies they found in the temples as the pitiless work of a familiar Devil. We know they drew comfort in the worst circumstances of individual and group disaster from the ample space for misfortune in Christian cosmology: while God sits securely in His heaven, all manner of things can be wrong with His world. Those miserable men held for sacrifice in Texcoco after the Spanish expulsion who left their forlorn messages scratched on a white wall ("Here the unhappy Juan Yuste was held prisoner") would through their misery be elevated to martyrdom.[20]

Even against that ground Cortés's faith was notably ardent, especially in his aggressive reaction to public manifestations of the enemy religion. In Cempoalla, with the natives cowed, he destroyed the existing idols, whitewashed the existing shrine, washed the existing attendants and cut their hair, dressed them in white, and taught these hastily refurbished priests to offer flowers and candles before an image of the Virgin. There is an intriguing elision of signs here. While the pagan attendants might have been clad suitably clerically, in long black robes like soutanes, with some hooded "like Dominicans," they also had waist-long hair clotted with human blood, and stank of decaying human flesh. Nonetheless he assessed them as "priests," and therefore fit to be entrusted with the Virgin's shrine.[21] Then having preached the doctrine "as well as any

---

[20] Cortés, "Third Letter," 184.
[21] Díaz, *Historia*, chap. 52. For a discussion see Richard C. Trexler, "Aztec Priests for Christian Altars: The Theory and Practice of Reverence in New Spain," in Paola Zambelli, ed., *Scienze credenze occulte livelli di cultura* (Florence, 1982), 175–96.

priest today," in Díaz's loyal opinion (filtered though it was through the halting tongues of two interpreters), he left daily supervision of the priests to an old crippled soldier assigned as hermit to the new shrine. Cortés moved on.[22]

The Cempoallan assault was less than politic, being achieved at the sword's point against the town on whose goodwill the little coastal fort of Vera Cruz would be most dependent. Cortés was not to be so reckless again, being restrained from too aggressive action by his chaplain and his captains, but throughout he appears to have been powerfully moved by a concern for the defense of the "honor" of the Christian god. It is worth remembering that for the entire process of the Conquest Cortés had no notion of the Spanish king's response to any of his actions. Only in September of 1523, more than two years after the fall of Tenochtitlan, and four and a half years after the Spanish landfall, did he finally learn that he had been appointed captain general of New Spain. It is difficult to imagine the effect of that prolonged visceral uncertainty, and (especially for a man of Cortés's temperament) of his crucial dependence on the machinations of men far away in Spain, quite beyond his control. Throughout the desperate vicissitudes of the campaign, as in the heroic isolation of his equivocal leadership, God was perhaps his least equivocal ally. That alliance required at best the removal of pagan idols and their replacement by Mary and the Cross, and at the least the Spaniards' public worship of their Christian images, the public statement of the principles of the Christian faith, and the public denunciation of human sacrifice, these statements and denunciations preferably being made in the Indians' most sacred places. Cortés's inability to let well alone in matters religious appears to have effected the final alienation of the Mexican priests and their demand for the Spaniards' death or expulsion from their uneasy perch in Tenochtitlan.[23] Cortés's claim of his early, total, and unresisted transformation of Mexican religious life through the destruction of their major idols was almost certainly a lie. (He had to suppress any mention of Alvarado's massacre of the warrior dancers in the main temple precinct as the precipitating factor in the Mexican "revolt" as too damaging to his story, for the Mexican celebrants would have been dancing under the serene gaze of the Virgin.) But the lie, like his accommodation to the cannibalism of his Tlaxcalan allies, was a strategic necessity impatiently borne. With victory all obligations would be discharged, and God's honor

[22] Díaz, *Historia*, chaps. 51, 52.
[23] Ibid., chap. 107.

vindicated.[24] That high sense of duty to his divine Lord and his courage in its pursuit must have impressed and comforted his men even as they strove to restrain him.

None of this undoubted flair makes Cortés the model of calculation, rationality, and control he is so often taken to be. There can be some doubt as to the efficacy of his acts of terror. It is true that after the "mutilated spies" episode the Tlaxcalans sued for peace and alliance, but as I will argue, routine acts of war in the European style were probably at least as destructive of Indian confidence of their ability to predict Spanish behavior as the most deliberate shock tactics.[25] The Spaniards' attack on the people of Cholula, the so-called "Cholula massacre," is a muddier affair. Cortés certainly knew the therapeutic effects of a good massacre on fighting men who have lived too long with fear, their sense of invincibility already badly dented by the Tlaxcalan clashes, and with the legendary warriors of Tenochtitlan, grown huge in imagination, still in prospect. As other leaders have discovered in other times, confidence returns when the invisible enemy is revealed as a screaming, bleeding, fleeing mass of humanity. But here Cortés was probably the unwitting agent of Tlaxcalan interests. Throughout the first phase honors in mutual manipulation between Spaniard and Indian would seem to be about even. The Cempoallan chief Cortés hoaxed into seizing Moctezuma's tax gatherers remained notably more afraid of Moctezuma in his far palace than of the hairy Spaniards at his elbow. Tricked into defiance of Moctezuma, he immediately tricked Cortés into leading four hundred Spaniards on a hot and futile march of fifteen miles in pursuit of phantom Mexican warriors in his own pursuit of a private feud, a deception that has been rather less remarked on.[26] There are other indications that hint at extensive native manipulations, guile being admired among Indians as much as it was among Spaniards, and Spanish dependence on Indian informants and translators was total. But they are indications only, given the relative

[24] In the ordinances he proclaimed in Tlaxcala in December 1520, preparatory to the great campaign against the lake cities, Cortés emphasized the necessary disciplines of war (no private booty, no gambling of weapons, no breakaway attacks, no insults or brawling in the ranks). But he prefaced it with the declaration that justified all: that the Spaniards' principal motive was to destroy idolatry and to bring the natives to the knowledge of God and of the Holy Catholic Faith. Without that primary justification, the war to come would be unjust, and everything taken in it liable to restitution: "Ordenanzas militares dadas por Hernando Cortés in Tlaxcallan," in Mario Hernandez Sánchez Barba, ed., *Hernán Cartés: Cartas y documentos* (Mexico City, 1963), 336–41.

[25] Cortés, "Second Letter," 60–62.

[26] Díaz, *Historia*, chaps. 46, 47, 51.

opacity and ignorance of the Spanish sources as to what the Indians were up to. Here I am not concerned to demonstrate the natives to have been as great deceivers as the Spaniards, but simply to suggest we have no serious grounds for claiming they were not.

Cortés's political situation was paradoxically made easier by his status as rebel. That saved him from the agonizing assessment of different courses of action: once gone from Cuba, in defiance of the governor, he could not turn back, save to certain dishonor and probable death. So we have the gambler's advance, with no secured lines back to the coast, no supplies, no reinforcements, the ships deliberately disabled on the beach to release the sailors for soldiering service and to persuade the faint-hearted against retreat. Beyond the beach lay Cuba, and an implacable enemy. The relentless march on Mexico impresses, until one asks just what Cortés intended once he had got there. We have the drive to the city, the seizing of Moctezuma – and then the agonizing wait by this unlikely Micawber for something to turn up, as the Spaniards, uncertainly tolerated guests, sat in the city, clutching the diminishing resource of Moctezuma's prestige as their only weapon. That "something" proved to be the Spanish punitive expedition, a couple of providential ships carrying gunpowder and a few reinforcements, and so a perilous way out of the impasse. Possibly Cortés had in mind a giant confidence trick: a slow process of securing and fortifying posts along the road to Vera Cruz and, then, with enough gold amassed, sending to the authorities in Hispaniola (bypassing Velázquez and Cuba) for ships, horses, and arms, which is the strategy he in fact followed after the retreat from Tenochtitlan.[27] It is nonetheless difficult (save in Cortés's magisterial telling of it) to read the performance as rational.[28]

It is always tempting to credit people of the past with unnaturally clear and purposeful policies: like Clifford Geertz's peasant, we see the bullet holes in the fence and proceed to draw the bull's-eyes around them. The temptation is maximized with a Cortés, a man of singular energy and decision, intent on projecting a self-image of formidable control of self and circumstance. Yet that control had its abrupt limits. His tense self-mastery, sustained in face of damaging action by others, could collapse into tears or sullen rage when any part of his own controlling analysis was exposed as flawed, as with his fury against Moctezuma for his "refusal"

[27] Ibid., chap. 95.
[28] As John Elliott puts it: "It would be hard to think of a crazier strategy." J. H. Elliott, *New York Review of Books*, 19 July 1984.

to quell the uprising in the city after Alvarado's attack on the unarmed dancers.[29] He had banked all on Moctezuma being the absolute ruler he had taken him to be. He had seized him, threatened him, shackled him to establish his personal domination over him. But whatever its normal grounds and span, Moctezuma's capacity to command, which was his capacity to command deference, had begun to bleed away from his first encounter with Spaniards and their unmannerliness, as they gazed and gabbled at the sacred leader.[30] It bled faster as they seized his person. Durán's account of Moctezuma pictured in native chronicles as emerging shackled from his first meeting with Cortés is "objectively" wrong, but from the Indian perspective right: the Great Speaker in the power of outsiders, casually and brutally handled, was the Great Speaker no longer.[31] Forced to attempt to calm his inflamed people, Moctezuma knew he could effect nothing; that his desacralization had been accomplished, first and unwittingly by Cortés, then, presumably, by a ritual action concealed from us; and that a new Great Speaker had been chosen while the old still lived: a step unprecedented to my knowledge in Mexican history.

Cortés could not acknowledge Moctezuma's impotence. Retrospectively he was insistent that his policy had been sound and had been brought down only through the accident of the Mexican ruler's final unreliability. Certainly his persistence in its defense after its collapse in debacle points to a high personal investment: intelligence is no bar to self-deception. Nonetheless there must have been some relief at the explosive end to a deeply uncanny situation, where experience had offered no guide to action in a looking-glass world of yielding kings and arrogant underlings; of riddling speech, unreadable glances, opaque silences. The sudden collapse of the waiting game liberated him back into the world of decisions, calculated violence, the energetic practicalities of war – the heady fiction of a world malleable before individual will.

His essential genius lay in the depth of his conviction, and in his capacity to bring others to share it: to coax, bully, and bribe his men, dream-led, dreamfed, into making his own gambler's throw; to participate in his own

---

[29] Díaz, *Historia*, chap. 126.

[30] Sahagún's informants emphasize physical contact far beyond Spanish reports, "recalling" Moctezuma as being prodded and pawed by any and all of the newcomers, with the disgrace of the unabashed glance marked equally keenly: "They caressed Moctezuma with their hands"; they "looked at him; they each looked at him thoroughly. They were continually active on their feet; they continually dismounted in order to look at him"; *Florentine Codex*, 12.16.43–46; Díaz, *Historia*, chap. 88.

[31] See note 30 above.

desperate personal destiny. Bernal Díaz recorded one of Cortés's speeches at a singularly low point on the first march to the city. With numbers already dangerously depleted, the remaining men wounded, cold, frightened, the natives ferocious, Cortés is reported as promising his men not wealth, not salvation, but deathless historical fame.[32] Again and again we see Cortés dare to cheat his followers in the distribution of loot and of "good-looking Indian women," but he never discounted the glory of their endeavors. Not the least factor in Cortés's hold over his men was his notary's gift for locating their situation and aspirations in reassuringly sonorous and legalistic terms: terms necessary to please the lawyers at home, who would finally judge their leader's case, but also essential for their own construction of an acceptable narrative out of problematical actions and equivocal experience. But he also lured them to acknowledge their most extreme fantasies; then he persuaded them, by his own enactment of them, that the fantasies were realizable.[33]

So Cortés, his men regrouped, his strategies evolved, stood ready for the second phase of the attack. What he was to experience in the struggle to come was to challenge his view of himself and his capacities, of the Mexican Indian, and of his special relationship with his God.

II

Analysts, save for military historians, have overwhelmingly concentrated on the first phase of the Conquest, assuming the consummation of Spanish victory to be merely a matter of applying a technological superiority: horsemen against pedestrian warriors, steel swords against wooden clubs, muskets and crossbows against bows and arrows and lances,

[32] "Recorded" is putting it rather too high: here we have to take the "captain's speech" for the literary convention it is. But it is, at best, close to what Cortés claims he said: at worst, the gist of what Díaz thought a man like Cortés ought to have said on such an occasion; Díaz, *Historia*, chap. 61, e.g., "Now and from henceforth, through God, the history books will make much more of this than of anything done in the past.... The most famous Roman captain has not achieved such great things as we have." Cf. "Second Letter," 63.

[33] For a contrary view of the whole conquest phenomenon as very much more pragmatic and routinized, see James Lockhart, *The Men of Cajamarca* (Austin, Tex., 1972). On the importance of the model of the Mexican Conquest for later conquerors: "[The Conquest of] Mexico had no major impact on Peru merely by virtue of some years' precedence.... Pizarro was certainly not thinking of Cortés and Moctezuma when he seized Atahualpa; he had been capturing *caciques* [chiefs] in Tierra Firme long before Mexico was heard of"; James Lockhart and Stuart B. Schwartz, *Early Latin America* (Cambridge, 1983), 84.

cannon against ferocious courage. I would argue that it is only for the second phase that we have sufficiently solid evidence to allow a close analysis of how Spaniards and Indians made sense of each other, and so to track down issues that must remain will-o'-the-wisps for the first phase. I would also argue that the final conquest was a very close-run thing: a view in which the combatants on both sides, as it happens, would agree. After the Spanish ejection from Tenochtitlan the Mexicans remained heavily favored in things material, most particularly manpower, which more than redressed any imbalance in equipment. Spanish technology had its problems: the miseries of slithering or cold-cramped or foundering horses, wet powder, the brutal weight of the cannon, and always the desperate question of supply. Smallpox, introduced into Mexico by one of Narváez's men, had swept through the native population, but its ravages had presumably affected Spanish "allies" equally with the Mexicans.[34] The sides were approximately matched in knowledge: if Cortés was to profit from his familiarity with the fortifications and functioning of the lake city, the Mexicans at last knew the Spaniards as enemies, and were under the direction of a ruler liberated from the ambiguities that appear to have bedeviled them earlier.

We tend to have a *Lord of the Flies* view of battle: that in deadly combat the veils of "culture" are ripped away, and natural man confronts himself. But if combat is not quite as cultural as cricket, its brutalities are nonetheless rulebound. Like cricket, it requires a sustained act of cooperation, with each side constructing the conditions in which both will operate, and so, where the struggle is between strangers, obliging a mutual "transmission of culture" of the shotgun variety. And because of its high intensities it promises to expose how one's own and other ways of acting and meaning are understood and responded to in crisis conditions, and what lessons about the other and about oneself can be learned in that intimate, involuntary, and most consequential communication.

The sources for the second phase are sufficiently solid. Given it is cultural assumptions we are after, equivocation in recollection and recording matter little. Cortés edits a debacle on the Tacuba causeway, where more than fifty Spaniards were taken alive through his own impetuosity, into a triumph of leadership in crisis; Díaz marvels at Spanish bravery under

---

[34] Skin afflictions were commonly understood as coming from Tezcatlipoca, the Mexican interventionist deity, but we do not know if the Mexicans identified smallpox pustules with more familiar lesions. As always, they noted the month of the epidemic's coming and of its diminishing (a span of sixty day signs), but smallpox does not appear in the *Florentine Codex* list of Spanish-related events (12.27–29.81–83).

the tireless onslaughts of savages; both are agreed as to the vocabulary through which they understand, assess, and record battle behavior. Sahagún's informants, able to report only bitter hearsay and received myth on the obscure political struggles of the first phase, move to confident detail in their accounts of the struggle for the city, in which at least some of them appear to have fought, naming precise locations and particular warrior feats; revealing through both the structure and the descriptions of the accounts their principles of battle. Those glimpses can be matched against admittedly fragmentary chronicles to yield the general contours of Indian battle behavior.

Here the usual caveats of overidealization apply. If all social rules are fictions, made "real" through being contested, denied, evaded, and recast as well as obeyed, "rules of war," war being what it is, are honored most earnestly in the breach. But in the warrior societies of Central Mexico, where the battlefield held a central place in the imagination, with its protocols rehearsed and trained for in the ordinary routines of life, the gap between principle and practice was narrow. War, at least war as fought among the dominant peoples of Mexico, and at least ideally, was a sacred contest, the outcome unknown but preordained, revealing which city, which local deity, would rightfully dominate another.[35] Something like equal terms were therefore required: to prevail by mere numbers or by some piece of treachery would vitiate the significance of the contest. So important was this notion of fair testing that food and weapons were sent to the selected target city as part of the challenge, there being no virtue in defeating a weakened enemy.[36]

The warriors typically met outside the city of the defenders. Should the attacking side prevail, the defenders abandoned the field and fled, and the victors swept unresisted into the city to fire the temple where the local deity had its place. That action marked victory in occurrence and record; the formal sign for conquest in the painted histories was a burning temple. Free pillage continued until the increasingly frantic pleas of the spokesmen for the defeated were heard, and terms of tribute set. Then the victors withdrew to their home city with their booty and their

---

[35] Wars of conquest waged against distant "barbarians" were a rather different matter. For an exhaustive description from a steadfastly pragmatic perspective, see Ross Hassig, *Aztec Warfare: Imperial Expansion and Political Control* (Norman, Okla., 1988). Dr. Hassig is persuaded that "in fact, Aztec [warrior] practices were shaped by political realities and practical necessities" (10). The question is to discover what the Aztec/Mexican understood those "realities and practical necessities" to be.

[36] Durán, *Historia*, chap. 34.

captives, including not only the warriors taken in the formal battle but "civilians" seized during the period of plunder. Their most significant captive was the image of the tutelary deity of the defeated city, to be held in the "god captive house" in Tenochtitlan. Defeat was bitter because it was a statement and judgment of inferiority of the defeated warriors, who had broken and run; a judgment the victorious warriors were only too ready to reinforce by savage mockery, and which was institutionalized by the imposition of tribute.[37]

The duration of the decision remained problematic. Defeated towns paid their tribute as a regular decision against further hostilities, but remained independent and usually notably disaffected, despite the conquering city's conviction of the legitimacy of their supremacy. Many towns in the valley, whether allied or defeated or intimidated by the Mexicans, paid their token tribute, fought alongside the Mexicans in Mexican campaigns, and shared in the spoils, but they remained mindful of their humiliation and unreconciled to their subordination. Beyond the valley the benefits of empire were commonly smaller, the costs greater, and disaffection chronic. The monolithic "Aztec empire" is a European hallucination: in this atomistic polity, the units were held together by the tension of mutual repulsion. (Therefore the ease with which Cortés could recruit "allies," too often taken as a tribute to his silver tongue, and therefore the deep confusion attending his constant use of that meaning-drenched word *vassal* to describe the relationship of subject towns first to Tenochtitlan, and later to the Spanish crown.)

If war was a sacred duel between peoples, and so between the "tribal" gods of those peoples, battle was ideally a sacred duel between matched warriors: a contest in which the taking of a fitting captive for presentation to one's own deity was a precise measure of one's own valor and one's own fate. One prepared for this individual combat by song, paint, and adornment with the sacred war regalia. (To go "always prepared for battle" in the Spanish style was unintelligible: a man carrying arms was only potentially a warrior.) The great warrior, scarred, painted, plumed, wearing the record of his victories in his regalia, erupting from concealment or looming suddenly through the rising dust, then screaming his war cry, could make lesser men flee by the pure terror of his presence: warriors

---

[37] Cf. the deliberate humiliation of the Tlatelolcan warriors, discovered hiding in the rushes after the Mexican victory, and ordered to quack. "Even today," Durán noted, decades after the debacle, "the Tlatelolca are called 'quackers' and imitators of water fowl. They are much offended by this name and when they fight the name is always recalled"; *Historia*, chap. 34, p. 264.

were practiced in projecting ferocity. His rightful, destined opponent was he who could master panic to stand and fight. There were maneuverings to "surprise" the enemy, and a fascination with ambush, but only as a device to confront more dramatically; to strike from hiding was unthinkable. At the outset of battle Indian arrows and darts flew thickly, but to weaken and draw blood, not to pierce fatally.[38] The obsidian-studded war club signaled warrior combat aims: the subduing of prestigious individual captives in single combat for presentation before the home deity.

In the desperation of the last stages of the battle for Tenochtitlan, the Mexican inhibition against battleground killing was somewhat reduced: Indian "allies" died, and Spaniards who could not be quickly subdued were killed, most often, as the Mexicans were careful to specify, and for reasons that will become clear, by having the backs of their heads beaten in. But the priority on the capture of significant antagonists remained. In other regards the Mexicans responded with flexibility to the challenges of siege warfare. They "read" Spanish tactics reasonably accurately: a Spanish assault on the freshwater aqueduct at Chapultepec was foreseen, and furiously, if fruitlessly, resisted. The brigantines, irresistible for their first appearance of the lake, were later lured into a carefully conceived ambush in which two were trapped. The horses' vulnerability to uneven ground, to attack from below, their panic under hails of missiles, were all exploited effectively. The Mexicans borrowed Spanish weapons: Spanish swords lashed to poles or Spanish lances to disable the horses; even Spanish crossbows, after captive crossbowmen had been forced to show them how the machines worked.[39] It was their invention and tenacity that forced Cortés to the desperate remedy of leveling structures along the causeways and into the city to provide the Spaniards with the secure ground they needed to be effective. And they were alert to the possibilities of psychological warfare, capitalizing on the Spaniards' peculiar dread of death by sacrifice and of the cannibalizing of the corpse.[40] On much they

---

[38] Contrast the fate of Spaniards when faced with the arrows projected from the short powerful bows of the Chichimeca, the Indians of the northern steppes whose territory lay athwart the road to the silver mines; Philip Wayne Powell, *Soldiers, Indians and Silver* (Tempe, Ariz., 1975).

[39] Díaz, *Historia*, chap. 153; Durán, *Historia*, chap. 77.

[40] Indian cannibalism is a vexed question. In very brief, insult displays pivoted on the threat of eating and being eaten. While the eating of the flesh of a warrior's sacrificed captive was hedged by ritual, more casual references suggest its debasing function, and it is possible that battlefield behavior was more relaxed. For ritual cannibalism, see *Florentine Codex*, 2.25.49–54; and Inga Clendinnen, "The Cost of Courage in Aztec Society," *Past and*

could be innovative. But on the most basic measure of man's worth, the taking alive of prestigious captives, they could not compromise.

That passion for captives meant that the moment when the opponent's nerve broke was helplessly compelling, an enemy in flight an irresistible lure. This pursuit reflex was sometimes exploited by native opponents as a slightly shabby trick. It provided Cortés with a standard tactic for a quick and sure crop of kills. Incurious as to the reason, he nonetheless noted and exploited Mexican unteachability: "Sometimes, as we were thus withdrawing and they pursued us so eagerly, the horsemen would pretend to be fleeing, and then suddenly would turn on them; we always took a dozen or so of the boldest. By these means and by the ambushes which we set for them, they were always much hurt; and certainly it was a remarkable sight for even when they well knew the harm they would receive from us as we withdrew, they still pursued us until we had left the city."[41] That commitment bore heavily on outcomes. Had Indians been as uninhibited as Spaniards in their killing, the small Spanish group, with no secured source of replenishment, would soon have been whittled away. In battle after battle the Spaniards report the deaths of many Indians, with their own men suffering not fatalities but wounds, and fast-healing wounds at that: those flint and obsidian blades sliced clean. It preserved the life of Cortés: time and again the Spanish leader struggled in Indian hands, the prize in a disorderly tug of war, with men dying on each side in the furious struggle for possession, with each time the Spaniards prevailing. Were Cortés in our hands, we would knife him. Mexican warriors could not kill the enemy leader so casually: were he to die, it would be in the temple of Huitzilopochtli, and before his shrine.[42]

If the measurable consequences of that insistence were obvious and damaging, there were others less obvious, but perhaps more significant. We have already noted the Spanish predilection for ambush as part of a wider preference for killing at least risk. Spaniards valued their crossbows and muskets for their capacity to pick off selected enemies well behind the line of engagement: as snipers, as we would say. The psychological demoralization attending those sudden, trivializing deaths of great men painted for war but not yet engaged in combat must have been formidable. (Were the victim actively engaged in battle, the matter was

---

Present 107 (May 1985): 44–89, esp. 56–60 and 69; for the debasing function, see Durán, *Historia*, chap. 9.

[41] Cortés, "Third Letter," 230.

[42] E.g., the attack on Cortés in the Xochimilco battle, and the desperate rescue, Cortés sustaining a "bad wound in the head"; Díaz, *Historia*, chap. 145.

different. Then he died nobly; although pierced by a bolt or a ball from a distance, his blood flowed forth to feed the earth as a warrior's should.) But more than Indian deaths and demoralization were effected through these transactions. To inflict such deaths – at a distance, without putting one's own life in play – developed a Mexican reading of the character of the Spanish warrior.[43]

Consider this episode, told by a one-time conquistador. Two Indian champions, stepping out from the mass of warriors, offered their formal challenge before a Spanish force. Cortés responded by ordering two horsemen to charge, their lances poised. One of the warriors, against all odds, contrived to sever a horse's hooves, and then, as it crashed to the ground, slashed its neck. Cortés, seeing the risk to the unhorsed rider, had a cannon fired so that "all the Indians in the front ranks were killed and the others scattered." The two Spaniards recovered themselves and scuttled back to safety under the covering fire of muskets, crossbows, and the cannon.[44]

For Cortés the individual challenge had been a histrionic preliminary flourish: he then proceeded to the serious work of using firepower to kill warriors and to control more territory, which was what he took war to be about. Throughout, Spaniards measured success in terms of body counts, territory controlled, and evidence of decay in the morale of the "enemy," which included all warriors, actively engaged in battle or not, and all "civilians" too. Cortés casually informed the king of his dawn raids into sleeping villages and the slaughter of the inhabitants, men, women, and children, as they stumbled into the streets: these were necessary and conventional steps in the progressive control of terrain, and the progressive demoralization of opposition. To an Indian warrior, Cortés's riposte to the Indian champions' challenge was shameful, with only the horses, putting themselves within reach of the opponents' weapons, emerging with any credit. Cortés's descents on villages are reported in tones of breathless incredulity.[45]

---

[43] Spaniards valued muskets equally with crossbows, a musketeer being allocated the same share of the spoils as a crossbowman, yet oddly muskets are mentioned infrequently in Indian accounts, perhaps because the ball could not be followed in flight, while crossbow bolts whirred and sang as they came; *Florentine Codex*, 12.22.62. For a succinct and accessible account of sixteenth-century cannon, in their enormous variety, see Pagden, *Cortés*, 507–8. Most of the small guns used in America could fire a ball of twenty pounds over some four hundred meters (ibid., n. 59). For a more extended account, see Alberto Mario Salas, *Las armas de la Conquista* (Buenos Aires, 1950).

[44] Durán , *Historia*, chap. 72, pp. 529–30.

[45] E.g., on the Spanish retreat from Tenochtitlan they "quickly slew the people of Calacoaya . . . [they] did not provoke them; without notice were they slain. [The Spaniards]

There is in the *Florentine Codex* an exquisitely painful, detailed description of the Spaniards' attack on the unarmed warrior dancers at the temple festival, the slaughter that triggered the Mexican "uprising" of May 1520. The first victim was a drummer: his hands were severed, then his neck. The account continues: "Of some they slashed open their backs: then their entrails gushed out. Of some they cut their heads to pieces.... Some they struck on the shoulder; they split openings. They broke openings in their bodies."[46] And so it goes on. How ought we interpret this? It was not, I think, recorded as a horror story, or only as a horror story. The account is sufficiently careful as to precise detail and sequence to suggest its construction close after the event, in an attempt to identify the pattern, and so to discover the sense, in the Spaniards' cuttings and slashings. (This was the first view the Mexicans had of Spanish swords at work.) The Mexicans had very precise rules about violent assaults on the body, as the range of their sacrificial rituals makes clear, but the notion of a "preemptive massacre" of warriors was not in their vocabulary.

Such baffling actions, much more than any deliberately riddling policy, worked to keep Indians off balance. To return to an early celebrated moment of mystification by Cortés, the display of the cannon to impress the Mexican envoys on the coast with the killing power of Spanish weapons: the men who carried the tale back reported the thunderous sound, the smoke, the fire, the foul smell – and that the shot had "dissolved" a mountain, and "pulverised" a tree.[47] It is highly doubtful that the native watchers took the intended point of the display, that this was a weapon of war for use against human flesh. It was not a conceivable weapon for warriors. So it must have appeared (as it is in fact reported) as a gratuitous assault upon nature: a scrambled lesson indeed. Mexican warriors learned, with experience, not to leap and shout and display when faced with cannon fire and crossbows, but to weave and duck, as the shield canoes learned to zigzag to avoid the cannon shot from the brigantines, so that with time the carnage was less.[48] But they also learned contempt for men who were prepared to kill indiscriminately,

---

vented their wrath upon them, they took their pleasure with them"; *Florentine Codex*, 12:25:73.

[46] *Florentine Codex*, 2.20.55. It appears from the funerary rites accorded the fragmented corpses of the warrior dancers that the Mexicans somehow decided that the victims had found death in a mode appropriate to warriors.

[47] Ibid., 12.7.19.

[48] Ibid., 12.30.86.

combatants and noncombatants alike, and at a secure distance, without putting their own lives in play.

What of Spanish horses, that other key element in Cortés's mystification program? We have early evidence of swift and effective warrior response to these exotics, and of a fine experimental attitude to verifying their nature. A small group of Tlaxcalan warriors having their first sight of horses and horsemen managed to kill two horses and to wound three more before the Spaniards got the upper hand.[49] In the next engagement a squad of Indians made a concerted and clearly deliberate attack on a horse, allowing the rider, although badly wounded, to escape, while they killed his mount and carted the body from the field. Bernal Díaz later recorded that the carcass was cut into pieces and distributed through the towns of Tlaxcala, presumably to demonstrate the horse's carnal nature. (They reserved the horseshoes, as he sourly recalled, to offer to their idols, along with "the Flemish hat, and the two letters we had sent them offering peace.")[50]

The distribution of the pieces of the horse's flesh possibly held further implications. Indians were in no doubt that horses were animals. But that did not reduce them, as it did for Spaniards, to brute beasts, unwitting, unthinking servants of the lords of creation. Indians had a different understanding of how animals signified. It was no vague aesthetic inclination that led the greatest warrior orders to mimic the eagle and the jaguar in their dress and conduct: those were creatures of power, exemplary of the purest warrior spirit. The eagle, slowly turning close to the sun, then the scream, the stoop, the strike; the jaguar, announcing its presence with the coughing rumble of thunder, erupting from the dappled darkness to make its kill: these provided unmatchable models for human emulation. That horses should appear ready to kill men was unremarkable. The ferocity and courage of these creatures, who raced into the close zone of combat, facing the clubs and swords; who plunged and screamed, whose eyes rolled, whose saliva flew (for the Mexicans saliva signified anger) marked them as agents in the battle action, as had the charge of the two horses against their Indian challengers. In the Mexican lexicon of battle, the horses excelled their masters. They were not equal in value as offerings – captured Spanish swords lashed to long poles were typically used against horses to disembowel or hamstring them, but not against their riders, judged too valuable to damage so deeply – but their valor

[49] Cortés, "Second Letter," 58.
[50] Díaz, *Historia*, chap. 63.

was recognized. When the besieged Mexicans won a major victory over Cortés's men on the Tacuba causeway, they displayed the heads of the sacrificed Spaniards on the skull rack in the usual way, and below them they skewered the heads of the four horses taken in the same melee.[51]

There is one small moment in which we see these contrary understandings held in counterpoise. During a skirmish in the city some Spanish horsemen emerging from an unsprung ambush collided, a Spaniard falling from his mare. Panicky, the riderless horse "rushed straight at the enemy, who shot at and wounded her with arrows; whereupon, seeing how badly she was being treated, she returned to us," Cortés reported, but "so badly wounded that she died that night." He continued: "Although we were much grieved by her loss, for our lives were dependent on the horses, we were pleased she had not perished at the hands of the enemy, for their joy at having captured her would have exceeded the grief caused by the death of their companions."[52]

For Cortés the mare was an animal, responding as an animal: disoriented, then fleeing from pain. Her fate had symbolic importance only through her association with the Spaniards. For the Indians the mare breaking out from the knot of Spaniards, rushing directly and alone toward enemy warriors – white-eyed, ferocity incarnate – was accorded the warrior's reception of a flight of arrows. Her reversal, her flight back to her friends probably signaled a small Indian victory, as her capture and death among enemies would have signaled to the Spaniards, at a more remote level, a small Spanish defeat. That doomed mare wheeling and turning in the desperate margin between different armies and different systems of understanding provides a sufficiently poignant metaphor for the themes I have been pursuing.

Spanish "difference" found its clearest expression in their final strategy for the reduction of the imperial city. Cortés had hoped to intimidate the Mexicans sufficiently by his steady reduction of the towns around the lake, by his histrionic acts of violence, and by the exemplary cruelty with which resistance was punished, to bring them to treat.[53] Example-at-a-distance in that mosaic of rival cities could have no relevance for the Mexicans – if all others quailed, they would not – so the Spaniards resorted, as Díaz put it, to "a new kind of warfare." Siege was the quintessential

---

[51] Note also the offering of the entire skins of five horses, "sewn up and as well tanned as anywhere in the world," in Texcoco. These captives had been taken in a situation where they were riderless at the time of engagement. Cortés, "Third Letter," 184.

[52] Ibid., 252.

[53] Ibid., 192.

European strategy: an economical design to exert maximum pressure on whole populations without active engagement, delivering control over people and place at least cost. If Cortés's own precarious position led him to increase that pressure by military sorties, his crucial weapon was want.

For the Mexicans, siege was the antithesis of war. They knew of encircling cities to persuade unwilling warriors to come out, and of destroying them too, when insult required it. They had sought to burn the Spaniards out of their quarters in Tenochtitlan, to force them to fight after their massacre of the warrior dancers.[54] But the deliberate and systematic weakening of opposition before engagement, and the deliberate implication of noncombatants in the contest, had no part in their experience.

As the siege continued the signs of Mexican contempt multiplied. Mexican warriors continued to seek face-to-face combat with these most unsatisfactory opponents, who skulked and refused battle, who clung together in tight bands behind their cannon, who fled without shame. When elite warriors, swept in by canoe, at last had the chance to engage the Spaniards closely, the Spaniards "turned their backs, they fled," with the Mexicans in pursuit. They abandoned a cannon in one of their pell-mell flights, positioned with unconscious irony on the gladiatorial stone on which the greatest enemy warriors had given their final display of fighting prowess; the Mexicans worried and dragged it along to the canal and dropped it into the water.[55] Indian warriors were careful, when they had to kill rather than capture Spaniards in battle, to deny them an honorable warrior's death, dispatching them by beating in the back of their heads, the death reserved for criminals in Tenochtitlan.[56] And the Spaniards captured after the debacle on the Tacuba causeway were stripped of all their battle equipment, their armor, their clothing: only then, when they were naked, and reduced to "slaves," did the Mexicans kill them.[57]

What does it matter, in the long run, that Mexican warriors admired Spanish horses and despised Spanish warriors? To discover how it bore on events we need to look briefly at Indian notions of "fate" and time. We can compare the structure of the Indian and Spanish accounts of the final

---

[54] Díaz recalls them yelling, whistling, and calling the Spaniards "rogues and cowards who did not dare to meet them through a day's battle, and retreated before them"; *Historia*, chap. 126.

[55] *Florentine Codex*, 12.31.89. For an account of those exemplary battles, see Clendinnen, "Cost of Courage."

[56] E.g., *Florentine Codex*, 12.35.87.

[57] Ibid., 12.33.96; 12.34.99 (*tlacotli*, a secular slave performing lowly tasks, not *tlaaltilli*, those selected captives ritually purified to be especially acceptable to the gods).

battles, to discover the explanatory strategies implied in that structuring. The Spanish versions present the struggles along the causeways, the narrow victories, the coups, the strokes of luck, the acts of daring on each side. Through the tracing of an intricate sequence of action we follow the movement of the advantage, first one way, then the other. God is at the Spaniards' shoulders, but only to lend power to their strong arms, or to tip an already tilting balance. Through selection and sequence of significant events we have the familiar, powerful, cumulative explanation through the narrative form.

The Indian accounts look superficially similar. There are episodes, and they are offered serially: descriptions of group or individual feats, of contemptible Spanish actions. But these are discrete events, moments to be memorialized, with time no more than the thread on which they are strung: there is no cumulative effect, no significance in sequence. Nor is there any implication that the human actions described bore on outcomes. The fact that defeat was suffered declares it to have been inevitable.

The Mexicans, like Mesoamericans generally, conceptualized time as multidimensional and eternally recurrent, and men attempted to comprehend its complex movement through the use of intermeshing time counts, which completed their complex permutations over fifty-two years, a *Xiumolpilli* or "Bundle of Years." (Note how that word *bundle* denies any significance to mere adjacency.) Under such a system, each "day" was not the outcome of the days preceding it: it had its own character, indicated by its complex name derived from the time counts, and was unique within its Bundle of Years. It also was more closely connected with the similarly named days that had occurred in every preceding Bundle of Years than with those clustered about it in its own bundle. Thus the particular contingent event was to be understood as unfolding in a dynamic process modeled by some past situation. But just as those anomalous events presumably noted before the Spanish advent could be categorized as "omens" and their portent identified only retrospectively, the identification of the recurrent in the apparently contingent was very much an after-the-event diagnosis, not an anterior paralyzing certitude. The essential character of the controlling time manifested itself in subtle ways, largely masked from human eyes. Events remained problematical in their experiencing, with innovation and desperate effort neither precluded nor inhibited. In human experience outcomes remained contingent until manifested.[58]

---

[58] Rather too much has been made of the Mexican concern for "day signs," the determining authority of the auguries associated with one's day of birth over the individual's *tonalli*, or destiny. It is true that in some passages of the *Florentine Codex* – the only source with the

Nonetheless, some few events were accorded special status, being recognized as signs of the foretold. At a place called Otumba the Spaniards,
limping away from Tenochtitlan after the expulsion of the Noche Triste,
were confronted by a sea of Mexican warriors: a sea that evaporated
when Cortés and his horsemen drove through to strike down the battle
leader, and to seize his fallen banner. The "battle of Otumba" mattered,
being the best chance from our perspective for the Mexicans to finish off
the Spaniards at their most vulnerable. The Spanish accounts identify the
striking down of the commander as decisive, but while the fall of a leader
was ominous (and an attack on a leader not actively engaged in combat
disreputable) it was the taking of the banner that signified. Our initial
temptation is to elide this with the familiar emotional attachment of a
body of fighting men to its colors: to recall the desperate struggles over
shreds of silk at Waterloo, the dour passion of a Roman legion in pursuit
of its lost Eagle and honor.[59] There might have been some of this in the
Indian case. But the taking of a banner was to Indians less a blow to
collective pride than a statement: a sign that the battle was to go, indeed
had gone, against them.

Cortés reported his determined attack on "the great cue," the pyramid
of Huitzilopochtli, during the first struggle in Tenochtitlan, claiming that
after three hours of struggle he cleared the temple of Indians and put
it to the torch. He also noted that the capture of the pyramid "so much
damaged their confidence that they began to weaken greatly on all sides":
the sign noted.[60] Had the capture been as decisive as Cortés claims,
we could expect more than "weakening," but just how complete it was
remains problematical: in Díaz's account the Spaniards, having fired the
shrine, were then tumbled back down the steps. The event clearly mattered
to the Indians, Díaz remarking how often he had seen that particular battle
pictured in later Indian accounts. He thought this was because the Indians
took the Spanish assault as a very heroic thing, as they were represented as
"much wounded and running with blood with many dead in the pictures

kind of "spread" to make this sort of concept mapping viable – the individual is presented
as quite mastered by his or her "fate." That clarity blurs on broader acquaintance,
emerging as part of the characteristic stylistic movement of much of the codex between
firm statements of the ideal and the tempering qualifications necessary to catch the
messiness of actuality. Day signs had about as much determining power as horoscopes
hold today for the moderate believer. They mattered, but more as intimations or as
post-hoc diagnoses (and even then, one suspects, most readily invoked by others, not
the individuals concerned) than as iron determinants of fate. Cf. Todorov: "To know
someone's birthday is to know his fate"; *Conquest of America*, 64.
[59] John Keegan, *The Face of Battle* (New York, 1977). 184–86.
[60] Cortés, "Second Letter," 134–35.

they made of the setting afire of the temple, with the many warriors guarding it."[61] My thought is that what the representations sought to make clear was that despite the firing of the shrine the Spaniards had not achieved the uncontested mastery which would indeed have constituted and marked "victory." The vigor of the attack must have made even more urgent the putting of the temple to rights after the Spaniards' expulsion – that period when we, with our notions of strategy, wait in vain for the Mexicans to pursue the weakened Spaniards and finish them off, while they prepared instead for the set-piece battle at Otumba, "read" the message of the taking of the banner, and yielded the day.

Deep into the second phase of the conquest, Spanish banner carriers remained special targets, being subjected to such ferocious attack that "a new one was needed every day."[62] But the Mexicans had come to pay less heed to signs, because they had discovered that Spaniards ignored them. In the course of the causeway victory a major Spanish banner had actually been taken: "The warriors from Tlatelolco captured it in the place known today as San Martín." But while the warrior who had seized the banner was carefully memorialized, "They were scornful of their prize and considered it of little importance." Sahagún's informants flatly record that the Spaniards "just kept on fighting."[63] Ignoring signs of defeat, the Spaniards were equally careless of signs of victory. When a Spanish contingent penetrated the marketplace of Tlatelolco, where the Mexicans had taken their last refuge, they managed to fight their way to the top of the main pyramid, to set the shrines on fire and plant their banners before they were forced to withdraw. "The common people began to wail, expecting the looting to begin," but the warriors, seasoned in Spanish ways, had no such expectation. They knew the fighting would go on: these enemies were as blind to signs as they were deaf to decency. Next day from his own encampment Cortés was puzzled to see the fires still burning unquenched, the banners still in place. The Mexicans would respect the signs and leave them to stand, even if the barbarians did not, even if the signs had lost efficacy, even if the rules of war were in abeyance.

John Keegan has characterized battle as "essentially a moral conflict [requiring] a mutual and sustained act of will between two contending

[61] Díaz, *Historia*, chap. 126.
[62] Ibid., chap. 151.
[63] Miguel Leon-Portilla, *The Broken Spears* (Boston, 1962), 107. The captor was the *Tla-panecatl* Hecatzin – see *Florentine Codex*, 12.35.103, n. 2. For an earlier exploit of the Otomi warrior, see *Florentine Codex*, 101.

parties, and, if it is to result in a decision, the moral collapse of one of them."[64] Paradoxically, that mutuality is most essential at the point of disengagement. To "surrender," to acquiesce in defeat and concede victory, is a complex business, at once a redefinition of self and one's range of effective action, and a redefinition of one's relationship with the erstwhile enemy. Those redefinitions have somehow to be acknowledged by the opponent. Where the indicators that mark defeat and so allow "moral collapse" to occur are not acknowledged, neither victory nor defeat is possible, and we approach a sinister zone in which there can be no resolution save death.[65]

That, I think, came to be the case in Mexico. "Signs" are equivocal things, especially when they point not to a temporary submission of uncertain duration, but to the end of a people's imperial domination. The precarious edifice of "empire" had not survived the introduction of the wild card of the Spaniards – men without a city, and so outside the central plays of power and punishment. Its collapse had been proclaimed by Quauhtemoc, "He Who Falls Like an Eagle," who had replaced the dead Cuitlahuac as Great Speaker, when he offered a general "remission" of tribute for a year in return for aid against the Spaniards: tribute is a product of the power to exact it. In the final battles the Mexicans were fighting for the integrity of their city, as so many others had fought before. They knew the settled hatred of the Tlaxcalans and the envy of other peoples. Perhaps even against indigenous enemies they might have fought on, in face of the signs of defeat. Against the Spaniards, cowardly opportunists impossible to trust, who disdained the signs of victory and defeat, they lacked any alternative.[66] The Mexicans continued to resist.

The chronicles record the stories of heroic deeds: of warriors scattering the Spaniards before them, of the great victory over Cortés's troop, with terrified Spaniards reeling "like drunken men," and fifty-three taken for sacrifice.[67] Spanish accounts tell us that the victory that had given so many captives to the Mexican war god was taken at the time to indicate the

---

[64] Keegan, *Face of Battle*, 296.

[65] As in the interspecies mayhem described by Konrad Z. Lorenz, where signs of submission are not "understood" in the battle between the turkey and the peacock; *King Solomon's Ring* (London, 1961), 194–95.

[66] Cortés was desperate to treat with Quauhtemoc in the last days of the siege, but Díaz reports that the ruler would not show himself, despite all reassurances, because he feared he would be killed by guns or crossbows, Cortés having behaved too dishonorably to be trusted; *Historia*, chap. 155.

[67] *Florentine Codex*, 12.35.104.

likelihood of a final Mexican victory, hopefully prophesied by the priests as coming within eight days. (The Indian records do not waste time on false inferences, misunderstood omens.) Cortés's allies, respectful of signs, accordingly removed themselves for the duration. But the days passed, the decisive victory did not come, and the macabre dance continued.[68]

And all the while, as individual warriors found their individual glory, the city was dying: starving, thirsting, choking on its own dead. This slow strangling is referred to as if quite separate from the battle, as in the Mexican mind it presumably was. Another brief glory occurred, when Eagle and Ocelot warriors, men from the two highest military orders, were silently poled in disguised canoes to where they could leap among looting native allies, spreading lethal panic among them. But still the remorseless pressure went on: "They indeed wound all around us, they were wrapped around us, no one could go anywhere.... Indeed many died in the press."[69]

The Mexicans made their endgame play. Here the augury component, always present in combat, is manifest. Quauhtemoc and his leading advisers selected a great warrior, clad him in the array of Quetzal Owl, the combat regalia of the great Ahuitzotl, who had ruled before the despised Moctezuma, and armed him with the flint-tipped darts of Huitzilopochtli; thus he became, as they said, "one of the number of the Mexicans' rulers." He was sent forth to cast his darts against the enemy: should the darts twice strike their mark, the Mexicans would prevail. Magnificent in his spreading quetzal plumes, with his four attendants, Quetzal Owl entered the battle. For a time they could follow his movements among the enemy: reclaiming stolen gold and quetzal plumes, taking three captives, or so they thought. Then he dropped from a terrace, and out of sight. The Spaniards record nothing of this exemplary combat.

After that ambiguous sign another day passed with no action: the Spaniards, disreputable to the end, "only lay still; they lay looking at the common folk."[70] On the next evening a great "bloodstone," a blazing coal of light, flared through the heavens, to whirl around the devastated city, then to vanish in the middle of the lake. No Spaniard saw the comet of fire that marked the end of imperial Tenochtitlan. Perhaps no Indian saw it either. But they knew great events must be attended by signs, and

---

[68] Díaz, *Historia*, chap. 153; Cortés, "Third Letter," 242. Cortés for his part deletes any reference to the withdrawal of his Indian "vassals," the admission of such a withdrawal casting altogether too much light on the nature of their commitment to the Spanish cause.

[69] *Florentine Codex*, 12.38.117.

[70] Ibid., 12.38.118.

that there must have been a sign. In the morning Quauhtemoc, having taken counsel with his lords, abandoned the city. He was captured in the course of his escape, to be brought before Cortés. Only then did his people leave their ruined city.[71]

So the Mexicans submitted to their fate, when that fate was manifest. A certain arrangement of things had been declared terminated: the period of Mexican domination and the primacy of Tenochtitlan was over.

A particular section of the Anales de Tlatelolco is often cited to demonstrate the completeness of the obliteration of a way of life and a way of thought. It runs:

> Broken spears lie in the roads;
> we have torn our hair in our grief.
> The houses are roofless now, and their walls
> are red with blood.
>
> Worms are swarming in the streets and plazas,
> and the walls are splattered with gore.
> The water has turned red, as if it were dyed,
> and when we drink it,
> it has the taste of brine.
>
> We have pounded our hands in despair
> against the adobe walls,
> for our inheritance, our city, is lost and dead.
> The shields of our warriors were its defense,
> but they could not save it.[72]

And so it continues. But what is notable here (apart from the poetic power) is that the "lament" was a traditional form, maintaining itself after the defeat, and so locating that defeat and rendering it intelligible by assaying it in the traditional mode. If the Mexican vision of empire was finished, the people, and their sense of distinctiveness as a people, were not. The great idols in the temples had been smuggled out of the city by their traditional custodians before its fall and sent toward Tula, a retracing of their earlier migration route. A cyclical view of time has

[71] Ibid., 12.40.123.

[72] I offer Miguel Leon-Portilla's translation as the version most likely to be familiar; *Broken Spears*, 137–38. Cf. Leon-Portilla, *Pre-Columbian Literatures of Mexico* (Norman, Okla., 1969), 150–51; and Gordon Brotherston and Ed Dorn, *Image of the New World* (London, 1979), 34–35. For other songs in traditional form to do with the Conquest, see John Bierhorst, *Cantares Mexicanos* (Stanford, Calif., 1985), esp. no. 13, pp. 151–53; no. 60, p. 279 (obscurely); no. 66, pp. 319–23; no. 68, for its early stanzas, pp. 327–41; no. 91, pp. 419–25.

its comforts. And if the "Quetzalcoatl returned" story as presented in the *Florentine Codex* is a post-Conquest imposition, as is likely, and if indeed it does move away from traditional native ways of accounting for human action in the world, with Moctezuma's conduct described not merely to memorialize his shame but in order to explain the outcome of defeat, as I believe it does – then its fabrication points to a concern for the construction of a viable and satisfying public history for the con-quered, an emollient myth, generated in part from within the European epistemological system to encompass the catastrophe of Mexican defeat.

III

Now, at last, for the consequences.

There is something appealing to our sense of irony in the notion that the Spaniards' heroic deeds, as they saw them, were judged shameful by the Mexican warriors. But attitudes of losers have little historical res-onance. Attitudes of victors do. Here I want to pursue an impression. Anyone who has worked on the history of Mexico – I suspect the case is the same for much of Latin America, but I cannot speak for that – is painfully impressed by the apparent incorrigibility of the division between the aboriginal inhabitants and the incomers, despite the domestic prox-imity of their lives, and by the chronic durability, whatever the form of government, whatever its public rhetoric, of systemic social injustice grounded in that division. In Mexico I am persuaded the terms of the relationship between the incoming and the indigenous peoples were set very early. A line of reforming sixteenth-century missionaries and upright judges were baffled as much as outraged by what they saw as the wan-tonness of Spanish maltreatment of Indians: cruelties indulged in the face of self-interest. Spaniards had been notoriously brutal in the Caribbean islands, where the indigenes were at too simple a level of social orga-nization to survive Spanish endeavors to exploit them. Yet in their first encounters with the peoples of Mexico the Spaniards had declared them-selves profoundly impressed. Cortés's co-venture with the Tlaxcalans seems to have involved genuine cooperation, a reasonably developed notion of mutuality, and (not to be sentimental) some affection between individuals.[73]

---

[73] For example, Cortés approvingly noted the courage of the chief Chichimecatecle, who "having always gone with his warriors in the vanguard," took it as an affront when put to the rear in the transport for the brigantines: "When he finally agreed to this, he asked

Then something happened, a crucial break of sympathy. It is always difficult to argue that things could have been other than they turn out to be, especially in the political maelstrom of post-Conquest Mexico.[74] But despite the continuing deftness of his political maneuverings in the aftermath of the Conquest, I have a sense of Cortés relinquishing both his control over the shaping of Spanish-Indian relations and his naturally conservationist policies – a conservationism based in pragmatism rather than humanity, but effective for all that – earlier and more easily than his previous conduct would have us expect. His removal to Honduras in October 1524 was an extraordinary abdication of the official authority he had sought so long and had worn only for a year, and marked the end of his effective role in "New Spain." We tend to like our heroes, whether villains or saints or Machiavels, to be all of a piece: unchanging, untinctured emblems of whatever qualities we assign them, impervious to experience. But there are indicators in his writings as in his actions that Cortés was changed by his experience in Mexico, and that the change had to do with the obstinate, and to Spanish eyes profoundly "irrational," refusal or incapacity of the Mexicans to submit.

Cortés was sensitive to the physical beauty and social complexity of the great city of Tenochtitlan. It was the dream of the city that had fired his ambition, and provided the focus for all his actions. We must remember that Tenochtitlan was a marvel, eclipsing all other cities in Mesoamerica (and Europe) in size, elegance, order, and magnificence of spectacle. Cortés had contrived the complex, difficult strategy of the blockade, and pursued the mammoth task of implementing it, in order to preserve the city by demonstrating the futility of resistance. Then he watched the slow struggle back and forth along the causeways, as the defenders, careless of their own lives, took back by night what had been so painfully won by day. He moved his men onto the causeways, into physical misery and constant danger, and then was forced to undertake the systematic destruction of the structures along the causeways to secure the yards won, a perilous prolongation of a task already long enough.

So, with patience, access to the city was gained, and the noose of famine tightened. From that point victory was in Spanish (and our) terms inevitable. Yet still the resistance continued, taking advantage of every

that no Spaniards should remain accompanying him, for he is a most valiant man and wished to keep all the glory for himself"; "Third Letter," 185.

[74] For the multiple demands on Cortés in this period see J.H. Elliott, "The Spanish Conquest and the Settlement of America," in Leslie Bethell, ed., *The Cambridge History of Latin America*, vol. 1 (Cambridge, 1984), 149–206.

corner and rooftop. So the work of demolition went on. At last, from
the top of a great pyramid Cortés could see that the Spaniards had won
seven-eighths of what had once been the city, with the remaining people
crammed into a corner where the houses were built out over the water.
Starvation was so extreme that even roots and bark had been gnawed,
with the survivors tottering shadows, but shadows who still resisted.[75]

Cortés's frustration in being forced to destroy the city he had so much
wanted to capture intact is manifest, as is his bewilderment at the tenacity
of so futile a resistance: "As we had entered the city from our camp two
or three days in succession, besides the three or four previous attacks, and
had always been victorious, killing with crossbow, harquebus and field
gun an infinite number of the enemy, we each day expected them to sue
for peace, which we desired as much as our own salvation; but nothing we
could do could induce them to it." After another largely unresisted thrust
into the city, "We could not but be saddened by their determination to
die."[76]

He had no stomach to attack again. Instead he made a final resort to
terror. Not to the terror of mass killings: that weapon had long lost its
efficacy. He constructed a war-engine, an intimidatory piece of European
technology that had the advantage of not requiring gunpowder: the mar-
velous catapult. It was a matter of some labor over three or four days,
of lime and stone and wood, then the great cords, and the stones big as
demijohns. It was aimed, as a native account bleakly recorded, to "stone
the common folk." It failed to work, the stone dribbling feebly from the
sling, so still the labor of forcing surrender remained.[77]

Four days patient waiting, four days further into starvation, and the
Spaniards entered the city again. Again they encountered ghostly figures,
of women and gaunt children, and saw the warriors still stationed on the
rooftops, but silent now, and unarmed, close-wrapped in their cloaks.
And still the fruitless pretense at negotiation, the dumb, obdurate resistance.

Cortés attacked, killing "more than twelve thousand," as he estimated.
Another meeting with some of the lords, and again they refused any
terms save a swift death. Cortés exhausted his famous eloquence: "I said
many things to persuade them to surrender but all to no avail, although
we showed them more signs of peace than have ever been shown to

[75] Cortés, "Third Letter," 256.
[76] Ibid., 232–33.
[77] Ibid., 257; Diaz, *Historia*, chap. 155; *Florentine Codex*, 12.38.113.

a vanquished people for we, by the grace of our Lord, were now the victors."[78] He released a captured noble, charging him to urge surrender: the only response was a sudden, desperate attack, and more Indians dead. He had a platform set up in the market square of Tlatelolco, ready for the ceremony of submission, with food prepared for the feast that should mark such a moment: still he clung to the European fiction of two rulers meeting in shared understanding for the transference of an empire. There was no response.

Two days more, and Cortés unleashed the allies. There followed a massacre, of men who no longer had arrows, javelins, or stones; of women and children stumbling and falling on the bodies of their own dead. Cortés thought forty thousand might have died or been taken on that day. The next day he had three heavy guns taken into the city. As he explained to his distant king, the enemy, being now "so massed together that they had no room to turn around, might crush us as we attacked, without actually fighting. I wished, therefore, to do them some harm with the guns, and so induce them to come out to meet us."[79] He had also posted the brigantines to penetrate between the houses to the interior lake where the last of the Mexican canoes were clustered. With the firing of the guns the final action began. The city was now a stinking desolation of heaped and rotting bodies, of starving men, women, and children crawling among them or struggling in the water. Quauhtemoc was taken in his canoe, and at last brought before Cortés, to make his request for death, and the survivors began to file out, these once immaculate people "so thin, sallow, dirty and stinking that it was pitiful to see them."[80]

Cortés had invoked one pragmatic reason for holding his hand in the taking of Tenochtitlan: if the Spaniards attempted to storm the city the Mexicans would throw all their riches into the water, or would be plundered by the allies, so some of the profit would be lost. His perturbation went, I think, very much deeper. His earlier battle narratives exemplify those splendid Caesarian simplicities identified by John Keegan: disjunctive movement, uniformity of behavior, simplified characterization, and simplified motivation.[81] That style of high control, of magisterial grasp,

---

[78] Cortés, "Third Letter," 258.

[79] Ibid., 262.

[80] Díaz, *Historia*, chap. 156.

[81] Keegan, *Face of Battle*, 65–66. This is not to claim any direct classical influence; see Pagden, *Cortés*, xlvii; and Elliott, "Mental World of Cortés," for Cortés's slight acquaintance with classical authors. Caesar's *Commentaries* had been published in Spanish by 1498, and it is possible that Cortés had read them, although perhaps unlikely.

falters when he must justify his own defeat on the causeway, which cost so many Spanish lives. It then recovers itself briefly, to fracture, finally and permanently, for the last stages of his account of the battle for Tenochtitlan. The soldierly narrative loses its fine onward drive as he deploys more and more detail to demonstrate the purposefulness of his own action, and frets more and more over native mood and intentions.[82]

Cortés's strategy in the world had been to treat all men, Indians and Spaniards alike, as manipulable. That sturdy denial of the problem of otherness, usually so profitable, had here been proved bankrupt. He had also been forced into parodying his earlier and once successful strategies. His use of European equipment to terrify had produced the elaborate threat of the catapult, then its farcical failure. "Standard" battle procedures – terror-raiding of villages, exemplary massacres – took on an unfamiliar aspect when the end those means were designed to effect proved phantasmal, when killing did not lead to panic and pleas for terms, but a silent pressing on to death. Even the matter of firing a cannon must have taken on a new significance: to use cannon to clear a contended street or causeway or to disperse massed warriors was one thing; to use cannon to break up a huddled mass of exhausted human misery was very much another. It is possible that as he ran through his degraded routine of stratagems in those last days Cortés was brought to glimpse something of the Indian view of the nature and quality of the Spanish warrior.

---

[82] For the control: "While the alguacil-mayor was at Matalcingo, the people of [Tenochtitlan] decided to attack Alvarado's camp by night, and struck shortly before dawn. When the sentries on foot and on horseback heard them they shouted, 'to arms!' Those who were in that place flung themselves upon the enemy, who leapt into the water as soon as they saw the horsemen.... Fearing our men might be defeated I ordered my own company to arm themselves and march into the city to weaken the offensive against Alvarado" – and so on; Cortés, "Third Letter," 247. For the dislocation:

When we came within sight of the enemy we did not attack but marched through the city thinking that at any moment they would come out to meet us [to surrender]. And to induce it I galloped up to a very strong barricade which they had set up and called out to certain chieftains who were behind and whom I knew, that as they saw how lost they were and knew that if I so desired within an hour not one of them would remain alive why did not Guatimucin [Quauhtemoc], their lord, come and speak with me.... I then used other arguments which moved them to tears, and weeping they replied they well knew their error and their fate, and would go and speak to their lord.... They went, and returned after a while and told me their lord had not come because it was late, but that he would come on the following day at noon to the marketplace; and so we returned to our camp.... On the following day we went to the city and I warned my men to be on the alert lest the enemy betray us and we be taken unawares.

And so to more worried guesses and second guesses; ibid., 259–60.

His privilege as victor was to survey the surreal devastation of the city that had been the glittering prize and magnificent justification for his insubordination, and for the desperate struggles and sufferings over two long years, now reduced by perverse, obdurate resistance to befouled rubble, its once magnificent lords, its whole splendid hierarchy, to undifferentiated human wreckage. That resistance had been at once "irrational," yet chillingly deliberate.

He had seen, too, the phobic cruelty of the "allies," most especially the Tlaxcalans. He had known that cruelty before, and had used and profited from it. But on that last day of killing they had killed and killed amid a wailing of women and children so terrible "that there was not one man amongst us whose heart did not bleed at the sound."[83]

Those luxurious killings are at odds with what I have claimed to be the protocols of Indian combat. Tlaxcalan warrior-to-warrior performance had been conventional enough: we glimpse them exchanging insults and dueling with Mexican warriors; quarreling over the place of danger while escorting the brigantines over the mountains. It is possible that they came to judge the inadequacies of Spanish battle performance with the leniency of increased knowledge, or (more plausibly) that they thought Spanish delicts none of their concern. During the conquest process they performed as co-venturers with the Spaniards, associates in no way subordinate and, given their greater investment, probably defining themselves as the senior partners in the association.[84] It is in their attitude to Tenochtitlan and its inhabitants that their behavior appears anomalous. Cortés recalled that when he took the decision to raze the buildings of the city, a dauntingly laborious project, the Tlaxcalans were jubilant. All non-Mexicans would have longed to plunder Tenochtitlan, had they dared, and all had scores to settle against Mexican arrogance. No victor would have left the city intact, built as it was as the testament of the Mexican right to rule. Nonetheless the Tlaxcalan taste for destruction was extravagant. Only the Tlaxcalans were relentless in their hatred of the Mexicans: other cities waited and watched through the long struggle for the causeways, "reading the signs"

---

[83] Ibid., 261.

[84] The Tlaxcalans refused to participate in any expedition (like the sortie against Narváez) not in their direct interest; they withdrew at will, taking their loot with them; they required payment for aid given the Spaniards after the expulsion from Tenochtitlan, having considered the utility of killing them; Díaz, *Historia*, chap. 98. Their self-representation as faithful friends and willing servants to the Spaniards, as pictured in the Lienzo de Tlaxcala, came a generation or more after the Conquest as part of a campaign for privileges.

in the ebb and flow of what we would call the fortunes of battle, moving, deft as dancers, in and out of alliance. Only the Tlaxcalans sought neither loot nor captives as they surged into Tenochtitlan, but to kill. Where is the exemption of nonwarriors, the passion for personal captures, for the limited aims of tribute exaction, in those killings? Is this a liberation into ecstatic violence after a painfully protracted and frustrating struggle?

Licensed massacres are, unhappily, unremarkable, but there are more particular explanations. The Tlaxcalans had signaled their peculiar hatred of the Mexicans early: on the Spaniards' first departure for the Mexican city the Tlaxcalans, warning of chronic Mexican treachery, offered chillingly explicit advice: "In fighting the Mexicans, they said, we should kill all we could, leaving no one alive: neither the young, lest they should bear arms again, nor the old, lest they give counsel."[85] Their long-term exclusion from the play of Mexican alliance politics, coupled with the massive power of the Mexicans, liberated them as underdogs from "normal" constraints. While other formidable Nahua-speaking cities and provinces were recruited into the empire, the Tlaxcalans were kept out. I have come to see their exclusion, their role as outsiders, not as an unfortunate quirk but a structural requirement, a necessary corollary, of the kind of empire it was. Asked whether he could defeat the Tlaxcalans if he so chose, Moctezuma was said to have replied that he could, but preferred to have an enemy against whom to test his warriors and to secure high-quality victims. I believe him.[86] How else, with campaigns increasingly fought far afield, to make real the rhetoric, the high glamor, the authenticity of risk of warriordom? The overriding metaphor of Mexican life was contest, and the political fantasy of destined dominance required a plausible antagonist/victim. That essential role had devolved onto the Tlaxcalans. They made absolutely no obeisance to the Mexican view of themselves, and they were proximate enemies, penned like gamecocks in a coop – until the Spaniards came. Those wandering men without a city could not be pursued, subdued, or incorporated: they could only be destroyed, and that Cortés's conservationist talents and the Mexican cultural predilection for capturing significant enemies alive combined to preclude. The house of cards structure of the wider empire had been rendered unstable by their mere presence. Then they challenged the mutuality of interest

---

[85] Ibid., chap. 79.
[86] Andrés de Tápia, "Relación hecha por el señor Andrés de Tápia sobre la Conquista de México," in Joaquin García Icazbalceta, ed., Colección de documentos para la historia de México, 2 vols. (Mexico City, 1858–66), 2:343–438.

bonding the valley city states, so opening Tenochtitlan to assault, and the Tlaxcalans took their chance to destroy people and city together.[87]

Writing later of that day of killing, and what he saw his Indian "friends" do there, Cortés was brought to make one of his very rare general statements: "No race, however savage, has ever practiced such fierce and unnatural cruelty as the natives of these parts."[88] "Unnatural" cruelty. Against nature. A heavily freighted term in early sixteenth-century Spain. He had described Moctezuma as a "barbarian lord" in his earlier letter, but he had done so in the course of an elaborate description of the Mexican city and its complex workings that demonstrated the Mexican ruler was a "barbarian" of a most rare and civilized kind. I think his view was changed by the experience of the siege. There he saw "fierce and unnatural cruelty," an unnatural indifference to suffering, an unnatural indifference to death: a terrifying, terminal demonstration of "otherness," and of its practical and cognitive unmanageability. Todorov has called Cortés a master in human communication. Here the master had found his limits.[89]

In the aftermath of the fall of the city the Spaniards expressed their own cruelties. There was a phobic edge in some of the things done, especially against those men most obviously the custodians of the indigenous culture. There was a special death for priests like the Keeper of the Black House in Tenochtitlan, and other wise men who came from Texcoco of their own free will, bearing their painted books. They were torn apart by dogs.[90]

I do not suggest that any special explanation is required for Spanish or any other conquerors' brutalities. All I would claim at the end is that in the long and terrible conversation of war, despite the apparent mutual intelligibility of move and counter-move, as in the trap and ambush game built around the brigantines, that final nontranslatability of the vocabulary

---

[87] It was possibly in the decimation of native leaders who had learned how to deal with each other that the smallpox epidemic had its most immediate political effect.

[88] Cortés, "Third Letter," 262.

[89] Those limits were to be drawn more narrowly through the shaking experience of the Honduran expedition. The Cortés who early in the Mexican campaign could dismiss "omens" in the confidence that "God is more powerful than Nature" learned in Honduras how helpless men are when Nature, not men, opposes them, and where God seems far away. There he discovered that God is bound by no contract, and that he, like all men, must wait upon His will. The "Fifth Letter" reads like a mournful antiphon to the sanguine assurance of Cortés's early Conquest accounts.

[90] *Anales de Tlatelolco: Unos anales historicos de la Nación Mexicana*, prepared by Heinrich Berlin (Mexico City, 1948), 371–89, 74–76.

of battle and its modes of termination divided Spaniard from Indian in new and decisive ways. If for Indian warriors the lesson that their opponents were barbarians was learned early, for Spaniards, and for Cortés, that lesson was learned most deeply only in the final stages, where the Mexicans revealed themselves as unamenable to "natural" reason, and so unamenable to the routines of management of one's fellow men. Once that sense of unassuageable otherness has been established, the outlook is bleak indeed.

3

Disciplining the Indians

Franciscan Ideology and Missionary Violence in Sixteenth-Century Yucatán*

SOME YEARS AGO T. O. BEIDELMAN WROTE AN ARTICLE WHICH, JUDGING from the flurry of responses it provoked, touched a nerve.[1] Noting that social anthropologists had for too long neglected the study of colonial groups, Beidelman asked that missionaries and mission stations be investigated; that we should break out of our traditional fixation with the "native" side of the equation to recognize our fellow Europeans as fit subjects for "wonder and analysis".

It is true that ethno-historians, while ready enough to exploit missionary writings, have given scant attention to the missionaries themselves, tending to dismiss them as interfering outsiders who came, saw little, and (whether they managed to convert anyone or not) irretrievably changed the societies they intruded upon. While we have perhaps suspected that solitary missionaries dumped down among barbarous tribes might well have had difficulty in sustaining their sense of self and their sense of purpose unimpaired, organized groups of missionaries – most especially those whose group organization long preceded the mission enterprise, as with members of Catholic orders – are typically seen as effectively insulated

---

* I am indebted to Greg Dening of the University of Melbourne who in a remarkable work *Islands and Beaches* (Melbourne, 1980) explores, among a great many other things, how missionaries must struggle to make real their message, rendered thin and problematical by its separation from the sustaining cultural context of the native land.
[1] T. O. Beidelman, "Social Theory and the Study of Christian Missions in Africa", *Africa*, xlvi (1974), pp. 235–49.

from their alien environment. We assume disquiets and cognitive quivers to be evoked in the native communities by the mere missionary presence; the missionaries themselves we treat as men rendered impervious by ideological armouring.

In what follows, I want to present as "subjects for wonder and analysis" a particular group of Franciscan missionary friars who worked among the Maya Indians of the Yucatán peninsula in the middle decades of the sixteenth century. Rigorously trained in their Rule, and heirs and custodians of an explicit ideology of "conversion", which had been consciously monitored and modified in response to accumulated Franciscan experience in the Mexican mission field, they moved with energy and clear purpose to root out and punish idolatry when they discovered it to have been covertly practised by their most trusted Indian converts. Then they found their vigorous prosecution of the inquisition and their punishment of the delinquents denounced as unjustified and excessively cruel not only by Spanish laymen, but by fellow missionary Franciscans.

Throughout the ensuing conflict – a conflict made the more bitter and painful by being conducted within the terms of a shared rhetoric – the Yucatán friars remained persuaded of the righteousness, and indeed the prescriptive necessity, of all their actions. Their brothers' denunciations they saw as outrageous betrayals. Clearly, what had been a shared understanding of the world had, somehow, ceased to be shared. My concern is to trace how the new challenges and new experiences in the Mexican missionary situation subtly shifted emphases within enduring themes of Franciscan ideology, and to identify what it was in the particular context of Yucatán which brought those new emphases to strong expression, so that we, if not the contending friars, can understand how the confusion, and the cruelty, came about.

I

At the beginning of the conversion it happened in the city of Tlaxcala that those who governed the land had committed a grave offence requiring punishment, but as they were at that time such great lords, who had never had to bend their necks or know anything of punishment, there was no one who would speak to them about it and even the guardian [of the Franciscan monastery], who was anxious to resolve the matter and punish them, did not dare to do so... [Therefore] he had all the culprits – who were the four chief lords, and other lords who were their accomplices – called together... in the chapter of the monastery, where he began to speak of their offence and sin, condemning it as he well knew how to do... So great was his persuasive power that he brought them to acknowledge and confess their offence, and he urged them to redeem themselves to gain God's pardon, by scourging themselves, and so that they should not think he was angry or offended with them, he wished to scourge himself together with them...and taking a *disciplina* from his sleeve, he put aside his habit and began to lash himself with great vigour and severity. The Tlaxcalans, seeing him thus stripped and scourging himself for an offence he had not committed, but of which they knew themselves to be guilty, were thus abashed and amazed, and flinging themselves to the ground each began to scourge himself...and they struck strongly, for a very long time, until the guardian, judging it was sufficient, indicated that they stop...[2]

So, at least, the story goes. Although hagiographic, as is so much of the material relating to the early years of the Franciscan mission in "New Spain", it is perhaps true. For the first few years after the Mexican conquest the Tlaxcalan lords clung to their roles as allies, and therefore equals, of the Spaniards, and their disciplining was a delicate matter. More significant for our purposes is the guardian's technique of bringing the culprits to a proper penitence through tender preaching, identification with the wrongdoers, and exemplary self-flagellation. Here we see replicated the sensitive style of authority practised within the Spanish Franciscan province of San Gabriel – poor, remote, and strictly Observant – which had provided the leader, Fray Martín de Valencia, and all but one of the "Twelve Apostles" of the first official Franciscan mission to Mexico. Fray Martín himself, as provincial of San Gabriel, had demonstrated the style on his first round of visitations. Entering the chapel where an assembled community awaited his interrogation, he got down on his knees, and began the painful recitation of his own faults, before taking the discipline in the sight of all. He then kissed the feet of the friars. Thus through a ritual display of personal unworthiness he intimated the actual legitimacy of his new authority.[3]

Reliance on example and circumspect avoidance of the direct exercise of power, while edifying in interchanges with fellow Franciscans, might seem an inappropriate model for dealing with a mass of newly conquered heathen, but it is clear that the Mexican missionaries had been initially determined to follow it. In his formal "Obedience" and "Instructions" their minister general had charged them to convert by "word and example", and while his rhetoric bristled with military metaphors – shields of faith, breastplates of justice, blades of the spirit of salvation, helmets

[2] Juan de Torquemada, *Monarquia indiana*, 3 vols. (Mexico, 1975), iii, pp. 233–4. "Friary" is of course more correct than "monastery" for the establishments of the mendicant orders in colonial New Spain, but the latter has become respectable through usage.

[3] *The Oroz Codex*, trans, and ed. Angelico Chavez, O.F.M. (Washington, D.C., 1972), p. 179. See also "Vida de Fr. Martín de Valencia escrita por su compañero Fr. Francisco Jimenez", ed. P. Anastasio Lopez, *Archivo ibero-americano*, xxvi (1926), p. 59.

and lances of perseverance – force was to be no part of the Franciscan armoury. Christ and his disciples, and then St. Francis and his chosen Twelve, had disarmed the world by their eloquence and the grace of their being. The new apostolic church of the Indies would also rest solely upon the coercive power of the word and the infectiousness of example. It was as holy fools that the Twelve would conquer:

treading and trampling upon the glory of the world, despised for littleness and idiocy, possessing the sublimest poverty, and in such a way that the world should regard you with mockery and contempt, and the very picture of contempt and derision, and should consider your life as madness, and your end without honour. For, thus become madmen to the world, you might convert the world by the foolishness of your preaching.[4]

Arriving in what remained of the Aztec capital of Tenochtitlán a mere three years after its surrender, and confronting for the first time the surviving Indian lords – lords who had been rounded up by armed Spaniards – the friars in their opening exhortation demonstrated their commitment to their minister general's vision: when the lords politely declined to abandon their traditional gods, the friars were content to exhort them afresh, and to threaten them only with the wrath of God.[5] But the Indians remained obstinate, and after "one or two years" of preaching, teaching and verbally rebuking them, to little effect, the friars capitulated, and formally resolved to punish recalcitrant Indians corporally.[6] It must have been a painful decision – at least one of the Twelve could never bring himself to punish his Indians – but once taken, force quickly became integrated into the standard repertoire of missionary strategies used by Franciscans, by members of the other orders which followed them to Mexico, and by secular clerics as well. When in 1539 the heads of the three orders working in Mexico met together with Bishop Zumárraga (himself a Franciscan) in a *junta eclesiastica*, they officially laid down

---

[4] "The Obedience and Instruction Given to Fray Martín de Valencia and his Twelve Companions by Fray Francisco de los Angeles, Minister General of the Order of Minors", the Instruction dated 4 Oct. (St. Francis's Day) 1523, the Obedience dated 30 Oct. 1523, in *Oroz Codex*, ed. Chavez, appendix 1, pp. 347–60.

[5] Bernadino de Sahagun, "Colloquios y doctrina christiana con que los doze frayles de San Francisco enbiados por el Papa Adriano sesto y por el Emperador Carlos quinto convertieron a los indios de la nueva Espanya en la lengua Mexicana y Española", in Zelia Nuttall, "El libro perdido de las platicas o coloquios de los doce primeros misioneras de Mexico", *Revista mexicana de estudios anthropologias*, i (1927), pp. 101–54, esp. p. 131.

[6] *Motolinía's History of the Indians of New Spain*, trans. and ed. Elizabeth Andros Foster (Westport, Conn., 1977), pp. 48–9; "Vida de Fr. Martín de Valencia", ed. Lopez, pp. 67–8.

that missionaries could properly impose "light punishments" on their Indians, as appropriate to "the master with his apprentice, or the teacher with the person in his charge".[7] So persuaded did the regular clergy come to be of the necessity of that power that they were to resist bitterly all later secular and episcopal attempts to wrest it from them.[8]

Mexican missionaries physically punished their Indians: that is not at issue. But there is another charge which sounded steadily in the contemporary chorus of accusations against the missionary friars – that their punishments, far from being "light", were too often excessively brutal, and restrained neither by compassion nor respect for law. Vasco de Quiroga, the saintly bishop of Michoacán, spoke for many when in 1561 he complained that the members of the regular orders:

had inflicted and are now inflicting many mistreatments upon the Indians, with great haughtiness and cruelty, for when the Indians do not obey them, they insult and strike them, tear out their hair, have them stripped and cruelly flogged, and then throw them into prison in chains and cruel irons, a thing most pitiable to hear about and much more pitiable to see.[9]

Historians have, on the whole, discounted such charges. Robert Ricard, in his classic study of the spiritual conquest of Mexico, judged them to be more indicative of the bitterness of the semi-institutionalized rivalries of the colonial order (particularly between seculars and regulars) than descriptive of actual missionary behaviour.[10] Most later historians working specifically on Franciscans have given the matter even less attention, being content to draw their picture of missionary performance from

---

[7] "Capitulos de la junta eclesiastica de 1539", in Joaquín Garcia Icazbalceta, *Don Fray Juan de Zumárraga*, 4 vols. (Mexico, 1947), iii, pp. 149–84.

[8] For example, "Carta al Rey D. Felipe de los provinciales de las ordenes de Santo Domingo, San Francisco y San Agustín, justificandose de los excesos que se les atribuin", 25 Feb. 1561, in *Cartas de Indias*, ed. Ministerio de Fomento (Madrid, 1877), doc. xxx, p. 149; "El Orden que los religiosos tienen en enseñan a los indios la doctrina, y otras cosas de policia cristiana", in *Nueva colección de documentos para la historia de Mexico*, ed. Joaquín Garcia Icazbalceta, 5 vols. (Mexico, 1892), ii, p. 66; "Memorial de las cosas que se piden y suplican a Su Majestad por parte de los religiosos de la orden de Sanct Francisco que residen en la Nueva España, Año de 1569": *ibid.*, iv, pp. 102–4. For the complexities of competing inquisitional jurisdictions throughout the colonial period, see Richard E. Greenleaf, "The Inquisition and the Indians of New Spain: A Study in Jurisdictional Confusion", *Americas*, xx (1965), pp. 138–66.

[9] Vasco de Quiroga, quoted in Robert Ricard, *The Spiritual Conquest of Mexico: An Essay on the Apostolate and the Evangelizing Methods of the Mendicant Orders in New Spain, 1523–1572*, trans. L. B. Simpson (Berkeley and Los Angeles, 1966), p. 244.

[10] *Ibid.*, pp. 247–8.

what are in effect the official and authorized accounts of that performance offered in the letters and more substantial writings of the friars themselves.[11] Thus the missionary friars have enjoyed a curious immunity from the critical scrutiny to which the real as opposed to the claimed motives and actions of their lay compatriots are now routinely subjected. That immunity probably derives both from their persons and from their role. Even secular-minded men are attracted by the peculiarly appealing mix of humanity and mysticism of St. Francis and his followers. Then there is the undoubted fact of the heroism of the early missionaries. In the sorry tale of Spanish mistreatment of Indians one cannot be unmoved by the friars' self-forgetfulness, their courage, and their magnificent tenacity: sinister claims of missionary brutality appear as a meanspirited coda to the triumphant cantata of their achievement.

For the secularist historian, these inhibitions are real enough; for historians identified with the Order, they must be powerful indeed. Manuel Pazos, the Spanish Franciscan who has written specifically on the friars' system of punishment, contrives to read charges of cruelty as paradoxical testaments to the loftiness of Franciscan intentions and actions: the great bulk of the accusations he identifies as the malicious inventions of wicked men who, finding their disreputable interests frustrated by Franciscan vigilance, inflated "ten or twelve strokes laid on over clothing" for routine offences, like failure to attend the doctrine, into "unheard-of tortures, strait imprisonment and violent deaths".[12] Fray Pedro Borges, less sanguine, acknowledges that some friars exceeded proper limits, but points out that as the excesses were lamented by leading missionaries, they may be identified as "aberrations".[13] Thus he draws a clear line between Franciscans who correctly followed the tenets of their order, and those unhappy individuals who, through whatever innate pathological disposition or weakness under stress, violated those tenets.

---

[11] For example, see José Antonio Maravall, "La utopia politico-religiosa de los franciscanos en Nueva España", *Estudios americanos*, i (1949), pp. 199–227; Esteban de Palomera, S. J., *Fray Diego Valades, O.F.M., evangelizador de la Nueva España: su obra* (Mexico, 1962); José Maria Kobayashi, *L/t educación como conquista: empresa franciscana en Mexico* (Mexico, 1974); Edwin Sylvest Jr., *Motifs of Franciscan Mission Theory in Sixteenth-Century New Spain, Province of the Holy Gospel* (Washington, D.C., 1975).

[12] Manuel R. Pazos, O.F.M., "Los misioneros franciscanos de Mejico en el siglo XVI y su sistema penal respecto de los indios", *Archivo ibero-americano*, 2nd ser., lii (1953), pp. 385–440, esp. pp. 388–9.

[13] Pedro Borges, O.F.M., *Métodos misionales en la cristianización de América: siglo XVI* (Madrid, 1960), pp. 119–36, esp. p. 121.

It is a comfortable reading, and one which, given the fragmentary and polemical character of so much of the evidence, cannot be casually set aside. Yet the vehemence of the accusations, the reputability of at least some who make them, and even more, the compelling detail of descriptions of particular acts of violence, snare attention, and warrant the investigation of the contrary position: that violence and cruelty threaded too deeply into missionary Franciscan performance to be diagnosed as aberrant.

There are, of course, difficulties. First, if some members of all orders used violence against their Indians, why should Franciscans be singled out for enquiry? But if, as George Santayana has reminded us, the power of a religion "consists in its special and surprising message and in the bias that revelation gives to life",[14] then we must grant that each missionary order, however little distinctive to the uncommitted observer, was imbued with its own consciously separate and cherished "message" and "bias", its own manner of construing the world and of evaluating action. It is the distinctive Franciscan "vision-in-action" that we are pursuing. Secondly, there is the problem of material. Most of the sources on this issue are, as has been said, fragmentary and coloured, suggesting much, but yielding no clear pattern: we glimpse a face, a moment of frantic or steely anger, and then the veil falls again.[15] But the episode in Yucatán, which extended over several months and is richly documented, does permit the establishment of context and the tracing of actions and of attitudes through time.

II

Yucatán received its first permanent Franciscan mission of eight friars, four from Guatemala and four from Mexico, in 1545, a year before the last desperate resistance of the Maya was finally broken. The conversion programme followed the pattern already laid down in Mexico: sons of the nobles were taken into monastery schools and there taught until they were judged sufficiently secure in the faith to be returned to their

---

[14] George Santayana, *The Life of Reason* (New York, 1953 edn.), p. 180.

[15] For some moments of violence, see Testimony of Juan de Aldana, n.d., in *Don Diego Quijada, alcalde mayor de Yucatán, 1561–1565*, ed. France V. Scholes and Eleanor B. Adams, 2 vols. (Mexico, 1938), i, pp. 224–5; "Informacion que hizo el provisor de los indios naturales de Mexico, sobre la usurpación de jurisdición ecclesiastica que hacian los frailes de la orden de San Francisco, Mexico, 24 Julio 1574", in *Epistolario de Nueva España, 1505–1518*, ed. Francisco del Paso y Troncoso, 16 vols. (Mexico, 1939–42), xi, pp. 147–71. esp. pp. 148–169.

villages as Christian schoolmasters, where they were to lead their fellow villagers through simple routines of worship, and prepare them for special instruction given by visiting friars. Initially the friars could staff only three monasteries, two in the Spanish towns of Mérida and Campeche and the third in Maní, the Indian province which had allied itself with the Spaniards during the latter phases of the conquest. Careful expansion followed as recruiting drives to Spain increased the friars' numbers: in 1549 six or seven Franciscans arrived, in 1553 perhaps fifteen, and in 1561 ten more entered the peninsula. By the end of that year, eight monasteries were in operation.

The conversion programme appeared to go sweetly enough. Settler-Indian relations were less abraded in Yucatán than in most other parts of the Indies, as the terrain resisted attempts at commercial exploitation, but there was sufficient conflict for the friars to be able to identify themselves as the defenders and protectors of the Indians against Spanish avarice, and to fight, tenaciously and finally successfully, to have tribute and labour demands reduced. Yucatán was Franciscan territory: no other orders sought access to the peninsula, and under the concessionary terms of the bull *Exponi nobis* the handful of secular clerics were subject to the authority of the Franciscan prelate. Then, after seventeen years of effort, and on the eve of the arrival of the first bishop to take up the diocese, Franciscans at Maní were confronted by clear evidence that their "Christian" Indians, who had been the first to be offered the faith, had continued to cherish and worship their idols in secret.

On being rounded up and questioned, local Indians readily admitted their idolatries, and implicated other communities. Then the friars at the monastery – the guardian, and six other Franciscans posted to Maní monastery to improve their command of Mayan – proceeded to take the Indians in job lots of twenty or thirty, and to subject them to the torture known as the *garrucha*, or the "hoist". A Spanish eyewitness remembered:

when the Indians confessed to having so few idols (one, two or three) the friars proceeded to string up many of the Indians, having tied their wrists together with cord, and thus hoisted them from the ground, telling them that they must confess all the idols they had, and where they were. The Indians continued saying they had no more... and so the friars ordered great stones attached to their feet, and so they were left to hang for a space, and if they still did not admit to a greater quantity of idols they were flogged as they hung there, and had burning wax splashed on their bodies... [16]

---

[16] Testimony of Bartolomé de Bohorqués, 2 Jan. 1565, in *Don Diego Quijada*, ed. Scholes and Adams, i, p. 25. For an account of the inquisition, see France V. Scholes and Ralph L.

When they were finally let down, the Indians were sent off to collect as many idols as they had "confessed" to owning, and were then returned to gaol to await formal judgement and punishment.

The judgements were made by the recently elected provincial of the order, Fray Diego de Landa, who in the absence of a bishop invoked his authority to conduct an episcopal inquisition. There is no hint that Landa flinched from what had been done by his brothers, or urged a gentler course. Indeed he delayed his own arrival in Mérida to take charge of proceedings for almost a month. On his arrival, he maintained the procedures of mass arrest and savage unselective torture, and ordered the inquiry extended into the ranks of the Indian noble caste and into two adjacent provinces, where the violence of the tortures and the invention of the torturers appears to have been even more extravagant.[17] When, after sentence, Indian penitents were tied to the whipping-post to suffer their prescribed number of lashes, it was reported that their bodies were already so torn from the interrogations that "there was no sound part on which they could be flogged".[18] (We are far indeed from that early style of "discipline" through exhortation and exemplary self-flagellation.) A later official inquiry established that of more than 4,500 Indians put to the torture during the three months of the inquisition, 157 had died during or as a result of the interrogations. At least thirteen people were known to have committed suicide to escape the torture, while eighteen others, who had disappeared, were thought to have killed themselves. Many more had been left crippled, their shoulder muscles irreparably torn, and their hands paralysed "like hooks".[19]

Although Landa labelled it an episcopal inquisition, the inquiry was carried through with reckless disregard of established inquisitorial forms. In Bishop Zumárraga's inquisition into Indian idolatries in Mexico between 1536 and 1543, procedures had been carefully prescribed and as carefully adhered to, and where torture was employed it was narrowly regulated.[20] The Yucatán friars kept no records of their interrogations,

Roys, "Fray Diego de Landa and the Problem of Idolatry in Yucatán", in *Co-operation in Research* (Carnegie Institution, Pubn., no. 501, Washington, D.C., 1938), pp. 585–620.

[17] Order to Bartolomé de Bohorques from Don Diego Quijada, 3 June 1562, in *Don Diego Quijada*, ed. Scholes and Adams, i, pp. 31–2; orders to Bartolomé de Bohorques to imprison certain named *caciques* and *principales* of Maní province, various dates: *ibid.*, pp. 32–5; Fray Antonio de Tarancón to Fray Francisco de Bustamente, 26 Feb. 1563: *ibid.*, ii, p. 22.

[18] Testimony of Juan de Villalobos, 27 Feb. 1562: *ibid.*, i, p. 66.

[19] Report of Sebastian Vazquez, 25 Mar. 1565: *ibid.*, pp. 209–21, esp. pp. 212–14.

[20] For Bishop Zumárraga's inquisition, and a full discussion of the episcopal inquisition and the operations of the Tribunal of the Holy Office in the sixteenth century, see

nor was any control exercised over the degree and duration of the torture. The penalties imposed – further floggings, heavy fines, and periods
of forced labour of up to ten years' duration, and these only on lesser
offenders – were well in excess of the limits clearly laid down by the
Mexican ecclesiastical council of 1555.[21] The provincial was later to justify his and his friars' disregard of legal formalities on the grounds of the
desperate urgency of the situation, in that:

> all [the Indians] being idolaters and guilty, it was not possible to proceed strictly
> juridically against them...because if we had proceeded with all according to
> the order of the law, it would be impossible to finish with the province of Maní
> alone in twenty years, and meanwhile they would all become idolaters and go to
> hell.[22]

But the friars had responded with swift ruthlessness and startling violence
to the initial discovery, before the extent of the problem was known. Their
actions were judged by Spaniards who saw them as shockingly cruel: secular priests as well as lay colonists protested, and made desperate efforts to
intervene, at some risk to themselves. It is true that over the last few days
of the inquiry Landa himself had extracted some lurid "confessions" to
human sacrifices, with preliminary crucifixions of the victims, but while
these were used, belatedly, to justify Franciscan procedure, they cannot
be invoked to explain it. Nor did the friars' energies flag: despite the concerted appeals of local Spaniards – and despite having watched men die –
Landa had been intent on pursuing the inquiry even more vigorously
when his authority was abruptly abrogated by the arrival of the new
bishop.

   The bishop was himself a Franciscan, of twenty years service in Mexico. On his elevation, Fray Francisco de Toral had indicated his continued
loyalty to the regular orders in their struggle against the seculars by reit-
erating to the crown his conviction that the regular clergy had the right

   Richard E. Greenleaf, *Zumárraga and the Mexican Inquisition, 1535–1543* (Washington,
   D.C., 1962); Richard E. Greenleaf, *The Mexican Inquisition of the Sixteenth Century.*
   (Albuquerque, N.M., 1969). For the detailed records of one torture session, see "Proceso
   del Santo Oficio contra Miguel, indio, vecino de Mexico, por idolatria", in *Processos
   de indios idolatras y hechiceros* (Publicationes del Archivo General de la Nacion, iii,
   Mexico, 1912), pp. 134–9.
[21] For the regulations, see Francisco Antonio Lorenzana, *Concilios provinciales primero y
   segundo, celebrados en el muy noble y muy leal ciudad de Mexico presidiendo el Illmo.
   y Rmo. Senor D. Fr. Alonso de Montufar, en los años de 1555, y 1565* (Mexico, 1769).
[22] Petition of Fray Diego de Landa, 15 Sept. 1562, in *Don Diego Quijada*, ed. Scholes and
   Adams, i, p. 171.

and the duty to punish their Indians physically.[23] Nonetheless Toral came quickly to repudiate what his brothers had done in Yucatán. Judging the Indian "confessions" to blasphemous idolatries and to human sacrifice to be the pitiable inventions of tormented and desperate men, he decided the Indians to have been guilty of no more than the continuation of some of their old idolatries, as to be expected in a people so new to the faith. He believed Landa and his friars had grossly over-reacted to minor delinquencies, and to have been moved throughout the inquiry by anger, arrogance and cruelty. When Lorenzo de Bienvenida, a pioneer in the Yucatán mission field, but in the last years much absent on administrative duties, returned to the peninsula in November of that same year, he too denounced his colleagues' activities, declaring it to be "unheard of" that the custodians of a people so new to the faith should become "their judges, their torturers, even their executioners". Both men were in their turn denounced as traitors to the order.[24] Within three months of his arrival, the breach between the bishop and most of his erstwhile brothers was complete.

Even after Landa had returned to Spain to face an inquiry by a committee of the Council of the Indies, his fellow Franciscans remained obdurate in their opposition to the bishop, and obdurate in their conviction that their behaviour over the three months of the inquisition – despite its illegalities, despite the blood and violence, despite the opposition of the colonists – had been fitting and necessary. We are not dealing with a solitary missionary flaring into momentary rage, or with the sudden voiding of "natural" frustration. Here a group of perhaps fifteen to twenty friars either initiated, actively prosecuted or supported a programme of extreme physical punishment over a prolonged period of time.[25] Their behaviour

[23] For details of Toral's life, see Eleanor B. Adams, *A. Biobibliagraphy of Franciscan Authors in Colonial Central America* (Washington, D.C., 1953), pp. 78–9. For his view on the necessity of punishment, see Fray Francisco de Toral to the crown, 28 May 1562, in *Documentos para la historia de Yucatán*, ed. F. V. Scholes *et al.*, 3 vols. (Merida, 1936–8), ii, p. 23.

[24] Declaration made at the request of Bishop Francisco de Toral on how Fray Diego de Landa and other regular clergy exercised ecclesiastical jurisdiction in the province of Yucatán, Jan. 1563, in *Don Diego Quijada*, ed. Scholes and Adams, i, pp. 249–89; Fray Lorenzo de Bienvenida to the crown, 23 Feb. 1563: *ibid.*, ii, p. 8; Fray Antonio de Tarancón to Fray Lorenzo de Bienvenida, n.d.: *ibid.*, pp. 14–16; Fray Antonio de Tarancón to Bishop Toral, n.d.: *ibid.*, pp. 16–21.

[25] While the arrival of friars into the peninsula is reasonably well documented, many departures seem to have gone unrecorded. I have been unable to establish the precise number of Franciscans present in Yucatán in 1562. It was later claimed against Landa that he had driven several "venerable and learned" friars out of the province when he

was certainly a distortion of conventional procedures, as Toral's response demonstrates, but where so large a group is so passionately persuaded of the appropriateness of its conduct, the distortion cannot be dismissed as fortuitous. It is reasonable to hypothesize a systematic relationship between the Yucatán friars' collective response, and their shared, though not necessarily explicit, understanding of the nature of the missionary enterprise and of the prerogatives legitimately exercised by those who pursued it.

That understanding had been built from the friars' own experience in the field, from the mental and moral attitudes shaped by their training within the order, and from the legends which had already come to cluster around the doings of the heroic first Twelve. The task is to trace the connections between the Yucatán friars' behaviour, the approved model of conduct in the field as developed by the pioneer missionaries, and the official Franciscan ideology from which that model was derived. Here "ideology" is being used in no pejorative nor in any limited political sense. Borrowing from Clifford Geertz, I take ideologies to be integrated structures of interrelated meanings, which function as "maps of problematical social reality and matrixes for the creation of collective conscience".[26] Geertz sees these maps being required when social reality is threatened, as when changes in the polity call received traditions into question. I would argue that in the course of the Observant Franciscans' constantly renewed struggle to reject the "received traditions" of their own wider society their attitudes crystallized to that degree of coherence, order and consciousness which warrants their identification as an ideology.

What, then, were the significant elements of Franciscan ideology as maintained by the men of San Gabriel? Most obviously, it was oppositional. St. Francis himself had rejected "received traditions" of his own

---

became provincial: Declaration made at the request of Bishop Francisco de Toral . . . Jan. 1563: *ibid.*, i, pp. 257–8, 262, 270–1, 283. Even so one friar at least, Juan de Herrera, was ready to denounce Landa's activities to the incoming bishop: Fray Antonio de Tarancón to Fray Francisco Bustamente, 26 Feb. 1563: *ibid.*, ii, p. 23. But a large majority were solidly behind the provincial: on 17 September 1562, in the thick of the flurry of the paper war between bishop and provincial, and shortly after the bishop had prohibited the use of torture, sixteen friars signed an accord devised by Landa declaring their refusal to administer the sacraments to the Indians of the province on the grounds of the "pertinacious idolatry" of so many Indians and the lack of a remedy for such activities. On the following day the friars declared they should man only five monasteries – three of them in Spanish towns and another in the already "purified" province of Maní. Despite their careful wording, the accords were clearly political acts. *Ibid.*, i, pp. 177–9.

[26] Clifford Geertz, "Ideology as a Cultural System", in his *The Interpretation of Cultures* (New York, 1973), p. 220.

society, most dramatically in the famous episode appropriately staged in the square before the bishop's palace in Assisi where, in the presence and in repudiation of his father, Francis stripped himself of all his clothing, so in one economical gesture symbolically divesting himself of family, of possessions, and of personal dignity as conventionally understood. Francis and his followers had moved through the world as "strangers and pilgrims", emphasizing their separateness with acts of calculated *naiveté*, embracing the humiliations heaped upon them, and narrowly escaping official definition as madmen or heretics.[27] To be a Franciscan in early sixteenth-century Spain was to be secure in official approval, but it was still, in an important sense, to choose exile in one's own land. To preach the beauty of poverty and humility in an expansionist, gold-dazzled, rank-mad world was to reject the values which most powerfully moved other men. But the Franciscans were still Spaniards, and their challenge to those values was expressed in the shared cultural idiom of theatrical gesture and escalation of contest. Spanish lay society identified rank and worth with the conspicuous display and consumption of material wealth; in sumptuous dress, lavish feasting and lordly giving. The Franciscans countered with an equally deliberate display of poverty and austerity; with conscientiously mean garments, competitive fasting, and total dependence on charity. To the Spanish passion for title, personal honour and pride in family, the friars opposed abandonment of family and title for the egalitarian brotherhood of Christ, and developed a powerful rhetoric of word and gesture to celebrate humility. Fray Martín de Valencia provides one among many examples of Franciscan counter-theatre, when, embarked on a visit to his natal village, he came to reflect – when already too far from the monastery to return, we are told – on the propriety of his action:

when he saw that it was something wordly and without profit – so as to bring vengeance upon himself and punishment upon his fault, greatly desiring to attain humility and contempt personally while wishing to be regarded as a madman by men for the love of God – he took off his habit before entering the village and, naked in the flesh except for underclothing and with a cord around his neck, he ordered his companion to lead him behind him like a malefactor through the streets of Valencia up to the church, and to lead him through a street where most of his relations lived. After this was done, and without visiting anyone, they returned the way they had come, whereby the relatives and inhabitants of that village scorned and despised him.

[27] For an attractive and long-needed brief account of the early days of the Franciscan order, and a useful collection of central documents, see Rosalind B. Brooke, *The Coming of the Friars* (New York and London, 1975).

He did this, his chronicler informs us, "for the love of Jesus Christ and to conquer himself", but we may legitimately note that not all private scruples are so publicly and painfully displayed.[28]

Thus the Franciscan ideal mirrored, but in reversed and opposed images, and indeed comprised a radical critique of, the Spanish secular world which the Observants came to believe they could not directly change. That belief justified their retreat to the eremitical life of San Gabriel. The peculiar delicacy with which authority was exercised within that province has already been touched upon. Ambivalence towards authority had marked the order from its earliest days. Francis had celebrated the beauty of the casting-aside of the will, and the joy of unreflecting submission. Yet for one individual to achieve that desired experience, another had to assume dominance. The tension of that paradox was reduced by distinctive strategies. The right to command obedience was not total: a brother could and should refuse an order which went against his heart and sense of the Rule. Further, if the inferior was bound to obedience, the superior was bound to total concern. Nor was authority permanently assigned, save to the minister general: lesser offices rotated by election, ensuring that the authority experience was transitory, and always followed by the antidote (and preferred) experience of powerlessness. The Franciscans so resisted the notion of a structural authority based on power rather than tenderness as to avoid the metaphor "father" in their characterization of those men who accepted the burdens of Martha to free their brothers to follow the way of Mary; they were rather the "servants", the "slaves", or – most characteristically of all – the "mothers" of their communities.[29] These were the complex understandings which shaped the delicate scrupulosity of Fray Martín's exercise of authority in San Gabriel.

For pope, crown and minister general to choose men who had withdrawn from their own world and who approached authority so gingerly as founders of the new church in the Indies might seem perverse, were

---

[28] *Oroz Codex*, ed. Chavez, p. 80.

[29] For example, "Those who wish to lead the religious life in hermitages let them go in threes and fours at most. Let two of them be the mothers and have two sons or one at least each; let the former lead the life of Martha, the latter of Mary": *Opuscula S. Patris Francisci Assisiensis*, ed., PP. Collegii S. Bonaventurae, 2nd edn. (Quaracchi, 1941), pp. 82–4. David Knowles offers a succinct and sensitive account of the distinctively Franciscan understanding of obedience, in his *From Pachomius to Ignatius: A Study in the Constitutional History of the Religious Orders* (Oxford, 1966), esp. pp. 80–8. For the constitutions of the order, see Rosalind B. Brooke, *Early Franciscan Government: Elias to Bonaventure* (Cambridge, 1959).

it not that along with the emphasis on submission, on austerities and on the minute regulation and examination of daily conduct, went a restless activism. Long before he was called to Mexico Fray Martín had sought to enter the mission field in emulation of his mentor Juan of Guadalupe. So profoundly was he moved when the thought first came to him that he stood enraptured for eight hours, so that even his fellow friars thought him deranged. The verse which triggered his ecstasy sounded a solemn millenarian note: "convertentur ad vesperam, et famen patientur".[30] In the minister general's exhortation to Fray Martín and the Twelve the millenarian and the activist notes sounded again; as he urged at this "eleventh hour... with the end of the world at hand", they go forth into the vineyard, for "if up to now, with Zaccheus up in the figberry tree sucking the sap of the Cross, you sought to see who Jesus might be, hurry down now to the active life".[31]

For Martín and his brothers, the New World was as liberating as it was for their lay countrymen: we ought not draw too sharp a line between missionaries and others attracted by the freedom of strange lands. Spirits which had chafed in the cloister, and energies which under the restrictions of the old world too easily soured into fretfulness, found joyful fulfilment in the massive and absorbing task of tending their new flock. The hardships and privations, elaborately contrived and artificially protected in Spain, were in New Spain part of their daily lot: in the weary distances travelled, always on foot; in the strange food and stranger diseases; in the exhaustion of the constant struggle to identify, in a flow of mere sound, the contours and intentions of human speech. They embraced the active life, and there was joy in it: one of his companions later recalled that Martín:

more highly regarded the services he had rendered to God our Lord in the two years that he had laboured in this Apostolate, and judged them more worthy of merit, than the thirty years he had spent within the order in Spain, although he spent these in much prayer and divine contemplation, in many penitential practices of fastings, scourgings, nakedness and barefootedness, and other holy exercises.[32]

There were, of course, costs. Even for Franciscans accustomed to self-exile within their home society the transition was profound. One

[30] *Oroz Codex*, ed. Chavez, pp. 174–5; Fray Geronimo de Mendieta, *Historia ecclesiástica indiana*, ed. Joaquín Garcia Icazbalceta (Mexico, 1971), bk. 5, ch. 4, pp. 577–9.
[31] *Oroz Codex*, ed. Chavez, p. 350.
[32] *Ibid.*, p. 183.

recognized loss was full participation in communal life. Alone among the missionary orders of New Spain, the Franciscans seem to have accepted eviction from the security and control of the community with equanimity. While the Dominicans and Augustinians came only unwillingly to the conclusion that the exigencies of missionary life precluded the maintenance of the old mode of living, the Franciscan minister general, while acknowledging that it would be "best" for his friars "to be together in one city", was prepared to accept from the outset that the community might be able to meet only once a year. He was, however, insistent that the friars work always in pairs, or groups of four. He recalled "the example of our father St. Francis, who when travelling made a superior of his companion, so as to be always under obedience".[33] That dyad of one who orders and one who obeys was the essential unit of the Franciscan structure: where it was, so was the order.

It might seem that the minister general's confidence in the ordering power of the Rule, even in an unfamiliar world, was not misplaced. Although the community was physically dispersed, it was present still in the steady and unchanging rhythm of daily observances, marking the hours with the familiar prayers, and the sacrifice of the mass. The very meagreness of Franciscan possessions, even to the familiar patches of the habit which served as blanket by night and garment by day, must have woven a web of security around the immediate environment unknown to those who travel amid a clutter of refractory possessions. New situations called for new strategies, but innovations were bound into the myths of the order: when a friar taught his Indians to count out the syllables of the essential prayers by stones, or to recite the names of the seven sins by naming three to the thumb, and one for each finger, he knew he was following the routines developed by the heroic Twelve, already legends in their lifetime. The Franciscan chronicler Geronimo de Mendieta, memorializing fifty years of missionary activity over the vast and various terrain of Mexico, was so confident that Franciscans remained rule-governed men, even when the rules had to be self-imposed and self-interpreted, as to dismiss any need to investigate the conversion experiences of particular villages or provinces: he was persuaded that "all were cut with the same scissors, and came to receive the faith in the same way".[34]

---

[33] Borges, *Métodos misionales en la cristianización de América*, p. 346 n. 35; *Oroz Codex*, ed. Chavez, p. 359.
[34] Mendieta, *Historia ecclesiástica indiana*, ed. Garcia Icazbalceta, bk, 3, ch. 23, p. 258.

Despite Mendieta's confidence, there had been and continued to be changes. We have already seen one early, deliberate adjustment, on the question of corporal punishment. The missionaries had little opportunity to reflect on, or even to note, other, more subtle shifts in their condition: when they could meet together, the comfort of shared religious observances and the press of urgent political business consumed the time. But that changes are not reflected upon does not make them less profound.

In one portentous regard Franciscan experience was irretrievably transformed. At home, in their self-contained communities, the problem of the proper limits of dominance and submission had been tenderly handled. In the New World, their peculiar responsibility towards the Indians, and their constant and intimate interaction, brought their charges within the boundaries of the Franciscan world. Yet in that crucial and continuing relationship the friars were placed of necessity in a position of permanent authority. There could be no rotation of office, no repeated antidote experience of powerlessness after power in that association. Nor was recognition of the claims of individual conscience likely to inhibit coercion, as it did when dealing with brother friars. As neophytes so recently in the thrall of the Devil any failure in obedience on the part of Indians could spring only from ignorance, confused understanding, or the residual influence of their old master.

That novel, inescapable, unilateral authority was rendered palatable and legitimate by the crystallization of the metaphor which was to shape Franciscan attitudes to Indians for the rest of the century and beyond. While there was some dispute as to their precise nature – gifted or backward, transparent or devious – the friars came to agree that the Indians were as children.[35] The identification defined the friars' role. They would be as fathers to their Indian charges, protecting, teaching, and where necessary chastising them. The paternalist metaphor of authority so long resisted within their own order was now irresistibly descriptive of the Franciscan-Indian relationship.

---

[35] The indispensable starting-point for any study of Franciscan thought is John Leddy Phelan, *The Millennial Kingdom of the Franciscans in the New World*, 2nd edn. (Berkeley and Los Angeles, 1970), esp. ch. 6, "The Indians, Genus Angelicum". Even in Franciscan relations with the Spanish laity, the "paternal" metaphor remains peripheral: the Franciscans who shaped the missionary venture to Mexico had withdrawn from such contact in Spain, and in the New World relations between the missionaries and the laity were played out, at least in the early years, in terms set by their conflicting interests in the Indians.

The "Indian as child" image was sufficiently complex, and its implications sufficiently serious, for it to be worth taking the time to sort out
some of its resonances. The friars had never known the Indians as warriors: they knew them only in defeat, defenceless as children before the
rapacity of lay Spaniards. The bitter experience of the gangster regime of
Nuño de Guzmán structured into Franciscan consciousness their role as
the defenders of those children. The Indians had been even more helpless before the terrible energy and invention of the Devil, who had ruled
them uncontested until the friars had come, like knights in an old story,
to set them free. The Devil's task had been made easy by the "natural"
docility of his victims, which so distinguished them from the Spaniards
as almost to make them a separate species – "small dogs" before the
Spaniards' "mighty lions" or, as Motolinía, one of the original Twelve,
put it:

by nature timid and very bashful so that it seems as if they were born to obey.
If one puts them in a corner, there they stay as if they were nailed there . . . What
one can say of these people is that they are temperamentally very different from
us, for we Spaniards have a heart that is big and ardent as fire, and these Indians,
and all the animals of this land, are by nature tame . . .[36]

The apparent docility and patience of Indians under the lash of disease
and of incessant Spanish demands, their uncomplaining acceptance of
acute poverty and physical hardship, and above all their seeming lack of
interest in material things, led many friars to read in Indian behaviour
evidence of remarkable innate qualities. Where we would see a people
shaken by defeat and exploitation, but still living within a cultural system
of complex reciprocities and highly elaborated deference rules, the friars
saw men and women "naturally" humble and submissive, and free of
the vices of pride, avarice and envy. The poignancy of that example for
Franciscans need not be laboured. When Motolinía wrote his *History*,
extolling twenty years of missionary activity and achievement, he warned
any newcomer friar noted for his penitential life in Castile that in New
Spain he would be no more than a river flowing into the sea, for "here the
whole community lives very poorly and keeps every rule that can be kept".
They did so because before them was always the example of the Indians,
"miserably dressed and barefooted, their beds and dwellings exceedingly
poor and their food more meagre than that of the strictest penitent, so
these newcomers will find nothing on which to pride themselves". Even

---

[36] *Motolinía's History of the Indians of New Spain*, ed. Foster, pp. 136–7. For examples
of the devil's audacity, see *ibid.*, pp. 131–2.

for long-resident friars, contemplation of the Indians induced humility, "for the Indians exceed them in penance, and in being scorned by men".[37] Geronimo de Mendieta, writing at the end of the century, had come to see the Indians as the meek of the Sermon on the Mount: theirs would be the kingdom of heaven, while Spaniards lay wailing.[38] Finally, the apparent ineffectuality and *naiveté* of Indians faced with the alien Spanish world–their "childishness", as we might put it – resonated with another aspect in the Franciscans' own preferred self-image. For them the child image, suffused as it was by the radiance of the Christ-child, was especially compelling, as they had sought to retrieve spontaneity and simplicity of soul by casting away the ephemera of this world to become the childlike simpletons of God. Mendieta found it peculiarly moving, because peculiarly fitting, that the first friars found their own best teachers to be the Indian children, who led them, stumbling and trusting, into the intricacies of the native tongues.[39]

As children, Indians were to be punished as children. "Fathers and teachers" in Spain had exercised their natural authority rigorously indeed, as Richard Kagan's accounts of routine floggings of schoolboys attest,[40] but for Indians – by nature more malleable, responsive, docile – less extreme, if more sustained, punishment was required. Their childhood was not a stage, but a state: for them, tutelage was to be permanent. The "soft wax" image, common enough in pedagogical literature, caught precisely what the friars saw as an Indian characteristic: quick to take an impression, they were equally quick to lose it, unless the impress were repeated again and again. Mendieta, persuaded of the beauty of the Indian soul, still knew they needed the whip:

the whip is as necessary to them as is bread to the mouth, and . . . to natural they could not live without it, and they themselves admit that, like children, they are lost without it, for if an Indian gets drunk or takes a concubine or beats and abuses his wife without reason, or if she runs away from her husband, or if they don't want to come to the mass or if they don't know the essential prayers, if they lie about the forbidden degrees of marriage, or do other similar things . . . then with a dozen lashes the matter is settled . . . and without it not only would it go unremedied, but they would go on to other major offences.[41]

---

[37] *Ibid.*, p. 194.

[38] Mendieta, *Historia ecclesiástica Indiana*, ed. Garcia Icazbalceta, *passim*, esp. bk. 3, ch. 41, pp. 281–93, and bk. 4, ch. 21, pp. 437–42.

[39] *Ibid.*, bk. 3, ch. 16, pp. 219–20.

[40] Richard Kagan, *Students and Society in Early Modern Spain* (Baltimore, 1974), esp. pp. 7–8.

[41] Fray Geronimo de Mendieta to the crown, 15 Apr. 1587, in *Nueva colección de documentos para la historia de Mexico*, ed. Garcia Icazbalceta, v, p. 9.

If the paternal metaphor legitimated the friars' new authority in the most human and reassuring terms, it also caught some of the emotional content of the Franciscan response to their charges. The friars were men who had abandoned the ties of kin for the fellowship of their brothers in Christ. In the New World, part of that companionship was denied those who committed themselves to active work in the mission field. In recompense, some found sustained relationships with particular Indian communities, especially as the hierarchy recognized that slow and painfully acquired expertise in a particular language should not be lightly set aside. At least for some friars, the hollow shape of "paternalism" was filled with the warm blood of human experience and affection. Further, that authority, unsought and therefore untainted, carried with it a great promise. Franciscans were of course free from that requirement, which was to lie so heavily on so many Protestant missionaries, of exemplifying, amid the perturbations and confusions of an alien world, the harmonious order of Christian family life. They had extricated themselves from the distracting tangles of familial and sexual relationships: their concern was with the soul's relationship to God. The way of life they celebrated, they knew, transcended ordinary human impulses. Those who chose to live by the Rule did so in the sure knowledge that the way to virtue lay through the defiance of natural instincts, the more systematic and vigorous the defiance the better. Franciscans confronted by the societies of the New World were not led to reflect on the relativity of social arrangements: their concern was to scrutinize social forms in terms of their approximation to the Christian ideal. Here, as we have seen, some aspects of Indian social behaviour and Indian "nature" appeared excitingly promising. The behaviour of their own compatriots – their pride, their avarice, their sloth, their sensuality – was no embarrassment, for it could be made to serve not as example, but as object lesson. The "authority" the military achievements of those same compatriots had thrust upon them was rendered legitimate, and could only be rendered legitimate, if it were seen as exclusive, absolute, and directed solely towards the shaping and moulding of their Indians into a triumphantly Christian social order.

Again and again through Franciscan explanations and justifications of their treatment of the Indians the same note sounds: as fathers and teachers of their charges, they claimed the autonomy necessary for the proper fulfilment of those roles, insisting that affection, responsibility, and their conscientious repudiation of the desire for power or for material goods provided complete protection against abuse. Only they could be trusted to discharge the conscience of the king; all other Spaniards' motives were suspect. The power to direct and to punish, once perceived as so dangerous, had become sanctified through its identification with an authority at once natural, human and divine.

Those claims (constantly reiterated by the official spokesmen of the order) could have made them ruthless social legislators indeed. But in most areas of New Spain the crown policy of overlapping jurisdictions, and of ranging one administrative hierarchy against another in dynamic tension, worked to prevent the dominance of any single group: the missionary friars were regularly and forcefully reminded that other groups also insisted on their right to intervene in Indian affairs. In the radically simplified frontier situation of Yucatán no such complex equipoise was possible. There the Franciscans enjoyed a monopoly of the mission field. No other order challenged their account of the Indians, or jealously assessed Franciscan performance. Nor did the secular government significantly restrict Franciscan pretensions. After the crown, with its usual mistrust of those who had served it too well, deprived Yucatán's conqueror Francisco de Montejo of all his authority, secular government passed through the hands of a sequence of undistinguished local colonists. Only in 1561, less than a year before the "idolatry trials" erupted, had an *alcalde mayor* from outside been appointed. By that time the political dominance of the Franciscans, under the leadership of their new provincial, Diego de Landa, had been effectively established, not least by the deliberate and systematic destruction of an overly-confident colonist who had dared to challenge Franciscan authority.[42] The incoming *alcalde mayor*, Diego Quijada, early identified Landa as a "choleric man" who "intends to rule in both spiritual and temporal matters";[43] three months later, by threats and the force of his passionate righteousness, Landa had reduced Quijada to the status of docile lieutenant.[44] Given political ascendance, standard Franciscan rhetoric of autonomous control over Indians could appear to be descriptive of reality, and could be made to be so. Strong emotional commitment was also present. The friars believed the

---

[42] "*Proceso* against Francisco Hernandez before the Ordinary Inquisition for Offences against the Friars of St. Francis, 1556–1562", in *Archivo de la historia de Yucatán, Campeche y Tabasco*, ed. J. Ignacio Rubio Mañé, 3 vols. (Mexico, 1942), ii, pp. 7–334. Rubio Mañé outlines the events in his Introduction: *ibid.*, i, pp. xxi–xxxiii; as does France Scholes in his Introduction to *Don-Diego Quijada*, ed. Scholes and Adams, i, pp. xx–xxvi.

[43] Don Diego Quijada to the crown, 15 Apr. 1562, in *Cartas de Indias*, doc. no. lxviii, pp. 380–91.

[44] For a clue to the intimidation of Quijada, see petition of Fray Diego de Landa to Don Diego Quijada, 4 July 1562, in *Don Diego Quijada*, ed. Scholes and Adams, i, p. 70.

Indians had ratified their own self-definition as their protectors and chosen custodians. Landa recalled that from the early days of the mission,
when the Indians:

saw all they [the friars] endured, without any private interest, and the freedom
which resulted from their efforts ... they did nothing without informing the friars
and taking their advice, and this gave cause for the [lay] Spaniards to be envi-
ous, and to say the friars had acted in this way to have the government of the
Indies ... [45]

"Paternalism" is a comfortably capacious metaphor: we would be
mistaken if we saw its content as necessarily or solely benevolent. There
are fathers and fathers. Some "loving" fathers punish most tenaciously.
Indeed the profound ambivalence of the consciously loving father towards
his child-victim is only now beginning to be explored.[46] In the very violence of the response of the Yucatán friars to the discovery of the "treachery" of their Indians we see the emotion-charged punitive rage of the
betrayed parent. Landa's own pain and bitterness are clear:

The provincial said that he had been among these Indians for fourteen years,
that he spoke their tongue, and had taught them the doctrine, and that no one
had a higher opinion of them than he, until they had disillusioned him ... and
he knew the whole land was damned, and that without compulsion they would
never speak the truth.[47]

He had trusted them, and believed them to have reciprocated that
trust, but they had wilfully deceived him; in all outward things they
had appeared to be Christian, yet secretly they cherished their old faith,
for "while they seem a simple people they are up to any mischief, and
obstinately attached to the rites and ceremonies of their forefathers".[48]
Their apparent recognition of the natural authority of the friars, their
apparent devotion, had been exposed as fraudulent, while their loyalty to

---

[45] *Landa's Relación de las cosas de Yucatán: A Translation*, trans. and ed. Alfred M. Tozzer
(Cambridge, Mass., 1941), p. 72.

[46] There is much to resist in Lloyd Demause's opening essay "The Evolution of Childhood",
in Lloyd Demause (ed.), *The History of Childhood* (New York, 1974), pp. 1–73. However, his brief analysis of the projective and reversal responses triggered in the parent by
the existence, not the behaviour, of the child is compelling, and he does much to explain
how severe floggings can be administered by parents who believe themselves to be loving,
and who suffer grievously as they flog.

[47] Statement made by the marques del Valle, 27 Nov. 1562, in *Don Diego Quijada*, ed.
Scholes and Adams, i, p. 186.

[48] Information given at the request of Provincial Diego de Landa before Dr. Quijada,
Jan. 1563: *ibid.*, p. 296.

their traditional lords was such that they could be burned alive before they would publicly speak against them. Returned to Spain, and answering charges made against him by a committee acting for the Council of the Indies, Landa was wrestling still with the painful paradox of his own earlier patience and gentleness in rebuking and forgiving Indians for their backsliding, when all the while they were exploiting his tenderness so as to deceive him further. He had finally come to realize, he said, that only through punishment could such a people be improved.[49]

The administering of that punishment had helped assuage his anguish: whimpering under the lash, men are made children again. Writing later of the affair, he was able to dismiss it briskly. The Maya had, after a promising beginning, yielded to the exhortations of their old chiefs and priests, and returned secretly to their old ways; they had been punished for it, and after punishment "in general they all showed deep repentance and readiness to become good Christians".[50]

III

On the first day of 1562, in the monastery at Toluca, Geronimo de Mendieta completed a long letter to his commissary general. Over its many pages he rehearsed, with the eloquence which comes not from art alone but from passionate conviction, the themes which have become familiar through the course of this essay. The great achievements of the past, the peace and Christian order of the kingdom, were hanging in the balance. Everywhere Indians were falling back into drunkenness and idolatry. There were endless debates between the orders, between secular clergy and religious, between ecclesiastical and secular authorities. The remedy was simple. All authority over the Indians (under the eye of the viceroy) should be vested in the friars. Mendieta admitted no anxiety as to how that authority would be used: while acknowledging that "perhaps three or four" friars might in the past have been guilty of "follies and extravagances", he knew the friars, unlike their compatriots, had been drawn to the new lands only to save souls, and to discharge the conscience of the king. There was for them no pleasure in domination. Left unrestrained, the Indians were as restive and ungovernable as beasts of the forest: under the exclusive authority of the friars – without lawyers,

---

[49] Responses of Fray Diego de Landa to the charges made by Fray Francisco de Guzmán, n.d.: *ibid.*, ii, p. 416.
[50] *Landa's Relación de las cosas de Yucatán*, ed. Tozzer, p. 80.

without notaries, without judges and bishops – they could be restored to a pure and simple faith.[51] It is a moving letter, and it expresses, five months before the chance discovery which led Landa and his friars to initiate their inquisition, the vision of the world which for them justified all their actions.

The Yucatán affair, where a group of Franciscans embarked on a course of action which seemed, to all but themselves, gratuitously savage, and where in an inversion of expected roles Franciscans tortured and enslaved, while colonists protested and protected, cannot be dismissed as an aberration.[52] The friars themselves saw their behaviour as continuous with the professed ideology of their order, and so, I suggest, must we. The experience in the New World, with its emphasis on activism, and its unsought but exhilarating ascription of authority, transformed the Franciscans' social role, however unaware they may have been of the precise dimensions or directions of that transformation. Traditionally they had learned to look scornfully at lay Spaniards' reading of the world, and that scorn had been powerfully fed by their experience in the New World, and celebrated in the legends which came to cluster around the intransigence in face of secular government of the first friars in the heroic early days after the conquest. These myths, and the heady rhetoric in which they were framed, served to maintain Franciscan morale by providing an ideal vision of sanctified autonomy against which individual experience and performance could be measured. In Yucatán no competing accounts of the world blurred that vision, which was allowed to serve as a guide to action. Conventional Franciscan rhetoric of privileged propriety control

---

[51] Fray Geronimo de Mendieta to Padre Francisco de Bustamente, 1 Jan. 1562, in *Nueva colección de documentos para la historia de Mexico*, ed. Garcia Icazbalceta, i, pp. 1–34.

[52] Pazos's strategy on the affair is interesting. He refers to it only in a footnote. After stating that his study dealt with "the system and method of punishment followed by the Franciscan missionaries in Mexico, without descending to details and particular cases", and claiming that where individuals were over-rigorous all blame attaches to the individual, "not to the collectivity to which he belonged nor the mission system adopted", he allows that in so wide an area there were occasional excesses, and refers to the Yucatán case which he allows was horrifying – as painted by some authors. But he excludes the case from discussion on the grounds that as an inquisitorial proceeding it was not a matter of "normal" punishment. Pazos, "Los misioneros franciscanos de Mexico en el siglo XVI y su sistema penal respecto de los indios", p. 435 n. 78. It is a hollow defence: the "inquisition" was initiated and conducted solely by Franciscans, who (as has been demonstrated) totally disregarded established inquisitorial procedures, and pursued their own notion of appropriate action. Pedro Borges, who offers no discussion of the Yucatán friars' behaviour, makes only passing reference to "el celebérrimo caso de 1560 [sic]": Borges, *Métodos misionales en la cristianización de América*, p. 292.

over Indians was there translated into the rejection of all outsiders' claims
to intervene. And it was precisely their "special relationship" with their
Indians which justified intransigence, and what others saw as cruelty:
abstract notions of law could not be permitted to deflect the intensity of
that commitment. For Toral, in new territory, long separated from "his"
Indians; for Lorenzo de Bien-venida, one-time missionary in the Yucatán
field, but long absorbed in peripatetic administration, their conduct was
outrageous – perhaps in part because both men could glimpse in it the
dark parody of their own cherished convictions. Martín de Valencia,
scourging himself to warm cold hearts to shame, the minister general
urging his "holy fools" into the fray, or Mendieta begging that Franciscans be given untrammelled authority over their Indians, would not
willingly have recognized Landa and his fellow friars, embarked on a
three-month-long reign of terror and torture, as their brothers. But their
brothers they were.

The Yucatán situation was, as are all situations, unique. There, insti-
tutional restraints were unusually weak. Personalities mattered: Landa
was a man of formidable energy and moral passion. Those circumstances
facilitated the full acting out of the new understandings (glimpsed in more
fragmentary sources elsewhere) which had come to inform the Franciscan
missionary vision. The episode reminds us that a stable rhetoric may give
an illusion of continuity, while meanings – manifested in action – change,
and that if "ideology" may be made to serve as a shield against experience, it is also, as a mode of grasping and interpreting that experience, in
constant interplay with it.

4

Ways to the Sacred

Reconstructing "Religion" in Sixteenth-Century Mexico

The Spanish conquest of Mexico in 1521 was followed almost immediately by the ardent attempt by picked bodies of missionary friars to
convert the Mexican Indians to Christianity, or more precisely, given
the friars' view of things, to liberate the natives from their miserable
servitude to the Devil.[1] I will be concerned in what follows not with
recording the early missionaries' ambitions and apparent early triumphs,
which perspective has tended to dominate much of the writing in the
field, but rather to uncover some part of the 'concealed and mysterious
dialectics' of European and native interactions,[2] in order to discover how
the 'religion' practised by Mexican Indians in the later sixteenth century,

---

[1] There is a large literature on the early missionary effort. For the organization of the
venture, see Pedro Borges, O. F. M., *Métodos misionales en la cristianización de América:
siglo XVI*, Madrid, 1960; for the intellectual milieu in which it was pursued John Leddy
Phelan, *The Millennial Kingdom of the Franciscans in the New World* 2nd. ed., University
of California Press, Berkeley and Los Angeles, 1970 and Anthony Pagden, *The fall of
natural man*, Cambridge University Press, 1982.

[2] For a brief but penetrating discussion of how such histories ought to be managed, see
Terence Ranger, 'An Africanist Comment', *American Ethnologist* 14:1, Feb. 1987, 182–
185. Partly because of the way the sources cluster, partly to restrict a topic already too
large, I will restrict discussion to the Nahuatl-speakers of the Valley of Mexico and the
Puebla-Tlaxcala valley, with a special focus on the people of the great city of Tenochtitlán-
Tlateloco, whom we know as the 'Aztecs'. I will call them 'Mexicans', to escape some of
the freight 'Aztec' has come to bear. Following Spanish colonial usage, I call the generality
of indigenous peoples 'Indians'.

Article originally published as "Ways to the Sacred: Reconstructing 'Religion' in Sixteenth
Century Mexico," in *History and Anthropology*, Vol. 5 (1990): 105–141. © 1990 Harwood
Academic Publishers GmbH.http://www.informaworld.com. Reprinted with permission.

when the main conversion thrust was over, can best be understood. If the enquiry incorporates rather more consideration of awkward and inconclusive theoretical issues than historians readily tolerate, that is because the enterprise requires it.

First, the sources. In Mexico there is a baffling hiatus in documentation for the first twenty years or so after the conquest. Systematic records are a reflex of stability, and the memorializing impulse depends on the sense that some phase in a great story is over. Authority had been slippery in Mexico, in an unstable context of a restless and rapidly dispersing Spanish population and a demoralized and rapidly diminishing Indian one, but with the installation of the first Viceroy in 1535 both the steady record-keeping and the memorializing effectively began. Within a year of the Viceroy's coming the Archbishop of Mexico launched his first Episcopal Inquisition, which functioned from 1536 to 1541, producing and preserving detailed records of all its cases, including those of the Indian 'backsliders' caught in its nets.[3] In 1541, a mere two decades after the fall of the imperial city of Mexico-Tenochtitlán to Cortés and his men, the Franciscan Toribio de Motolinía, one of the legendary 'Twelve Apostles to the Indies', had completed his 'History of the Indians of New Spain', in which he celebrated the total triumph of Christianity in what he was ready to call (in face of the Inquisition's findings) the 'new Jerusalem' of Mexico. In the same year an elaborate, delicately drawn and coloured pictorial record of life as it had been lived in Mexico-Tenochtitlán before the Spaniards came was presented to the Viceroy, and named for him the 'Codex Mendoza'. The Spanish rush to fix and order the past (and so to control their present) had begun.

At about the same time Indian communities, drawing on the skills of mission-trained youths, began to keep their own records in their own Nahuatl tongue written in European script. Remarkable work has been done over the last years to decipher some of these extraordinary Indian texts. Municipal records, wills, lawsuits, sermons, or anything else written in a native tongue by a native speaker have been scanned for

[3] Fr. Toribo Motolinía, O. F. M., *Memoriales é Historia de los indios de la Nueva España*, Estudio preliminar por Fidel de Lejarza, O. F. M., Madrid, Ediciones Atlas, 1970, hereafter *Memoriales* or *Historia*, with appropriate part or book and chapter number; James Cooper Clark, (ed.), *Codex Mendoza* 3 vols., Waterlow & Sons, London, 1938. For the standard account of Mexican manuscript paintings, see Donald Robertson, *Mexican Manuscript Painting of the Early Colonial Period: The Metropolitan Schools*, New Haven, Conn., Yale University Press, 1959. For the 'Indian' inquisition, see 'Procesos de indios idólatras y hechiceros', *Publicaciones del Archivo General de la Nación* 3, 1912–13.

adaptations of Spanish organisations, native uses of Spanish law, the composition of households, preferred systems of land tenure and inheritance,
and so on.[4] But the more interior experience of conquest and colonisation,
most particularly native response to their attempted 'spiritual conquest'
by the missionary friars, has remained something of a no-go area for
historians.[5] In part the avoidance has arisen from justifiable epistemological anxieties, the scholar who wrote the classic pioneer study of the
heroic endeavors of the first missionary friars finally abdicating the issue
of native response with the disarming disclaimer: 'who can flatter himself
that he knows what takes place in the dark minds of the natives?' (Ricard
1966:277). More recently the enquiry has also been inhibited by what
passes for ideological struggle in the quiet encampments of historians.
There has been a tendency to denigrate the use of Spanish-derived texts
for illumination on matters Indian, and to elevate the milking of Nahuatl
texts, however small the yield, however thin the milk, as the narrow way
to legitimate 'knowledge'. While there is much of how the world is and
ought to be embedded in those Nahuatl municipal records and letters
and petitions; in the changing use of the language, in variations in the
formulaic structure of wills, in the indications of individual and group
strategies and obsessions,[6] they can shed only a shifting and refracted
light on Indian religious sensibility. I want, unfashionably, to turn again
to Spanish accounts of Indian religious observances, to see what they can
be made to yield about that crucial and obscure zone.[7]

---

[4] This approach was pioneered by Arthur J. O. Anderson, Frances Berdan and James
Lockhart, with their *Beyond the Codices: The Nahua View of Colonial Mexico*, Los
Angeles, 1976 and *The Tlaxcalan Actas: A compendium of the Records of the Cabildo
of Tlaxcala (1545–1627)*, Salt Lake City, Utah, 1986. See also S. L. Cline and Miguel
Leon-Portilla (eds.) *The Testaments of Culhuacán*, Los Angeles, 1985.

[5] Charles Gibson in his magisterial study of the circumstances of life of Aztecs under Spanish
rule left such questions strictly alone. Charles Gibson, *The Aztecs under Spanish Rule*,
Stanford, Stanford University Press, 1964. But see the work of J. Jorge Klor de Alva, e.g.
his 'Spiritual Conflict and Accommodation in New Spain: Towards a Typology of Aztec
Responses to Christianity', in George A. Collier, Renato I. Rosaldo and John D. Wirth
(eds.), *The Inca and Aztec States 1400–1800*, Academic Press, 1982, pp. 345–366.

[6] See e.g. James Lockhart and Frances Karttunen, *Nahuatl in the Middle Years: Language
Contact Phenomena in Texts of the Colonial Period*, Berkeley, California, 1976, and their
The Art of Nahuatl Speech: The Bancroft Dialogues, UCLA Latin American Publications,
Los Angeles, 1987; James Lockhart, 'Views of Corporate Self and History in Some Val-
ley of Mexico Towns', in Collier *et. al*, *The Inca and Aztec States, 1400–1800*, and
'Some Nahua Concepts in Post-Conquest Guise', *History of European Ideas*, VI, 1985,
pp. 465–482; Serge Gruzinski, *La Colonisation de l'imaginaire*, Gallimard, Paris, 1987.

[7] There are, of course, other routes to Indian religious understandings. See e.g. the elegant
and ingenious strategy of analysis of baptismal records devised by William Taylor in his

There are of course problems with the Spanish texts. The records of the Episcopal Inquisition of 1536–1541 yield clear and detailed descriptions of actions and interactions, in the usual way of Inquisition records, but most are seriously lacking in context. Consider the famous case of Ocelotl, a native 'sorcerer' in the inquisitors' eyes, a resistance fighter to one recent commentator (Klor de Alva 1981: 128–141), a confused opportunist, 'the first of those petty native messiahs' (Lafaye 1976: 20–22) to another.[8] For close on two decades after the conquest Ocelotl served an extensive and aristocratic Indian clientele in the heartland of the Spanish presence, through his talent for foretelling individual catastrophes like deaths and collective ones like famines, as well as through the usual range of 'cunning man' skills of finding lost or stolen objects and curing sick animals. (His therapeutic effect on ailing humans seems to have derived primarily from his reassurances that they were not – yet – due to die.) Ocelotl amassed significant property and moved freely and publicly through central Mexico with apparently slight regard for or hindrance from the Spaniards. He was well known to the local friars who, I think, feared him: they certainly failed to act against him until the episcopal inquisitor gave the lead. The identification of his precise preconquest role is difficult, neither friars nor their youthful native assistants quite knowing what to make of those ambivalent sorcerer-magicians spangling what they studiously represented as a priestly system, while any confident characterization of his post-conquest role is impossible. Was he one of a very few native religious specialists still surviving, his role and his skills expanding to fill a post-conquest vacuum? Or did he remain a specialist in individual and long-term collective crises, while other practitioners about whom we know nothing were providing reduced but adequate routines of traditional religious activity? Given the dispersed and fragmentary evidence of the Inquisitorial records we cannot know, so the clue breaks in the hand.

The great 'practising missionary' histories, most notably Motolínia's, then later in the century works by the Dominican Diego Durán and the

---

enquiry into the relative popularity of the Guadalupe cult among Spaniards and Indians in the late colonial period. William B. Taylor, 'The Virgin of Guadalupe in New Spain: an inquiry into the social history of Marian devotion', *American Ethnologist* 14:1, February 1987, 9–33.

[8] For the case against 'Martín Ucelo' or Ocelotl see 'Procesos de indios idólatras y hechiceros', pp. 17–51. For the organisation and work of the Episcopal Inquisition, Richard E. Greenleaf, *Zumárraga and the Mexican Inquisition, 1536–1543*, Washington D.C., Academy of American Franciscan History 1961.

Franciscan Bernardino Sahagún, along with the later reports of secular clerics, have their own difficulties. They are not 'official' histories, and so happily retain idiosyncracy of perspective and observation, and as it happens their writers drew on much the same geographical zone, with some temporal overlap. Nonetheless, they disagree as to the nature of what they were observing. Motolinía was enchanted by his new flock, whom he tirelessly compared with his compatriots, always to the Spaniards' disadvantage. Unlike Spaniards, who knew the evil they did, he judged the Mexicans blameless for their earlier vile actions, for then they had been in helpless servitude to the Devil. Their delectable docility in face of Spanish brutality, their patient misery in this world, their readiness to share the little they had, identified them as the meek who would inherit the golden kingdom. He dismissed the Inquisition's findings of less than Christian behaviour as the mud-stirrings of officious troublemakers.[9] His Indians not only suffered with exemplary Christian patience but sought baptism with single-minded intensity, and revelled in Christian observances, seizing on the simplest Spanish scripts to make plays of infatuated devotion. He therefore knew them to be Christian by way of natural temperament and passionate religiosity.

The Dominican Diego Durán, who had come to Mexico as a small child and probably spoke Nahuatl pretty much 'like a native', watched those same extravagant 'Christian' performances with a notably cooler eye. He allowed that the Indians were enthusiastic enough. Enthusiasm was not the issue. What account of the world were they celebrating? He knew them to have been well taught, indeed better taught than any other people in the world, some of them into the third generation. Yet there was a troubling fecklessness about their Christianity. And everywhere he saw intimations of the old faith, in all the rhythms and routines of life: 'in sowing, in reaping, in storing grain, even in plowing the earth and building houses; in wakes and funerals, in weddings and births . . . in their dances, in their market places, in their bathhouses, in the songs they chant, in their repasts and banquets', and penetrating deep into their so-called 'Christian' performances too. The contamination of paganism and idolatry was everywhere. Durán thought there was some degree of deliberate concealment from the Spaniards, some element of deception, but he identified the deepest spring of Indian delinquency not as wilfulness, but fear. He had come to see them as a broken people, like wild creatures too long hunted 'which everything intimidates into flight'. Even before

---

[9] Motolinía, *Historia*, book 3, chapter 20.

the Spaniards came they lived 'filled with the shadows of retribution and death.' Then, with the coming of the Faith, 'the shadows increased beyond measure. From that time on these people have been afflicted with nothing but death, toil, trouble and anguish'.[10] Their terror of the Spaniards rendered them devious and incapable of learning. Durán's Indians were characterised by chronic fear, and a profound melancholy and oppression of spirit.

Bernardino de Sahagún, who came to Spain as a young Franciscan in 1529 and died there at a ripe age in 1590, and to whose efforts we owe most of what we know about pre-conquest Mexico, essentially concurred with Durán's account of the situation, but he differed from his diagnosis. For Sahagún the traditional social order had worked because it had been sufficiently strict to counter the corrupting force of climate. With the Conquest that order had been broken, largely unwittingly but probably by necessity, the things of idolatry being so inextricably mixed into it. But no new discipline of equivalent rigour had been introduced, and chaos had entered in: Indians drank to stupor, and were fit for nothing. And the friars had lost their access to the native communities. Where once the lads trained in the mission schools were eager agents of the friars and were feared by their own people, now those few who were ready to serve as the friars' agents were themselves fearful. The doors of the villagers were closed against Spaniards, and informers were made to suffer. Sahagún judged the situation to be almost hopeless: 'if the Indians were abandoned to their own devices, in less than fifty years there would be no trace of the preaching they have received' (Nicolau D'Olwer 1987:105). The only remedy was to destroy the corrupting order, and to start the heartbreaking labour again. With increasing years came deeper bitterness, and the conviction that even apparently orthodox Christian worship was no more than a mask for clandestine idolatry.[11] For Sahagún the Mexicans were finally characterised by indiscipline, sensuality, sloth, and deceit.

---

[10] Fr. Diego Durán, *Historia de las Indias de Nueva España e Islas de la Tierra Firme*, 2 vols. with Atlas, ed. José F. Ramirez, Mexico D.F., Editoria Nacional, 1967; El Calendario Antiguo, Epístola, vol. 2, pp. 68–71; 250.

[11] See especially Fr. Bernardino de Sahagún, O. F. M., 'Calendario mexicano, latino y catellano' and the 'Arte Adivinatoria', both published in Joaquín García Icazbalceta, *Bibliografía mexicana del siglo XVI. Catálogo razonado de los libros impresos en México de 1539 a 1600, México*, 1866, pp. 314–323. See also the 'Prologues' to the twelve books of his 'Florentine Codex', Fray Bernardino de Sahagún, *The Florentine Codex: General History of the Things of New Spain*, translated from the Nahuatl by Arthur J. O. Anderson and Charles E. Dibble, 13 vols., Santa Fé: School of American Research, 1950–1982, Vol. I.

What we gain from all this is the recognition that however reverent we might wish to be towards the expertise of 'men on the spot', we cannot work from their conclusions, because the men on the spot failed to agree on Indian intentions, if not Indian conduct. So what is to be done? Does the longevity of certain customs make the case for the dominance of the old ways?

Certainly Durán, sixty years after the conquest, and others forty years later again attested that traditional rites of passage, individual and collective, were still being enacted in Indian communities. But longevity of custom need not imply simple continuity of meaning. One dispirited Nichoacan priest described midwives' manipulations of fire and water during the naming of newborn infants, and reported 'seers' who gazed into water and told the people what they saw (as he grimly commented, 'although it be a lie, they believe them'); of men well paid to chase hail away from the tender crops. But his account makes clear that 'Christian' incorporations abounded too, although he understandably took small comfort from them. Indians swallowing hallucinogens like peyote or decoctions of morning glory seeds were sometimes brought to see 'Our Lord or His angels,' and chickens were ritually decapitated and their blood sprinkled on the fire in celebration of the days of Christian saints. (The flesh was then prepared as a food offering, to be divided impartially between the fire and at the altar of the church, with the 'church people', the local office-bearers, consuming the churchly share.)[12]

---

[12] Pedro Ponce, Appendix A, 'A Brief Relation of the Gods and Rites of Heathenism', in Hernando Ruiz de Alarcón, *Treatise on the Heathen Superstitions and Customs That Today live Among the Indians Native to This New Spain*, 1629, translated and edited by J. Richard Andrews and Ross Hassig, University of Oklahoma Press, 1984, *passim.* but esp. p. 218. Ponce was curate of a small Michoacán town at the time of writing, but offered a rather broader composite picture of 'Indian' religion. Note here William Christian's account of lay professionals who circulated through the sixteenth-century Castilian countryside selling their services to individuals or communities to ward off disease, locusts, other insect pests or hailstorms. Known variously as necromancers, enpsalmers, or conjurers of clouds, they competed directly with the priests of the parishes: indeed Christian comments that from the Inquisition records it would appear many of them were clergy or religious . . . 'In some places the wizards would hold matches with the local clergy to see who could best deal with the clouds'. William Christian *Local Religion in 16th century Spain*, Princeton University Press, 1981, pp. 29–30. John Bossy comments that the Counter Reformation attempt to impose a uniform religious practice in order to foster interior Christian faith and behaviour 'meant, on the popular front, turning collective Christians into individual ones'; an endeavour he believes to have failed. John Bossy, 'The Counter-Reformation and the People of Catholic Europe', *Past and Present* 47, May 1970, 51–70, p. 62.

The temptation when faced with this kind of material is to resort to playing with that familiar mix and match model of 'syncretism'. We look for the belief, the theological principle we take to be encapsulated in the particular action, and struggle to sort these items of behaviour into their category of origin – this for Indian, that for Spanish, this rapidly expanding category for 'undecided' – with the implication that we can somehow quantify just how 'Christian' these neophytes were. Here we tread the painful path of the missionary, forced by the nature of his peculiar vocation to subject a lived faith to vivisection, carving it into transportable, stateable, teachable propositions: a disturbing, dispiriting, and finally disabling business. Of the three missionaries discussed, Motolinía, with his marvellous insouciance concerning what he regarded as intellectualist trivia, probably suffered least, being insulated from despair by his recognition of the authenticity of Indian religiosity, and by his confusion of native etiquette and social ethics with specifically 'Christian' virtues. Both Durán and Sahagún sensed the incorrigibility of the cultural, the intractability of a profoundly different way of conceptualising the world and of man's place within it, and suffered accordingly.[13] But single items of behaviour, particular actions dislocated from their context in performance, can give no access to the meanings which may have informed them. Such analysis – into – fragments denies the fact that rituals are wholes, their meanings carried in the structure and the logic of their progression.

'Religion' is a notoriously protean beast, resistant to being pinned down, and all strategies are finally inadequate. But my conviction is that the 'belief analysis' approach, indeed the whole intellectualist emphasis in matters religious, however sanctified by convention, is mistaken.[14] The notion of a 'belief' as a proposition to which the individual assents does

---

[13] For a more extended account of missionary dilemmas, see Inga Clendinnen, 'Franciscan missionaries in Sixteenth-Century Mexico', in *Disciplines of Faith: Studies in Religion, Politics and Patriarchy*, edited by Jim Obelkevich, Lyndal Roper and Raphael Samuel, Routledge and Kegan Paul, London and New York, 1987, pp. 229–245. For rather different categorizations, Tzvetan Todorov, *The Conquest of America: The Question of the Other*, translated from the French by Richard Howard, Harper and Row, New York, 1984, esp. sections 3 & 4.

[14] Here I follow William Christian, *Local Religion*, in his concentration on observances over theology, and on local practices over clerical prescriptions. Christian's differentiation between 'local' and 'translocal' religion and religious sensibility (Intro, and esp. chapter 5) connects with Dell Hymes' distinction 'between knowledge what and knowledge how'. Dell Hymes, 'Breakthrough into Performance', in Dan Ben-Amos and K. S. Goldstein, eds., *Folklore and Communication*, Paris, 1975, p. 19.

not catch the quality of a lived faith, where 'belief' has as much to do with affect emotional, moral and aesthetic as with propositions. I therefore prefer to look to action, and its concomitant experience, to seek 'religion' in observances. The strategy requires rituals to be understood as performances devised to lead participant men and women through particular experiences: choreographed sequences of sculpted emotions developed out of a repertoire of prescribed actions which open a particular way to the sacred. The approach assumes the usual chicken-and-egg mutual fusing, with context, action and cause confounded: 'we know this to be the sacred because this is the way we've got here'; 'we know this is the way because the sacred is at the end of it'. It does not assume any mechanical efficacy: given that individuals, moods and susceptibilities differ, the degree and constancy of engagement will presumably be various and variable. Nonetheless I think it is this 'religion as performed' perspective which is most likely to yield some sense of how Indians managed the world before and after the dark days of the conquest. If we can learn something of the work – the quality of the physical and emotional labour – expended in ritual action, and grasp the dramatic structuring of that work, we should be able to retrieve something of the distinctive experience built into flesh and mind and imagination through those particular sequences of action. The task is to recover and compare the experiential scripts, the cultural texts, of Mexican religious performances before and after the conquest, to discover how far the same kind of sacred experience was being constructed and pursued.[15]

To do the retrieving we need to resist our notions of what legitimately 'religious' emotions and sentiments are, and be alert to the great range of sensory and emotional experiences which may be associated with encounters with the sacred. Contrast the conventional modern Christian habituation to passive listening or silent talking as major religious modes with the distinctive kinetic experience of the sacred in many cultures: those

---

[15] Therefore we have to seek 'the final and completed revelation of the paradigmatic structure of the ritual action which has continually informed the logic of its progression.' Bruce Kapferer, 'Performance and the Structure of Meaning and Experience', in Victor W. Turner and Edward M. Bruner, (eds.) *The Anthropology of Experience*, University of Illinois Press, Urbana and Chicago, 1986, p. 194. My debt to the work of Clifford Geertz is pervasive and, I hope, apparent. It is certainly too encompassing to be usefully specified, but see his 'Religion as a Cultural System' in his *The Interpretation of Cultures*, Basic Books, Stanford, 1973, pp. 87–125. For an example of the enlistment of familiar emotional experiences by stylised cues in the resolutely non-illusionist public theatre of Iran, see Roy Mottahedeh, *The Mantle of the Prophet: Religion and Politics in Iran*, Simon and Schuster, New York, 1985, pp. 174–179.

whirling dervishes balanced on the turning point of the world, or the rhythmic rocking of the devout Jew at prayer, or the neat self-inversion of the normally strenuously upright Muslim before Allah, or indeed the shout-and-dance Christians of other livelier traditions.[16]

Victor Turner has written of the ritual in tribal societies as constituted by 'an immense orchestration of genres in all available sensory codes: speech, music, singing; the presentation of elaborately worked objects, such as masks; wall paintings, body paintings; sculptured forms; complex; multitiered shrines; costumes, dance forms with complex grammars and vocabularies of body movements, gestures and facial expressions'. He also notes that such 'ritual' is freer than we might expect, and likely to contain 'plastic and labile phrases as well as fixed and formal ones' (Turner 1984: 19–41; Ravicz 1980: 115–133). That – ducking the awkward word 'tribal' – just about gets it right for the Mexicans.[17] Yet this emphasis on action as generative of religious experience, and, indeed, as constituting it, is not all a current notion among historians, including those working on simpler societies: most of us remain professionally fixated on the narrowest identification of 'religion' with 'belief'. For example, John McAndrew produced a notable study of the churches of sixteenth-century Mexico, those great stone texts of Spanish-Indian encounter. He paced the huge open courts; grassy wastes today but built to contain jostling or dancing crowds; the posas mutely marking the stations of great ambulatory movements of devotion. Nonetheless he tranquilly declared: 'It was only in safely secondary matters that the friars would allow no great break with past customs: in dancing, parading, wearing costumes, making offerings of flowers, or decorating shrines.' McAndrew went on to make the theologian's move: 'Here what was done could be similar to the old ways with propriety as long as it was made clear that the reason for doing it had changed' (McAndrew 1965: 61–62). The 'doing', by implication, is no more than pretty play. Possibly the message about changed reasons

---

[16] On the import of *Davening* see Riv-Ellen Prell-Foldes 'The reinvention of reflexivity in Jewish prayer: The self and community in modernity', in *Semiotica: Special issue: Signs about Signs: the Semiotics of Self-Reference* ed. Barbara Babcock, Vol. 30, 1/2, 1980, pp. 73–95.

[17] I am also ducking for the moment the great question of different cultural notions of the self and of the person, clearly crucial if we are to understand the 'who' doing the performing, but too expansive an issue to discuss here. See Michael Carrithers, Steven Collins, Steven Lukes, (eds.) *The category of the person*, Cambridge University Press, Cambridge, 1985, for an indispensable set of essays. For rich anthropological perspectives to the crucial zone of constructed experience, see *The Anthropology of Experience*, ed. Victor W. Turner and Edward M. Bruner.

could have been communicated, although given the primitive nature of missionary techniques I very much doubt it. But those matters dismissed as 'safely secondary' are in my view primary: the performances which crucially constituted individual and group experience.

Such a claim opens the kind of Pandora's box of philosophical problems historians usually manage to keep discreetly closed. It begins by requiring the rejection of the notion of emotions as eruptions, affects or manifestations of unconscious movements; the 'hydraulic theory of the passions,' as Robert Solomon dubs it, and its replacement by the recognition of emotions as activities, not occurrences (Solomon 1976: 170). It further requires the recognition that the emotions are culturally shaped[18], and as being particularly susceptible to shaping through the focussed intensities of collective ritual. Part of the 'how' of that particular efficacy may well be neurophysiologically based (Schechner 1986: 344–369). More must come through 'learning' and repetition. But for historians made restless by the attempt to trace the links between neurophysiology and action, or by the enterprise of sorting the instinctual responses of the human from the reflexive responses of the cultural, let me offer a concrete example of the kind of sculpting and shaping effect I am talking about, through the native account of a pre-contact Mexican ritual written down by the friar Sahagún.[19]

Every four years in the traditional Mexican seasonal calendar, at the festival of Izcalli, the most recent crop of children (probably those weaned over the four years since the last festival, and so ranging from about two to six years) were formally presented to the local community and to formal religious observances. On the day before the presentation there had been food-sharing among neighbours and kin, with much mutual visiting and feasting. The parents had also selected honorary 'aunts' or 'uncles', enlisting their cooperation by gifts. These men and women, not

---

[18] For the delicate exposure of distinctive culture mixes, see Michele Rosaldo, *Knowledge and Passion: Ilongot notions of self and social life*, Cambridge, Cambridge University Press, 1980, or on the Balinese emotion of 'lek', Clifford Geertz, 'Person, Time, and Conduct in Bali', in his *The Interpretation of Cultures*, Basic Books, New York, 1973, pp. 360–411, esp. 401–403.

[19] Sahagún, *Florentine Codex* Book 2, chaps. 37 & 38. The marvellously detailed descriptions of precontact ceremonial Sahagún recorded were spoken by one-time participants: old men at the time of their recording, with little to gain from the new order, save the poignant pleasure of recalling the old. The accounts are geographically focussed: they describe the great linked feasts of the seasonal calendar, along with those of particular sacred days, which laced individual households and neighbourhoods to the central temple precinct of Tenochtitlan.

kinsfolk, and chosen for their distinction, were almost certainly strangers to the children. On the eve of the appointed day the little ones, presumably already in a high state of nervous excitement, were kept awake until midnight, and then handed over to their ritual aunts and uncles and hurried through the dark streets to the local temple. There priests bored holes in their ears with a bone awl, and drew through the hole a thread of unspun cotton before pasting soft yellow parrot down on their heads. (The children squirmed and wailed all through this, 'raising a cry of weeping'.) Then the old men of the temple held each child in turn over a fire dense with the smoke of the native incense. They were then taken back to their houses by their unfamiliar custodians, there to be kept awake until dawn, 'when the barn swallow would sing' and the feasting could begin.

Throughout the morning hours there was dancing and singing in the home courtyard, with the children made to dance too, being held by the hands or (for the smallest) on the backs of their pseudo-kin. It was a celebratory occasion, at least for the adults, and even for the children there may have been some gratification, despite the fatigue and the shaking tensions of the night, as they displayed their bloodied wisps of cotton and their first awarded feathers. But they were allowed no rest. After that long night and day of no sleep and new experiences, they were taken to the great temple and a huge assembly of strangers, where they heard for the first time the surge and thunder of full Mexica ceremonial, the chants 'crashing like waves' around them.

Then the ceremony moved into its last phase. The drinking of pulque, an intoxicating beer made from the fermented juice of the maguey cactus, was strictly controlled in pre-contact Mexico, and penalties for unlicensed or private drinking were severe, but on this day of Izcalli, as with some other specified festivals, drinking to drunkenness was universal and obligatory.[20] Pulque ran like water through all of that long night. Children down to the babies on their cradleboards were made to swallow mouthfuls of the strange, sour milk while the newly-initiated children were given enough of the stuff to make them drunk.[21] Then the adults settled to the serious drinking. The children, exhausted, frantic for want of sleep, and after a night of fear and pain at the hands of strangers, watched

---

[20] It is possible that among the consciousness-altering drugs only pulque was available to the commoners, Muñoz Camargo claiming the use of psychotropic drugs like peyote, mushrooms and *tlapatl* (a form of datura) was largely restricted to the lords. Diego Muñoz Camargo, *Historia de Talxcala*, published and annotated by Alfredo Chavero, Guadalajara, Jal., Edmundo Aviña Levy, 1966, facs. ed. of 1892 ed., pp. 134–135.

[21] Sahagún, *Florentine Codex* 2; Appendix: 203.

as parents and familiar adults drank to strangeness. There was 'reddening of faces...glazing of eyes, quarrelling, tramping, elbowing', as men and women squabbled and boasted, or grabbed at each other in anger or sodden affection: all the normally disapproved conducts on drunken display. Then they staggered back to their houses for yet more drinking, and at last sleep.

The 'presentation of the children' immediately preceded the Nemontemi, the five unnamed days at the end of the yearly calendar round: a sinister period of 'time' beyond ritual control, and therefore a period when the human social world was most vulnerable to the intrusion of destructive because uncontrolled sacred forces. Through that dangerous non-time conduct was accordingly cautious: no fires were lit and all possible activity was suspended. (Children born during this period were so ill-omened as to be unlikely to survive.) Those hushed days gave a fine opportunity for men and women nursing broken heads and bruised relationships to meditate on the wisdom of acute self-control, the undervalued beauty of order, and the dark and decisively anti-social forces unleashed by the sacred pulque.

The children, deprived of the balm of normality, with household routines broken and adult conduct strangely muted, were unlikely to forget the sensations of their encounter with high religion and the sacred. It is of course impossible to be confident of the details of this kind of reconstruction, but the broad terms of the psychological engineering involved are clear enough. The temple had been presented as a place of excitement, glamour and terror. It was a place of isolation, where familiar protectors had failed to protect, and then had ceased to be familiar. Yet it was also a place where the initiated children had been made the focus of attention, and mysteriously elevated; where their bodies and selves had been invaded by the awls of the priests, by the choking smoke of the fire, by the sacred milk of the pulque, and transformed by that encounter with the terrible power of the sacred. The Izcalli experience *per se* would not be repeated, but those themes, and others, would be rehearsed through a multitude of other ceremonies.[22]

If pre-contact rituals are available to us in a sufficiently richly-textured form to allow some retrieval of experience, we have adequate if

---

[22] Along, of course, with others, some apparently incompatible. To grasp the dominant themes (which is probably all that can be done at our temporal and cultural distance) one needs to scan the whole spectrum of ritual action for the unobvious resonances between the performances.

thinner and more fragmentary descriptions of post-contact performances of largely Indian devising, as friars recorded the multiple ways in which Indian towns elaborated the skeletal Christian scripts which had been their gifts to them. (The elaborations were the more welcomed and the more lovingly described because the friars had not specifically suggested them, and so took them as signs of spontaneity, which indeed they probably were.) The very closeness of the friars' engagement with those early Indian expressions of 'Christian' sensibility presents its own difficulty in interpretation. Even in the matter of innovations friars were rendered indulgent because Indian embroideries sufficiently resembled familiar forms of Spanish lay devotion. Spanish towns and villages too had their special festivals, their processions for which the whole village turned out, their saints paraded in litters. If Mexican saints came to be luxuriously manipulable, so too were some European images, with articulated limbs and other inventive physical detailing.[23] To fast, to keep vigil; so purified, to dress with special care in specially prepared garments; to carry offerings of fruit, flowers or green branches; to process specially venerated objects; to dance, to sing, to pretend the gods are accessible – surely these are the commonplaces of folk observances? Even the traditional penchant for the use of living images in religious performance had its European counterpart. 'On April 12, 1507, in the midst of the great 3 plague, the city (Barcelona) held an elaborate procession to found a chapel to the plague saint, Sebastian. In the procession walked a man dressed as Saint Sebastian, his clothes pierced with arrows, "and after him a group of children in shirts and barefoot, flagellating themselves. Saint Sebastian would turn to the children and ask them what they wanted, and they would fall to their knees and reply, 'We all ask our Lord God that we do not die so quickly from such a severe plague, and we say Lord God have mercy.' And those who said this wept with tears and lamentations so piercing that it almost broke the hearts of those who cried and those who heard them" (Christian 1981a: 220). Richard Trexler provides contemporary descriptions of remarkable 'sacred representations' in mid-sixteenth

[23] T. J. Schmitt notes that women of one village in a French diocese would come during pregnancy to invoke a papier maché statue of Our Lady in one of the chapels of their local church. After some set prayers and an offering, they would open the belly of the statue, gaze at an Infant Jesus there, and then close the belly-flap, hoping for a happy birth. 'When [in 1689] the curé was ordered not to tolerate the superstition he put an iron band round the statue, and then assured his superiors, prematurely perhaps, that the devotion was no longer practised.' Quoted Jean Delumeau, *Catholicism between Luther and Voltaire*, London, 1977, pp. 178–179.

century Florence, most particularly of the elaborate doings in the convent of San Vicenzo, built around the spiritually gifted Sister Caterina. Caterina, dressed as the Christ of Calvary in red gown, diadem, and 'a false beard on her chin', or as the twelve-year-old Christ 'with a lovely wig of real curly hair,' would in the course of her dressing be moved into a rapturous state, to the tender delight of her sisters, who also dressed for their parts in these peculiar theatrical realizations (Trexler 1980: 190–196). In post-conquest Mexico we have elaborate enactments of sacred plays and episodes by whole Indian communities, with extravagant outlays of time, invention, and scarce resources on elaborate costumes and complex naturalistic 'effects'. So how are we to distinguish 'Indian' performances from Spanish folk religiosity, or indeed from folk religiosity anywhere? How are we to determine what is 'Indian', and what is 'Catholic', in all that?

The human imagination being human, the general contours of ways to the sacred can be made to look isomorphic, but only if viewed from a sufficient height, or muffled in the grey blanket of middle level generalisation (which I have practised for demonstration purposes in the paragraph above). It is the precise configuration – in the Mexican case the detail of the dynamic pattern of action created out of the borrowings, the impositions, the elaborations – which constitute the distinctiveness.[24] What I am therefore concerned with is the dramatic structuring of the rituals, their practical aesthetics, and the experiential graph they prescribed for each category of participant. (The individual and idiosyncratic are clearly inaccessible by this method as with these sources: we are working with the public and the shared.)

So, at last, to the action, which given the exigencies of space will have to be tackled in altogether too piecemeal a fashion. One of the clearest maps to Indian innovation and undesired exuberance in the area of ritual is provided by the anxious edicts of sixteenth-century Mexican ecclesiastical juntas and synods, as they strove to restrain unacceptable enthusiasms. Yet it is something not complained of which yields the first clue: the eager and lavish expenditure by hard-pressed Indian communities on eminently perishable items of display.[25] Despite their steady impoverishment

---

[24] This is my quarrel with George Foster's vastly influential study of Spain's influence on America, where the detail, although beguilingly vivid, is insufficiently refined. George M. Foster, *Culture and Conquest: America's Spanish Heritage*, Quadrangle Books, Chicago, 1960.

[25] The distribution of the cost burden between individual and community is not possible to unravel for the early days after conquest. Charles Gibson has suggested that cofradías,

the towns and villages delighted in expenditure on the magnificently ephemeral, an aesthetic preference which picks up an important theme in pre-contact sensibility. The multiple arches heavy with costly imported 'roses' and the tireless elaboration of the physical settings also point to a developed pleasure in the prolonged collective engagement necessary for the staging of such performances: a cultural taste for the 'busywork' of ritual, as Clifford Geertz has called it. (Were this analysis to be properly exhaustive, the nature and texture of the getting ready and the cleaning up would have to be investigated equally with the performance phase.)

Such showy pleasures were presumably judged to be innocent. What we find being rebuked by the synods is a passion to perform, to participate; in music and dance, in drinking and processing and song. The first Mexican council of bishops in 1539, contemporaneous both with Motolinía's 'History' as with the Inquisitorial findings, and not yet habituated to the idiosyncracies of Indians, was carefully explicit. The bishops forbade the Indians to feast or drink the wine of Castile or to make unseemly music in the churches, or for too long in the hours of darkness outside them: such performances were inappropriate in Christian worship, and smacked of idolatry. They were not to burn copal, nor to keep fires burning through the night or in the daylight hours before the churchyard crosses. And they were to give up the private oratories and images which 'every Indian had'.[26]

once taken to be an early Indian borrowing, remained few until late in the sixteenth century, their multiplication being a seventeenth-century phenomenon. Charles Gibson, *The Aztecs under Spanish Rule*, p. 127. But note Motolinía's insistence that (by 1541) 'all of them [Indians], both men and women', belonged to the brotherhood of the Cross, scourging themselves on all the Fridays of the year as well as for three days in Lent, or when 'troubled by drought or illness or any other adversity'. Motolinía, *Historia*, Book 1, chapter XIII.

[26] They were also to desist from overly extravagant demonstrations of respect for the Christian clergy: the sweeping of the roads and erection of arches, the falling on the knees and the breast-beatings were declared to be excessive, at least for ordinary clergy on ordinary occasions. These displays of submissive respect, like the weeping hordes of commoners who begged to be baptised, suggest the desperate desire for a restored institutionalised way to the sacred. For the councils, Francisco Antonio Lorenzana, *Concilios provinciales primero y segundo, celebrados en el muy noble y muy leal ciudad de México presidiendo el illmo. y Rmo. D. Fr. Alonso de Montufar, en los Años de 1555 y 1565*, Mexico, 1796, and Jose A Llaguno, S. J., *La personalidad jurídica del indio y el III Concilio Provincial Mexicana (1585)*, Editorial Porrua, Mexico D. F., 1962. Note useful bibliography. For the articles of the first ecclesiastical junta of April 1539 see appendix. See also Joaquín García Icazbalceta, *Don Fray Juan de Zumárraga, primer Obispo y Arzobispo de México*, ed. Rafael Aguayo Spencer y Antonio Castro Leal, 4 vols., Mexico D. F., 1947, iii, pp. 149–184.

The thrust was not to awaken 'piety', but to sedate it. The effort failed. The Church continued to suffer a population explosion of musicians and singers, and a doubtfully holy cacophony of trumpets and drums and other unsuitable instruments.[27] The Indians persisted in making a song and dance of their religion, in tune with the de facto tolerance of their spiritual leaders. The extent of their tolerance is surprising. It is as if the massive dimensions of the task of conversion, and the apparently unequivocal evidence of enthusiasm for Christianity – Indians falling on their knees before the friars, weeping, moaning, begging for baptism – worked to disarm suspicion and cloud memory. Motolinía, for one, 'knew' a good deal about Indian sacred dance in the old world, before the Spaniards came. He knew that dancing before the gods had been an act of religious merit for all groups in Indian society; a 'penance' of a precise kind, and often obligatory for a particular group or age-set: 'in these festival and their dances, they not only called on and honoured and praised their gods with songs but also with the heart and the movements of the body. In order to do this properly, they had used many set patterns, not only with the movements of the head, of the arms and of the feet but with all their body they strove to serve and call on their gods, through such laborious care raising their hearts and senses to their devils, and of serving them with all the talents of the body, and in such labour they would continue a day and a great part of the night...'[28]

The old gods had been served through specific movements and kinetic experiences, and all their worshippers of all ages were obliged so to serve them. Yet Motolinía 'innocently' records an Easter dance of Indian infants, so young that he thought still not weaned, as no more than a pretty scene. He also cheerfully tells us of Indian nobles in their ritual regalia of white garments with feathered cloaks, garlanded with flowers, singing and dancing through the night as a standard feature of 'Christian' festivals.[29] As it happens there is a contemporaneous Inquisitorial account of a pagan lord and his followers, crowned with roses, dancing, chanting

---

[27] The synod of 1555 was still striving to banish 'unsuitable' instruments from the interior of the church, seeking to replace the collective racket with the seemly sonorities of a single organ. The easy adoption of Spanish instruments is unsurprising: there had always been a brisk traffic in songs, voice-styles, dance forms, regalias and ritual sequences within the valley and beyond. It is true that church office carried or was thought to carry exemption from tribute, and came in some provinces to hold high prestige: note the engrossment of all church duties down to the lowliest by the Tlaxcalan nobility. But the enthusiasm for participation was too widespread to be explained by such simple pragmatics.

[28] Motolinía, *Memoriales*, Part 2, chapter 27, Durán, *Historia*, Vol. 2, chapter 11.

[29] Motolinía, *Historia*, Book 1, chapters 13 & 14. For the first obligatory dance of infants in pre-conquest times, cf. Sahagún, *Florentine Codex* Book 2, chapter 38, p. 170.

and celebrating the old gods through a long night. Not content with drum and dance, the pagans were also drunk, which is a matter for later exploration, with the chief so elevated as to show neither fear nor deference to a shocked Spaniard who happened on the scene.[30] Yet Motolinía's complacency remained unruffled. Again we have the casual award of priority to the assumed directing 'reason' in disregard of the highly visible 'action'.

The capacity of translation to mask action and muffle difference also plays its part. Consider what Indians and Spaniards meant by what we call 'fasting', and how each understood its function, its location and its constitutive and associated experiences along the way to the sacred. For pre-contact Indians lay 'fasting' meant the taking of only one frugal meal of the blandest food (tortillas without chilli or salt) daily. In a 'night fast' one ate only at midday, in a 'day fast' one ate only in the middle of the night. Typically one fasted in company with the group who were preparing themselves for a particular festival, spending much of the nights in vigil with them. The fasting state also entailed abstinence from sexual intercourse, and the regular drawing of blood from the earlobe, tongue or the flesh of the thigh, often with the passing of tiny bundles of straws or 'twigs' through the hole.[31] The duration of fasts varied, with four days as a minimum, while one's preparation for a festival to which one owed special commitment could require a fast of twenty, sixty, or even eighty days. (In the case of the young warriors who had 'eaten the flesh of Huitziliopochtli' the austerities endured for a full year.) In preparation for occasions of high sacredness all might fast, but most fasts were not universally obligatory, falling rather on particular occupational or age groups. On occasion all of one's immediate society would be involved, as with a co-resident group like the salt workers; at other times the fasting group (as with warrior fasters) would be dispersed through the population for much of the day, meeting together to keep their vigil at night. That is, the burden was not sustained alone, but was defined as a duty not only to the deity, but to the collectivity.

If fasting for the general adult population could be strenuous, priests' austerities were raised to heroic levels. Tlaxcalan priests preparing for a

---

[30] Proceso y información que se toma contra Xpobal y su mujer, por ocultar ídolos y otros delitos, y contra Martín, hermano del primero (1 53), *Publicaciones del Archivo General de la Nación*, pp. 141–175. This is admittedly an odd and complex case, with the strong possibility of the corruption of the resident Spanish priest, but there is little doubt as to the chief's condition. On the priest, Richard Greenleaf, *Zumárraga and the Mexican Inquisition 1536–1543*, Academy of American Franciscan History, Washington D.C., 1961, p. 109.

[31] *Florentine Codex* 2: Appendix: pp. 193, 197.

great four-yearly feast for their major deity had their tongues pierced by obsidian blades, and then drew through the slit rods of smoothed wood, varying in thickness, we are told, from a thumb to 'the space one can encircle with the thumb and forefinger'. Senior priests were committed to forcing four hundred and five rods through their tongue in this way, and the more junior two hundred. This exercise initiated an eighty day fast, with the forcing of rods through the tongue repeated every twenty days. (It is difficult to imagine that deliberate breaking-open of the barely healed flesh.) For the second eighty day fast it was the turn of the common people, who imitated the priestly sacrifice at a less heroic level, being content to draw through their tongues 'little rods as thick as a duck's quill'.[32]

What was being offered here was not (or not primarily) pain, which where practicable was minimized: that first obsidian blade sliced cleanly, while the wood of the rods was carefully smoothed. Blood was the desired and measurable product, the bloodied rods being heaped in a special enclosure to be offered before the deity. There were other even more strenuous exercises, as for example the slitting of the penis and the passing through the slit of a rope some fathoms long. This could suggest the use of extreme pain to induce a vision, as with the Sun Dance, were it not that fainting was taken as a sign of disqualifying impurity.[33] The process looks to be rather one of ritual preparation. Through their performance the Tlaxcalan priests had been brought to a proper condition to encounter the god. Only those who had endured the fast were qualified to don their regalia and to celebrate his festival. The laity too had been brought to an adequate state to attend the deity, although they would not encounter the sacred power so closely.

For priests and laity alike the end of the fasting period saw a degree of skeletonization, the visible self refined, with the inner self also tuned to the proper pitch for the intensities of festival engagement. The lay

---

[32] Motolinía, *Historia*, Book One, chapter Ten. See also chapter Eleven for the pains of 'waiting on the god' in an eighty day vigil.

[33] Motolinía, *Historia*, Book One, chapter Nine. Cf. Schele and Miller who argue that the Maya bloodletting ritual was practised to secure visions, being in itself sufficient to procure visions 'without the help of other drugs' through 'blood loss and shock', the release of endorphins produced in the brain in response to 'massive blood loss' generating hallucinations, in the Maya understanding by the way of the 'Vision Serpent' connecting the supernatural and the human worlds. Linda Schele and Mary Ellen Miller, *The Blood of Kings: Dynasty and Ritual in Maya Art*, Kimball Art Museum, Fort Worth, 1986, p. 177. I am unpersuaded that the blood loss among the Aztecs was sufficiently great to trigger such a reaction, although the power of expectation ought not to be underestimated.

faster's depleted body would be painted by specialist painters who worked for hire in the marketplace, dressed in its ritual garments, and provided the requisite accoutrements of feathers or maizestalks or flowers, while the priests were garbed in their regalia with even greater ceremony. The fasters moved into the demanding, compelling rhythms of collective dance-and-chant. Participation was obligatory for all members of the group involved, with 'watchers' overseeing their movements.[34] All had been trained in adolescence in the 'House of Song', so there was no excuse for clumsiness.[35] The dancers were led by trained and ritually prepared drummers and singers, with any error punishable by death.[36] These formal dances were of a repetitive kind, with the beat most precisely marked, and prolonged over several hours, and a complex patterning inscribed again and again through the interweaving of the lines of dancers.[37] The inference is sufficiently clear: while dance could on occasion be no more than a diversion,[38] it was on formal occasions an essential element in the invocation of the deity. As Motolinía had said, through dance they 'called on their gods, raising their hearts and senses to their devils', serving them 'with all the talents of their body'. For the watchers, the festival unleashed chanting, constant movement, special festival foods – the kind of multiple assault on the senses we associate not with high reverence and

[34] E.g., *Florentine Codex* 2:27:101. There are resonances here with the dance-whippers of the Plains Indians, who vigorously policed the dancers, on specially solemn occasions allowing the dancers to leave the dance zone only to urinate.

[35] Durán, *Historia*, Book 1, chapter X. Warrior dances ought ideally to be discussed here, as avenues to the sacred. For a glimpse of their power and import – and the award of the lordly turquoise to one who excelled – see Don Francisco de San Antón Muñón Chimalpahin. Cuauhtlehuanitzin, *Relaciones Originales de Chalco Amaquemecan*, trans. and edited S. Rendón, Mexico-Buenos Aires, 1965, Séptima Relación, pp. 211–214.

[36] Even on 'secular' occasions, if any Mexican occasion can be so described, a singer took a pinch of incense from the incense gourd and tossed it into the fire as prelude to the song. So did a judge before making a formal pronouncement, which suggests the world-changing capacity of each statement: performative utterances indeed.

[37] *Florentince Codex* 2:8:56. The standard text on pre-Columbian dance remains Samuel Martí and Gertrude Prokosch Kurath, *Dances of Anáhuac: The Choreography and Music of Precortesian Dances*, Aldine Publishing Co., Chicago, 1964. See also José Acosta, *Historia natural y moral de las Indias*, ed. y preparada por Edmundo O'Gorman, México, Fondo de Cultura Económica, 1962, esp. Book 6, Chapter 28. The account given by Barbara Tedlock of the punctilious assessment of Zuñi song and of its compositional complexity picks up and amplifies the meagre clues regarding Aztec song. Barbara Tedlock, 'Songs of the Zuñi Kachina Society: Composition, Rehearsal, Performance', in *Southwestern Indian Ritual Drama*, ed. Charlotte J. Frisbie, Albuquerque, University of New Mexico Press, 1980.

[38] E.g. *Florentine Codex* 2:25:84. For non-obligatory participation, *ibid* 2:21:56.

'religion' but with Carnival. For the lay dancers the long preparation, the alteration in the sense of self through the fasting period, the distancing formalism of the painting and robing, then prolonged repetitive movement coupled with intense sensory stimulation almost certainly generated a trance experience. And only then, as the self evaporated and the choreographed excitements multiplied and the sensations came flooding in, did the god come.

Contrast that with Spanish Catholic fasting which, when collective, appears to have been more of a negotiation with a most attentive divinity, the food eaten and not eaten a measurable offering of penance and a calculable display of the potential for discipline of the very present self. When voluntary and solitary (and setting aside the extravagances of the heroic non-eaters) it was deeply sustained by the conviction that the fasting period itself, which was marked by other austerities and by intensified prayer, was a time of privileged intimacy with the deity.[39] Dances where they happened were at least by Indian standards brief and casual affairs, figuring not as a path towards but as a festive relaxation from the rough and stony way of the fasting period. Unhappily we do not have the sustained and detailed accounts of colonial Indian preparations for sacred performance which would allow close comparison with the precontact pattern, such things being concealed from the eyes of outside observers, but the glimpses we have of the public phase mimic the traditional mode very much more closely than they do the Spanish.

After the conquest Mexicans were to display an early, puzzling and enduring passion for the 'dances of the Moors and the Christians', the stylized military confrontations of Christians and non-believers. There was a great conquerors' event in Mexico City in 1538, when in celebration of the reception of the news of the Treaty of Aigues Mortes Spaniards enacted the capture of Rhodes. Later in that year at Corpus Christi Tlaxcala staged a dazzling enactment of the conquest of Jerusalem, with an all-Indian cast of at least hundreds, including 'armies' of Europeans and Moors and ten companies of Mexican warriors, each in its appropriate regalia. Famous individuals represented included the Pope, the Emperor, St. James and St. Hippolytus (the saintly patrons of Old and New Spain respectively), the Archangel Michael and the Great Sultan

---

[39] Among other things. Carol Walker Bynum, 'Fast, Feast, and Flesh': The Religious Significance of Food to Medieval Women', *Representations*, 11, Summer 1985, 1–87.

of Babylon and Tetrarch of Jerusalem. The whole stunning performance ended with the triumph of the Christians, not without supernatural intervention, and the mass baptism of the defeated and abashed 'Moors'.[40]

This 'theatre of conquest' has been diagnosed by Richard Trexler as an imposed theatre of humiliation, with the conquered being forced to enact and re-enact their defeat and painful submission: enactments communicating highly specific political and cultural messages. He is perhaps right as to Spanish expectations.[41] But for Indians? They drew on a very long ritual tradition in which contest themes abounded. In the great battle enactments staged in Tenochtitlan the non-Mexican roles (including those of the arch villains the Moon and the Uncounted Stars, the rivalrous siblings who sought to kill the unborn Sun) could be played with high zest by Mexican warriors. What I would rather emphasise is the steady Indian predilection for performances which incorporated passages in the contest mode, from oppositional dances to uninhibited brawling, desperate duels, or the strenuous elegancies of the ball-game. Those contests were nested within a wider category of interludes of vigorous male action: lightly scripted segments of licensed spontaneity inserted into the more formal ritual text. Pre-conquest performances had been punctuated by a remarkable range of such passages, from genial buffoonery, with transvestism and animal imitations, through playful chases and 'play' raidings to competitive races and contests. (Those most consequential displays of martial skill, the so-called 'gladiatoral' sacrifices, took up the

---

[40] Motolinía's 'set-piece' description of this and other great Tlaxcalan occasions have permeated the literature, being quoted extensively by Torquemada and Las Casas. Motolinía, *Historia*, Book 1, chapter 15. For a history of the dances in Spain and in Mexico, see Arturo Warman, *La Danza de Moros y Cristianos*, Secretaría de Educación Pública, Mexico, 1972.

[41] To say 'intentions' would be to put it too high. Richard C. Trexler, 'We Think, They Act: Clerical Readings of Missionary Theatre in 16th century New Spain', in Steven Kaplan (ed.) *Understanding Popular Culture: Europe from the Middle Ages to the Nineteenth Century*, Mouton, 1984, pp. 189–227. For the edifying plays, written by Spanish friars but staged and acted by Indians, which I lack space to discuss here, see Marilyn Ekdahl Ravicz, *Early Colonial Religious Drama in Mexico: From Tzompantli to Golgotha*, The Catholic University of America Press, Washington D.C., 1970, and Trexler, 'Clerical Readings'. See Ravicz' useful bibliography for the small but important literature on Mexican dramatic performances, before and after the conquest. For the song-poems, a dominant and continuing performance art, see John Bierhorst, ed. and translator, *Cantares Mexicanos: Songs of the Aztecs*, Stanford University Press, Stanford, 1985. For the long European roots of mock wars, as for a penetrating discussion of the form as developed by Spaniards and Indians, see Warman, *La Danza de Moros y Cristianos*, chapter 1.

contest theme but leached it of all play, formally framing its desperate urgencies as high art.)[42]

However little such episodes square with our notions of sacred etiquette, they were not incidental to the sacred action, but constitutive of it. Structurally they were often transition markers: between initial rather open 'parade' sequences and more formal and focussed processions; between processions and elaborately-framed, dramatic and presumably climactic 'spectacles', and between those spectacles and the period of detumescence and reintegration over the last phase of the action.[43] The processions, races and chases were themselves sometimes punctuated by more formally staged interludes, in which mythic moments were re-enacted, so that present violence resonated with violences past and eternal and a local topography transmuted into a sacred landscape: the familiar, reiterative astonishing miracle of ritual.[44] In the colonial period we see the same structure asserting itself; in looping and curling processions linking place to traditionally sanctified place, streaked with vivid eruptions of licensed spontaneity: with exuberant burlesque, races and mock 'battles' where sedate and controlled demeanours flared into dangerous glee.[45] Indians displayed a particular penchant for the liturgical dramas of Spain, and for the playlets written specifically for their edification, but again wrought their own transformations. In Spain religious

[42] For an analysis of the gladiatorial stone action see Inga Clendinnen, 'The Cost of Courage in Aztec Society', *Past and Present, 107*, May 1985, 44–89. These kinds of performances opened a rather different way to ecstasy, the escape from self-consciousness being effected by the total focussing of concentration on the perfect exemplification of the art, or the narrowed intensities of the game.

[43] E.g. for the first, the mock combat of women physicians which followed the silent 'parade' dance of the warriors in Ochpaniztli; for the second, the marathon run by Paynal, the victims' combat and the warriors' race which preceded the killings in Panquetzaliztli; for the last, the play-lootings which brought the action of Tlacaxipeualiztli to a close. The examples are multiple, with almost any ceremony yielding several.

[44] For example, the festival of Panquetzaliztli, the warrior festival marking the mid-point of the season of war, saw the staged re-enactment of the new-born Huitzilipochtli's first entry into the theatre of combat, the stages being nested in a breathless scenario of massed marathons, sprints and desperate battles.

[45] Present day 'Indian' performances are similarly marked by danger, as in the wild exuberance of the firework 'bulls', or the balletic whip-battle of the jaguar dance, while the mythification of the landscape continues. Raviez comments: The hillsides and church courtyards of the pueblos of contemporary Mexico still become stages for dramatic rituals during the most important fiestas; and processions, dances, music, mock battles, and the whole theatrical entourage are supported by patronage and the cooperation of cofradias and mayordomias just as they were in the sixteenth century'. Raviez, *Early Colonial Religious Drama*, p. 78.

dramas were typically enacted at first within, then later just outside, the churches, on small specially erected stages, or on wagons, and were rather static affairs: small sequences of highly mannered and stylised formalised moments, with explanatory speeches; more linked tableaux than drama.[46] Indians notably expanded both their geographical and their dramatic range, transforming them into fast-moving processual street-theatre, with the tableaux activated by the procession's arrival, and the action sometimes multi-level. Processions themselves expanded in directions alarming to those less sanguine than Motolinía: the first bishop of Mexico was complaining in the early fifteen forties of the profanities which already encrusted Indian processings of the Host, when in defiance of proper Christian solemnity 'men with masks, dressed as women, and dancing and leaping about shamefully and lasciviously, pranced in front of the sacred things.[47]

In such matters sequence is all; the distinctive patterning of movement and stasis, sound and silence, darkness and light, rhythm and reiteration. I suspect it is the narrative of ritual experience which most powerfully focusses feeling and channels desire, not only because of the ordering pulse of myth, but because of the transforming transitions and the force

[46] N. D. Shergold, *A History of the Spanish Stage from Medieval Times until the End of the Seventeenth Century*, Oxford, Clarendon Press, 1967, esp. pp. 104–7. The Spanish productions had their exoticisms – Shergold mentions a Gerona Corpus Christi festival which featured a giant, a dragon and an eagle (p. 105, n. 1) – and there was the usual pressing on the boundaries, the Visitor-General to the Archbishopric of Galicia complaining in 1617 of the presentation of 'algunas coplas indecentes y deshonestas en presencia del Santísimo Sacramento'. Shergold, p. 106, n.4. But serious anxiety seems to have focussed on the excesses of 'secular' theatre: see Shergold, pp. 151–2 and pp. 516–5. The interdependence between 'religious' and 'secular' theatre was complex, with theatres closing while professional actors performed autos during Corpus Christi. For the yearly pattern see pp. 542–543. Shergold notes that 'secular' plays were sometimes performed by professional actors within monasteries and convents, p. 536. I thank Dr. John Brotherston of the School of Spanish and Latin American Studies at the University of New South Wales for drawing my attention to a now-lost 16th century ms., *Abusos de comedias y tragedias*: 'Que se representaban en los templos ciertas composiciones devotas, pero mezclados con ellas entremeses indecentes y bailes deshonestas y esto se hacía hasta en los conventos de monjas'. E. Cotarelo y Mori, *Bibliografía de las controversias sobre la licitud del teatro en España*, Madrid, 1904, p. 45.

[47] Archbishop Zumárraga, quoted Marilyn Ekdahl Ravicz, *Early Colonial Religious Drama*, pp. 74–75. The next Archbishop attempted to prohibit all unlicensed performances within the churches, with licensed presentations restricted to the hours of daylight. Joaquín Garcia Icazbalceta, 'Representaciones religiosas de México en el siglo XVI', *Obras, opúsculos varios*, ii, Mexico, 1986, pp. 349–350. See also *Descripción del Arzobispado de México hecha en 1570 y otros documentos*, ed. Luis García Pimental, Mexico, Joaquín Terrazaz e Hijas, 1897.

of the cumulative narrative experience working within the individual and the group. The precise dramatic shape of ritual performance, the plotting of its intensities, is therefore crucial for the retrieval of any significant fraction of its meaning. The laconic insider style of the sources for pre-contact ritual can make it difficult to identify their dramatic shapes, while the imposition of one's own familiar narrative structure is fatally easy. Mexica ritual was also multi-level, with the counterpoint between those levels problematical. But it seems sufficiently clear that the day named as the major feast day in the monthly round saw the high point of the ritual action, most typically in a 'spectacle', with most of the participants turned onlooker, and the consumatory action playing around the fact or the possibility of human death.

The 'participants turned onlooker' shift raises the question of the meaning of that transition. Does absorbing, kinetically engaging 'ritual' become mere visual 'ceremony', instructive, but not transformative, at that point?[48] If we are to claim any continuing mutual illumination between 'ritual' and 'society', that sudden space between audience and actors must somehow be bridged. Too often we span it only by the floating threads of intuition: by our powerful sense that watcher-listeners are somehow 'part of the action'. We have, after all, experienced the miracle ourselves: it is not necessary to be on stage with Lear to weep for him. Yet if experiencing is believing, it is not much help when we come to explaining. Here recent work on the emotionally infective power of expressions at the neuro-physiological level intriguingly illuminates just how this remarkable trick might be being done.[49] But human performances find

[48] Here I draw on Victor Turner's necessary distinction between 'ceremony', which he identifies as essentially confirmatory of the social world ('an impressive institutionalized performance of indicative, normatively structured social reality . . . both a model *of* and a model *for* social states and statuses') and 'ritual', which he claimes to be profoundly subversive of that accepted social reality, in that 'the cognitive schemata that give sense and order to everyday life no longer apply, but are, as it were, suspended – in ritual symbolism perhaps even shown as destroyed or dissolved'. Victor Turner, *From Ritual to Theatre: the Human Seriousness of Play*, Performing Arts Journal, Inc., New York, 1982 pp. 83–84. Or, more succinctly, 'Ceremony *indicates*, ritual *transforms* [author's italics]'. Turner, *From Ritual to Theatre* p. 80. See this section for a useful reconsideration of Sally Falk Moore and Barbara Myerhoff's distinctions in their introduction to *Secular Ritual*, ed. Sally Falk Moore and Barbara Myerhoff, Amsterdam, Royal van Gorcum, 1977.

[49] For a lucid exposition of the possible neuro-physiology see Richard Schechner, 'Magnitudes of Performance', in Turner and Bruner, *Anthropology of Experience*, 344–369. For a brilliant elucidation of the delicate practicalities of managing the distance between actor and self, actor and audience in different cultural modes, and the transformations of consciousness involved, see Schechner's *Between Theater and Anthropology*, University of Pennsylvania Press, Philadelphia, 1985, Chapter 1.

their efficacy, their variety and their flexibility well beyond this simple, if potent, level. Clifford Geertz's recognition of the primacy of what he calls 'cultural texts' remains central.[50] The men and women of any particular culture are trained in the great reflexive, reiterative texts of that culture; in myths and stories, in games and play, in common-sense pragmatics, in aesthetic and moral preferences; their imaginations stretched and shaped to particular themes and possibilities. It is the riches of these multiple prior texts which web the space between the mundane and the supra-mundane, and lace the world of ritual to the world of the everyday. (Geertz 1973: 3–30)

For all their careful framing, the climactic spectacles offered to Mexicans as participatory exercises for the imagination sustained and intensified the focus on dangerously uncontrolled action sequences pivoting on death-invoking arts: the exemplary 'gladiatorial' combats, 'dances' requiring a long step with death, and, of course, on the deliberate killing of humans. This phase of the performance and the nature of its attractive power was, obviously, complex, and only the most cursory elucidation can be offered here. It was marked by the peculiar excitements of the public doing of humans to death: excitements presumably most deeply grounded, whatever their collective gloss, in terrors regarding individual physical and existential integrity, but in Mexico also urgent with the conviction of the awakened hunger of the summoned god. And since the destined victims were typically only precariously controlled on and at that final stage[51] there was the added dramatic tension of the possibility of debâcle should they break out of role.

So the ritual makers were, most publicly, playing with fire. But the uncontrol of the victims signified very much more than a dramatic frisson. Here it is necessary to draw a distinction. Outsiders have tended to see the mass killings of humans as the central fact about Mexican high ritual throughout the Valley of Mexico and beyond. It is true that mass killing provided the major public spectacle of some major rituals and that for some individuals – the warrior offering a prized captive, the merchant a magnificently expensive slave – the killing of his particular offering

---

[50] For practical demonstrations, see almost any of his writings, although some of the interrelationships are perhaps traced most clearly in Geertz, 'Person, Time and Conduct in Bali', *The Interpretation of Cutlures*, pp. 360–411.

[51] Very occasionally the victims were bound, as with those trussed like deer who died in the Quecholli festival, and the men cast bound into the fire at Xocotluetzi. *Florentine Codex*, Book 2, chapter 29, for Xocotluetzi; Book 2, chapter 33 for Quecholli. It is unclear whether the captives cast into the fire during Teotleco were bound or not. *Florentine Codex* Book 2, chapter 31.

among those massed offerings probably marked the high point of the performance. But for most of the people most of the time I doubt these large-scale killings signified much beyond the arithmetic of power, with its attendant gratifications of inter-group rivalry. The men, women and children who died in those mass offerings died as sacrificial-stone fodder, their individual conduct of small moment.

The deaths and style of death which signified more deeply to the watchers were those of victims specially selected from among slaves and captives on grounds of physical beauty and grace; then trained and cosseted and coaxed to play the part of a god. These human figures fell within the Nahuatl category of *ixiptlas*,[52] or 'god-representations', and it was they who most powerfully compelled the watchers' attention. A characteristic movement shaped those individual performances. Initially their conduct was calculated, and closely controlled. Then through the exhaustion of dance or simulated combat, through relentless excitation, or, more economically, through drink or drugs, the god-representations were for their last and very public hours made open to the sacred power their slow adorning and ritual preparation had invoked. Increasingly invaded, and then obliterated by the sacred power, 'possessed' in the fullest possible sense, they had ceased to exist as persons well before they met their physical deaths. So they became what they were named: 'god representations'. The dancing puppets had become fleshly mirrors of the god, the hidden face of the sacred divined from their twitching flesh and opaque or flickering eyes.

God-representations were not understood to contain the sacred power: that would be to pretend to constrain it. Rather the force was first attracted by chant and drum, further lured by the facsimilation of its visual signs in the *ixiptla* details of paint, dress and regalia, then brought to invade the form of the *ixiptla* as its primary vehicle and locus. For the most critical and so most intensely engaging phase of the ritual, these dangerous, glamorous, infinitely compelling figures not only made it possible for men to glimpse the face of the sacred, but also to experience it.

It was the priests,[53] fortified and disciplined as we have seen by rigorous preparatory exercises of body and spirit, who could allow themselves

---

[52] More correctly, *ixiptlayo-tl* as given in Frances Karttunen, *An Analytical Dictionary of Nahuatl*, University of Texas Press, Austin, 1983, p. 115.

[53] It would be reasonable to object to the relentlessly masculine orientation of this discussion, when women (occasionally) died as victims, or wept for them; where women (rarely and briefly) dominated the ritual action; where some of the most formidable deities were

to be drawn most deeply into the potent zone around the *ixiptla*. From the sixteenth century on clerics and outside analysts have tended to mute the ecstatic and shamanistic aspects of the Mexican priesthood, choosing to emphasize Quetzalcoatl as exemplar of priestly knowledge over Tezcatlipoca, 'Smoking Mirror', with his seer's glass and his association with the jaguar, avatar of the sorcerer. Yet the priestly identifying emblems, apart from the bright flowers of blood blooming below the lacerated ears, were their tobacco pouches and incense bags of jaguar-skin. We have only recently been made aware of the importance of hallucinogenic drugs as a way to the sacred in the Mesamerican world, and it is worth remembering the consciousness-altering power of native tobacco, especially when taken in by a fasting, fatigued body.[54] Nonetheless, I doubt the priests were drug-tranced during these taxing public performances. As impresarios and main players in such chancy, precariously-balanced ceremonials, they would have needed their wits about them. More important, drugs were for them redundant when the final phase was reached: then they watched from the threshold as the *ixiptla*, in the full grip of the sacred, dazed, delirious, reeled through the shifting darkness to the brightness beyond. Then the survivors of this close encounter with the sacred took their long step back to the usual world, bearing ritual things marked by the sacred but most powerfully marked themselves, and the ritual, and the experience, was complete.

With the conquest high ritual ceased. The warrior cult too, with all its glamour and competitive intensities for the making of the self and the promise of liberation from the self, was abruptly eclipsed.[55] The panoply

female. But this was a warrior society, and precisely how that great fact impinged on women must be separately pursued.

[54] Peter Furst, working largely from visual representations, and drawing on his deep knowledge of drug use amongst modern Northern Mexican groups, has been a pioneer in this crucial area. See e.g. his 'Morning Glory and Mother Goddess at Tepantitla, Teotihuacan: Iconography and analogy in pre-Columbian Art', in Norman Hammond (ed.) *Mesoamerican Archeology: New Approaches*, London, Duckworth, 1979, pp. 187–216, and *Hallucinogens and Culture*, Chandler and Sharp, San Francisco, 1976. While peyote seems to have been used by the priesthood, the famous magic mushroom appears to have been reserved for more individual and 'secular' (that is less dangerously charged) occasions. Priestly trance was typically a priest-house or solitary experience.

[55] While trusted Indian groups continued to be recruited to fight in Spanish causes, any lustre quickly dimmed. See e.g. William Sherman's retrieval of the unhappy fate of Tlaxcalan 'allies' recruited into Pedro de Alvarado's service in Guatemala. William Sherman, 'Tlaxcalans in Post-Conquest Guatemala', *Tlalocan* 7:1, 1969, pp. 124–139. The rivalrous display element of the warrior cult seems to have been rather less decisively extinguished, though the hints are few enough: see e.g. Motolinía, *Memoriales* part 2, chapter 26. For

of exemplary 'game' performances of utter and fatal exertion, like the high displays of martial art in the gladiatorial combats of Tlacaxipeualiztli, which drew on the same deep cultural predilection for seeking the sacred through the extinction of the self, or, as we would most inadequately translate it, through 'ecstasy', were also terminated. What was left of the rich traditional constellation of paths to ecstasy in the new colonial reality, and what new Christian alternatives were opened?

One Christian way, the way of the mystics, was effectively closed to Indian neophytes.[56] The Franciscan Martín de Valencia, leader of the famous Twelve, could fall into a rigid trance lasting over hours or days at the mere power of the Word, to no more than the disquiet of his fellows.[57] Such behaviour in an Indian could only arouse intense suspicion. The way of self-inflicted austerities, through fasting, pain and blood loss, was perhaps still open. There is some temptation to equate traditional self-laceration with maguey spines and the making of blood-offerings with the vigorous self-flagellation which so quickly became part of the Indi-ans' post-conquest ritual repertoire.[58] But as we have seen, pre-conquest bloodletting was typically practised in seclusion and accompanied by rigorous fasting and vigil: that is, it appears as part of the preliminary ordering of one' relationship with the sacred powers before the public phase of the ritual performance. On those grounds I hesitate to equate it, despite the blood, despite the pain, with those public and collective pro-cessions of Indian flagellants which so impressed Motolinía twenty years after the conquest.[59] My present suspicion is that the attractive power of the flagellant experience lay in a new blend of old elements, with

the ecstasy of the pre-contact warrior yielding fully to his fate, see Clendinnen, 'The Cost of Courage in Aztec Society', *passim.*

[56] But see Motolinía, *Historia*, Book 2, chapter 8 for some (rather tentatively-reported) Indian 'visions'.

[57] Franciscan legend has it that one of his fellow friars, wistfully emulous, called out, when Martín was so transported, 'Martín, Martín, stay there! Don't come back!' Quoted Angelico Chavez, O. F. M., *The Oroz Codex*, Academy of Franciscan History, Wash-ington D.C., 1972, p. 192.

[58] Motolinía speaks of processions of flagellants numbering in some places 'five or six thousand and in others ten or twelve thousand' *Historia*, Book 1, chapter 8.

[59] Motolinía, *ibid* in the maguey-spine lacerations the overt 'reason' for the action was the drawing forth of blood, the associated physical experience being therefore a by-product. The 'reason' for Christian self-flagellation was presumably the experience of pain, in imitation of and in penance for Christ's suffering, with any blood drawn being therefore a by-product. Yet pain would be common to the practitioners of both spiritual exercises. Durán mentions an episode of what he calls 'flagellation' in the festival of Toxcatl, but I judge this to be a distortion in the Durán manner. Durán, *Historia*, Book 1, chapter IV. Note the priestly ordeal by burning resin described by Durán for the festival Huey

both the maguey-spine lacerations and the flagellations being stimulated and coloured by the excitements of in-group competition, while the rhythmic blows, the chantings and the parallel violation of physical integrity promised escape from 'self' through collective engagement.[60] For the engagement was obdurately collective: there was small interest among Indians in private flagellation.[61] It is possible that the flagellant performances also echoed the measured pulse of the obligatory dances which celebrated the self-defined ritual group in pre-contact times, but I do not know how closely regimented they were: on this the sources are mute. But the flagellants typically completed the exercise, Motolinía informs us, by taking sweat baths and eating of hot chilli peppers, which were the actions associated with post-ritual cleansing from the sacred in the traditional world, so the experience was brought to its conclusion in the traditional mode. Certainly there is scant indication that Indians were pursuing a Christian way of penitence.

One Indian way appears to have closed. Dreams for the Mexicans were not solitary voyages into individual interiority: they were rather communications, in a language more or less clear, from the 'real' world of the sacred. Books of dreams were among the Mexicans' most valued possessions, and dream-readers among their most honoured experts. Deities revealed themselves in dreams.[62] It is probable that dreams held something like the same significance for the traditional Mexicans as they did for the native peoples of North America. Belief in the predictive power of dreams remained sufficiently vivid to be denounced by Durán in the late fifteen-seventies, along with the tribes of 'soothsayers' he saw as infesting

---

Tecuilhuitl, where he claims burning copal resin was permitted to run down over the priest's flesh, to be torn off and burnt. Durán, *Historia*, Book 1, chapter XIII.

[60] On the issue of competition versus communitas, cf. Mottahedeh's discussion of initially competitive self-mutilation as a process through which 'the penitent loses not only his sense of self-protection but also his sense of separateness... the penitent has broken the boundary between himself and his fellow penitents and even – to some extent – between himself and the spiritual mode he seeks to imitate'. Mottahedeh, *The Mantle of the Prophet* pp. 174–176. For an outsider's view of a collective flagellant penance in which a kind of ecstasy seems to have been arrived at, Fanny Calderón de la Barca, *Life in Mexico: The Letters of Fanny Calderón de la Barca*, (1843) ed. Howard T. Fisher and Marion Hall Fisher, Doubleday, New York, 1966, chapter 26, pp. 336–338.

[61] e.g. Motolinía's examples of individual acts of devotion were performed publicly, within the churches. Motolinía, *Historia*, Book 2, chapter 5, See also Book 1, chapter 15.

[62] 'They had books of their dreams and their meanings, expressed in figures, and experts who interpreted them...' Motolinía, *Historia*, chapter 49, p. 67. See also the dedicatory letter, p. 2; Durán, *Historia*, Book 1, chapter XIII; Book II, chapter LXVIII, for dreams as augury and as intimations of the sacred.

all regions, but he gives no indication of highly specialised interpreters, so it is likely that dream-telling was becoming, as we would expect, a more individual and idiosyncratic matter.[63] There is a teasing glimpse in a treatise written nearly a century after the Conquest of something like a vision experience accorded men who had withdrawn to a remote place to offer their own blood to the gods.[64] But few Spaniards or acculturated Indians had much interest in reporting such matters, and we know almost nothing of them.

One wide and easy path was held open by Spaniards. In the course of his 'History' Motolinía casually noted the difficult early steps along the way to Christianity's triumph. He remembered the hostility of the Indians of Mexico-Tenochtitlan to the friars' earnest desire to bring them awareness of Christ and his Church. 'All the knowledge they wished', he wrote, 'was of how to give themselves over to vice and sin'; feasting, drawing blood from their ears and arms and tongues, and drinking: 'this land was a copy of hell, its inhabitants shouting at night, some calling on the devil, some drunk, some singing and dancing'. He remembered the Indians' great drinking bouts with the clarity of disgust. 'They ordinarily began to drink after vespers; they drank so steadily, in groups of ten or fifteen with the pourers never ceasing to pour, and ate so little that by the end of the evening they were losing their wits, now falling, now sitting down, singing and shouting and calling upon the devil.' Motolinía goes on to make his outsider's judgment: 'it was pitiable to see men created in the image of God become worse than brute beasts'.[65]

That was and continued to be the Spanish reading of Indian drinking.[66] Spaniards, taking drink to be an attribute of civilized living, sought to drink without losing 'self-possession'. Such was not the Indian understanding. For them the way to the sacred was opened precisely through losing 'possession' of the merely human self, and on designated ritual

---

[63] Durán, Book I, chapter VI.

[64] The local priest reports: 'they say that some even fainted or fell asleep, and in this ecstasy they would hear, or thought they heard, words from their idol who spoke to them, of which they would become very proud and seemingly certain they would be granted what they were requesting, which ordinarily was children, wealth, a long life, or health.' Ruiz de Alarcón, *Treatise*, p. 57.

[65] Motolinía, *Historia*, Book 1, chapter 2.

[66] On this key issue of different cultural understandings of drinking and its consequences (and for the exemplary analysis of uncooperative documents) see William B. Taylor's *Drinking, Homicide and Rebellion in Colonial Mexican Villages*, Stanford University Press, Stanford, 1979, on which much of the following discussion depends. See esp. chapter 2, pp. 41–43.

occasions, as in the festival of Izcalli earlier discussed, drinking had provided such a way.[67] There the festival state of drunkenness had taken the collectivity into the dangerous realm of the sacred, with its derangement of the senses, its disruption of the ordinary, its deliriously transforming powers.[68] The danger was inseparable from the experience. Ritual drunkenness could be invoked because it could be ritually controlled, while individual drunkenness was profoundly dangerous. We think of drunkenness as destructive of the social fabric and individual moral fibre. For pre-conquest Indians it tore the membrane between the mundane and the sacred, and to do that without ritual preparation was not only dangerous to the individual, but to society. In well-regimented Mexico-Tenochtitlán prostitution was frowned upon, but went unpunished. A woman drunk on an unsanctioned occasion, 'tumbled there, with hair streaming out', and as we might think doing no particular harm to anybody, attracted exemplary punishment, her drunken, insensate body doubly inviting invasion by the uncontrolled sacred.[69] Motolinía's drinkers, however uncontrolled they appeared to him, were drinking in a ritual context, as the groupings, the sunset hour, the ritual pourers, all indicate. When fully drunk, they 'called on the devil': on the sacred powers at last drawn near.

It would not do to exaggerate the collective and religious strand in Indian drinking throughout the three centuries of colonial rule. As William Taylor's remarkable study of colonial Mexican villages makes clear, much of the drinking in the late colonial period looks irredeemably 'secular'. But there are haunting themes in what remained distinctively Indian styles of drunkenness. Pulque, and pulque preferably locally rather than commercially produced, continued to be preferred over 'foreign' cane spirits for collective (and putatively Christian) ritual occasions, and on those occasions Indians drank to full inebriation. If Spaniards uneasily noted the transformation alcohol wrought on normally passive natives,

---

[67] Sahagún, *Florentine Codex* Book 2, pp. 170–171. On drinking, as on so much else, the Florentine Codex traces a characteristic movement between the 'hard rule' statement ('absolutely nobody drank') and its erosion by a multitude of scattered references to exceptions.

[68] Durán was well aware that pre-contact controls on drunkeness were because 'these people held the maguey to be something divine, celestial . . . [it] was not only an inebriating drink but also a god to be revered, [and] held to be a divine thing, because of its effects and power to intoxicate'. Durán, *Historia*, Book 1, chapter XIII. See also Ruiz de Alarcón, *Treatise*, p. 53 for a celebration of the first gathering of amaranth and the drinking to inebriation which concluded it.

[69] Sahagún, *Florentine Codex*, Book 4, chapter 5, p. 16.

thinking they made violent and dangerous drunks, the periodic community drinking bouts were typically genial, even jubilant, occasions, with festivals marked by exuberant mock combats and transvestism, and with broad tolerance of 'crazy' behaviour.[70] (Such occasions could also context drinking duels, which in that headily heightened world flared easily into violence.[71]) Indian attraction towards the disordering, or reordering, of the senses through alcohol, so often and easily translated as symptomatic of extreme social and psychological demoralization, speaks rather of a continued quest for the ecstatic sacred experience, to which other routes, like the ingestion of hallucinogens, or the addictive delights of warrior testing, had been largely closed.[72] If Spanish friars deplored Indian drinking, other Spaniards were happy to supply (and to tax) the drinkers. So the drinking continued and intensified, coming to be accepted as the denouement of all significant Indian collective engagements. Other zones, like that of 'fasting' and preliminary purification, are by their nature more masked from us, but the glimpses we have of the style of the ritual episodes and of their process – the ritual lexicon and grammar, to vary the metaphor – point to pre-contact modes.

[70] Taylor, *Drinking, Homicide and Rebellion*, esp. pp. 37–43. Taylor concludes that 'rules of social behaviour in the community were not dissolved by alcohol.' (p. 61) For Christian occasions, p. 60; for 'loco' conduct, p. 61.

[71] It would perhaps be opportunistic to interpret Indian claims to be innocent of crimes committed when drunk because 'out' of their senses as confirmation of my 'possession by the sacred' interpretation, especially as such pleas often mitigated punishment. Taylor, *Drinking, Homicide and Rebellion*, pp. 64–65.

[72] How effective the prohibition of plant-derived drugs had been I do not know. A century after the conquest Ruiz de Alarcón noted the practised use of hallucinogenic or narcotic materials, especially *ololiuhqui*, a decoction of the morning glory seed, for many exigencies of life among the Indians of his (admittedly somewhat remote) region. From this evidence it is impossible to know whether the Indians of more effectively supervised regions had forgotten such practices, or had merely learnt discretion. He recorded a native woman hiding her little basket of *ololiuhqui* and incense in a household oratory, which suggest an easy domestic association. Ruiz de Alarcón, *Treatise*, pp. 60–61. The vision of the sacred *ololiuhqui* yielded was not typically taken as 'Christian', especially as the *ololiuhqui* itself was understood to punish all who failed to treat it with respect, as Ruiz de Alarcón discovered to his chagrin when he fell ill after making a salutary public bonfire of it (p. 62). The incantations he records employ a distilled traditional ritual vocabulary, invoking traditionally and correctly-named deities, and deeply infused with traditional space-time understandings, but like Ocelotl these much later shamans seem to have incorporated 'Christian' figures in their range of spiritual helpers with no cognitive frisson: e.g. Ruiz de Alarcón pp. 66–67, for a woman shaman being taught curing rituals by her angelic spirit helper while nailed to the cross; pp. 184–187 for even more illustrious Christian teachers. Perhaps because of the difficulty of its procuring (and its formidable potency) peyote seemed to have been used almost exclusively by shamans.

A difficulty with an 'action' focus is that it requires both space and a most leisurely pace. For my arguments both theoretical and historical to be adequately demonstrated I would need to trace the trajectory of Indian collective ritual, before and after the conquest, in much more detail, and to map much more closely the sequences of physical experiences which Indians had come to associate with access to the sacred: the patterns of dance and drum etched in the senses, the smells, the sting and smart of the skin, the tension in the thinned belly and the muscles of thigh and chest and throat and tongue which signalled that a god was near. I would also need to subject Spanish religious performances to something like the same scrutiny, which is notably absent from what can be no more than a preliminary 'essay'. But for the last I want to glance briefly at a more static phenomenon: the Indians' care and use of Christian religious images, and the possible relationship between the use of those images and of pre-contact *ixiptlas*.

The European imagination is easily captivated by the drama and pathos of the human *ixiptlas*; those men and women who paraded, danced and died in the regalia of a god. But for Indians *ixiptlas* came in various media, in wood or clay or stone or maize dough, with no special priority accorded the human variant. The Mexica of Tenochtitlan concocted the greatest *ixiptla* of their own greatest warrior deity on a frame of wood, fleshing it magnificently with maize dough, girding it in paper regalia of gargantuan proportions, including a heroic loincloth, so building the god more hugely in the imagination that he ever could have been in flesh.

The criteria which established the Mexican category of *ixiptla* appear to have been threefold. *Ixiptlas* were impermanent. They were named for the sacred force or being or aspect of being they represented. They were made and unmade in the course of the ritual, the process of their construction and deconstruction being carefully prescribed.[73] It was the process of construction of the image – the preliminary purification of its builders and adorners; the slow sequence of its dressing in precisely detailed and prescribed regalia – which invoked the desired specific sacred presence. The completion of the image, and its naming, opened it as the habitation of the god. Then, after the celebration, and the experiencing,

---

[73] I have only recently thought to wonder about the status of the 'god-puppets' described by Sahagún; those elegantly dressed little figures the *teuquiquixti* (he who brings out and makes representations with the god figures') made perform in the market place or anywhere elsewhere he could get the fee, and which were then folded away in his bag. Bernardino de Sahagún, *Informantes de Sahagún*, trans. from the Nahuatl to Spanish by Angel María Garibay, *Tlalocan*, II, 3, 1947, p. 235.

of the 'presented' deity, the image was ceremoniously dismantled, the materials of its making, now charged with the sacred, reverently disposed of. The different media of flesh, clay, stone, wood, dough, were not much more than that: different frames on which the crucial construction could be built and unbuilt.[74]

So much for pre-conquest *ixiptlas*. Now to jump that couple of blurred decades after conquest to an inquisitorial case in 1539. A local 'chief' and his wife accused of idolatry had in their possession a small idol, which we are told they would dress on particular occasions in accordance with the instructions of a visiting 'calendar priest': in a huipil if the deity to be propitiated were female, in a mantle and breechclout if it were male.[75] This immediately suggests impoverishment of sacred paraphernalia, of religious specialists, of knowledge: a sad little do-it-yourself ritual, symptomatic of material and cultural impoverishment, the depleted ceremonial of a defeated people.

There are symptoms of impoverishment enough, in the admission of the chief's wife into responsibility for the maintenance of the ritual round, and in their dependence on a peripatetic priest, but I doubt the all-purpose image, 'made' female or male by its dressing, is one of them. In her illuminating study of post-conquest Mexican sculpture Elizabeth Weismann comments on early Indian dissatisfaction with the fully 'precast' Spanish Christian image, which came with garments and accoutrements formed into the wood or the clay. Indians insisted that a 'proper' image was most desirably a doll, with 'nothing . . . needed but a head, a pair of hands, and preferably adjustable arms', together with an extensive wardrobe, to be drawn on for suitable garments for particular occasions. That is, the image was ideally constructed according to the requirements of each occasion.

The Indian preference was noted, deplored and resisted by the Church. The ruling of the Third Council of the Mexican Church in 1585 was stern, clear and as usual lagging rather badly behind events: 'Images which are made from this time forward . . . shall be of such a kind that under no circumstances will it be necessary to adorn them with clothing' (Weismann 1950:178). But local convictions could not be denied. Through that

---

[74] Spaniards were to identify the dismembering and distribution for ritual consumption of the maize-dough ixiptla as an echo (or a Satanic parody) of Christian communion. The confusions encapsulated in that identification require separate exploration.

[75] Proceso e información qu se toma contra Xpobal y su mujer, por ocultar ídolos y otros delitos, y contra Martín, hermano del primero (1539), 'Procesos de indios idólatras y hechiceros', pp. 141–175.

complex process of exchange and mutual modification between 'popular' and 'elite' cultures which Roger Chartier has usefully named 'appropriation', the church hierarchy itself came to adopt the Indian view (Chartier 1984:229–253). Mexican holy images acquired elaborate wardrobes of suitable garments for particular occasions: as Weisemann comments, 'in Lent the Virgin must wear mourning; satin, tinsel, and jewells were hardly enough to bedeck her for Easter or Christmas; but immediately after the nativity, when at Holy Innocents she must flee with the child into Egypt, she must be equipped with travelling cape, pilgrim's hat, lunch basket and water gourd'. For the great miraculous images magnificent *camarines* – dressing rooms – were provided, where their raiment could be kept and cared for. By the midseventeenth century the Church had capitulated entirely. Images which could not be 'dressed' had come to be regarded as 'provincial, old-fashioned, and a little vulgar', and villagers were able to spend as much of their invention and their scarce resources as they could afford in the appropriate presentation of their local saints, to be dressed, processed, then 'retired' until the next occasion (Weismann 1950:176).[76]

This cultural predilection sheds an oblique light on another puzzle. The early Indian devotion to the Virgin Mary presents problems both for the 'belief' perspective, and for my kind of 'belief in action' analysis. Mary was temperamentally and physically notably unlike the great sacred females of the Mexican world. Yet hers was the ubiquitous figure in the private shrines Indians maintained in their houses, and her public devotion was extravagant. Her key attraction would appear to have been her (human) maternalism. The friars had initially borrowed the name 'To Nantzin', 'Our (honoured) Mother', from one of those formidable pre-contact sacred females for Mary, but by the late sixteenth century she had come to be called 'Tlaconantzin', 'Precious Mother', by

---

[76] Note also illustration 160 on the same page of the extraordinary little bald virgin propped on her four wooden legs, being what was left of Our Lady of Health of Pátzcuaro after the solid image had been covertly whittled into the desired 'frame' form. Just how enduring that preference has proved, at least at the village level, is beguilingly displayed in the hanging Christs in their decorative huipiles, and the robust little virgins in their straw hats and kerchiefs, ready for the fields, in Porter and Auerbach's photographic record of Mexican churches. Eliot Porter and Ellen Auerbach, *Mexican Churches*, University of New Mexico Pres, Albuquerque, 1987, *passim* for village church interiors but see esp. plates 48 and 49, from the church of Santa María de Coyotepec, Oaxaca, and the 'clothes-horse' saints, plates 54 and 55. Charles Gibson tells us of unofficial Indian cofradías supporting their favourite image in the local church (including three versions of the Virgin, and 'Santo Ecce Homo') from their cultivation of the saint's 'own' land, earnings being spent on candles, fireworks, flowers and gunpowder for the saint's fiesta. Gibson, *The Aztecs under Spanish Rule*, pp. 129–130.

her Indian devotees, which suggests a more tender warmth.[77] My own view is that the most likely bridging figures from pre-contact conceptualizations of sacred females towards this very much more human and domestic one were the little images of the goddesses of sustenance (of water and maize) typically represented as sedate young women, and particularly favoured, even mass-produced, for household shrines, to judge from the clay moulds which happen to have survived. (The maize goddess at least was invested with a kind of passive intercessory function, her stricken misery in time of drought being invoked to draw rain from her 'younger brother' the Rain God.[78]) The maternal and nurturant themes commingled. By the eighteenth century the Virgin was often identified with pulque, an identification which evokes at once sacred power and 'natural' generosity, and the shadow image of Mayahuel, one-time goddess of pulque, her multiple and super-abundant breasts endlessly flowing with the sacred milk.[79] But perhaps at least a subsidiary reason for the enthusiastic adoption of the image of the Virgin in so many villages was that she led so diverse and interesting a ritual life, providing constant challenges for her appropriate 'presenting'. This raises the intriguing possibility that images accorded particular devotion by Indians, and assumed by European clerics (and European analysts) to be stable entities with continuous personae, might not have been so understood by their devotees, but perhaps rather as sacred 'kits' to be variously activated for various occasions.

Crosses and crucifixes present different problems. We know from Motolinía of the extraordinary efflorescence of apparent devotion to the cross in Bishop Zumárraga's time – sprouting massively, first in wood, then in stone, on mountain tops, at springs, corners and crossroads, as well as in its official place in the village churchyard. We recollect the Tlaloc cross, and Mexican reverence for the Four Directions and the Fifth Direction of the Centre. We note the enduring Indian enthusiasm for curiously stylized representations of the stigmata, with the four wounds

---

[77] See e.g. the standard preamble to the testaments of Culhuacan, most being written between 1579–1582, in Cline and Leon-Portilla (eds.) *The Testamants of Culhuacán* and Ruiz de Alarcón, *Treatise*, p. 149. See also William Taylor, 'The Virgin of Guadalupe in New Spain', for Mary's rural worship as 'a unique mother of miraculous, spontaneous fertility'.

[78] Sahagún, *Florentine Codex*, Book 6, chapter 8, p. 35.

[79] For the identification of the Virgin (especially the Virgin of Guadalupe) with pulque, see Taylor, 'The Virgin of Guadalupe in New Spain', p. 19, and his *Drinking, Homicide and Rebellion*, p. 59.

formally disposed around the central heart,[80] which echoes the compass-rose form of the Four directions. So the cross-building may initially have been no more than an inadvertently licensed public manifestation of an enduring cult. But Indians also did new things with crosses in central Mexico. Weismann describes early Mexican crosses as typically absorbing the figure of Christ back into the structure, with the sudarium become a mask at the arms' juncture; the emblem of the passion – the ladder, the lash, the seamless garment – carved into the shaft; the nails and the crown of thorns driven directly into the wood. The practice of carving the emblems into the shaft, for which there was no European precedent, could have been a product of the friars' initial dependence on visual rather than verbal communication for teaching, as Weismann suggests. It is the eclipse of the human figure which holds more interest. Pre-conquest Mexicans had slight inclination to represent the human body. Their gods shared only a vestigially human basic architecture, typically being compilations of symbolic forms identified through the diagnostics of regalia and conventionalised gesture, not any nuance of feature or glance.[81] The forms beneath these regalias were frames, skeletal structures for the 'adornments' which constituted the persona: the direction taken after the conquest by those pared-down Christian images.[82] Something of the same process seems to be going on with the modification of the Cross: not so much the Cross itself being treated as 'equivalent to Christ', as Weismann suggests, but rather the (merely human) Christ subsumed into the more formidable non-human symbol.[83] (It is piquant that the same period of the sixteenth

---

[80] For churchyard crosses and the Five Wounds of Christ, Weismann, *Mexico in Sculpture*, pp. 7–11, plates 1–3; p. 28, plate 21. For the early enthusiasm, Motolinía, *Historia*, Book 1, chapter 3.

[81] The people of Michoacán are reported to have 'called the crosses [of the Christians] Holy Mary, because they did not know the doctrine and they thought the crosses were gods like those they had'. Fray Martín de Jesús de la Coruña (?), *Relación de las ceremonias y ritos y población y gobernación de los indios de la provincia de Mechuacán 1539–1541* (?), translated and edited as *The Chronicles of Michoacán* by Eugene R. Crane and Reginald C. Reindorp, University of Oklahoma Press, Norman, 1970, p. 88. Cf. Motolinía, recalling his first days in Mexico: 'up to that time they were naming God. They also used the name Saint Mary for all the Christian images they saw'. Motolinía, *Historia*, chapter 4. What we note is the potency of the giving of the name. (Spanish images in this conquest stage were presumably eminently portable and all-of-a-piece, and might well have appeared to be 'the same' to Indian eyes.)

[82] One apparent exception here, Xipe Totec, is not: the Flayed Lord wore his persona-defining skin over a naked form. The quiet girl maize-and-sustenance goddesses were intermediate, and as I have suggested probably mediating, figures.

[83] Note too the occasional insertion of an obsidian or jade disk in a hollow at the juncture of the arms, like the jade set in the centre torso of so many Mexican idols, and the cavity

century saw increasingly intense devotion to the Cross in Spain, and its increasing personification, in that its 'person' could suffer assault by the impious.) (Christian 1981b).

Christ figures appear to have enjoyed their Mexican vogue only after the close of the sixteenth century. It is difficult to date Mexican representations of the Christ, but easy to recognise them: they are typically marked by an intense focus on physical suffering, the bodies twisted, the wounds raw, the blood vivid.[84] Are the Indians recording an *ixiptla*-making process, marking the process of the 'making' (in Christ's case, the narrative of suffering) into the image? In the more settled and controlled situation of the evolved colony it is, paradoxically, more difficult to assess the degree of Spanish influence, and the images themselves, despite their overwhelming emotional eloquence, are mute witnesses to process.

The use of living images in sacred dramas had their European precedents, as we have seen, but despite some external resemblance they signified very differently. Barcelona's pretty ambulatory tableau of St. Sebastian with his entourage of weeping children was designed to touch a compulsively attentive and potentially compassionate deity with a predilection for children as innocents. Mexican gods were none of those things. The plays built around the entranced nun moving like a sacred somnambulist in her Florentine nunnery seem closer to Mexican *ixiptla* performances in their precise replications of details of appearance as a main element in the theatrical 'realization', but the scope, status and nature of the experience so constructed were profoundly unlike. Caterina's ecstatic elevation was a private and inward matter, her sisters being privileged to watch the outward signs of her tender union with Christ: edified spectators of her exaltation, they were not participant in it. By contrast the Mexican *ixiptla* was not 'participant', nor finally 'human' at all, the individual being quite eclipsed and consumed by the incandescent blaze of the sacred for which its living body gave point and focus. In that perilously constructed zone of sacred danger the immanent was brought to manifest itself, and men could bathe in its unearthly light.

---

in the breast of the Christ Child. Weismann, *Mexico in Sculpture* p. 13, plates 4 & 5; p. 109, plate 100.

[84] Weismann acknowledges the difficulty in dating Mexican figures, given the strong current of traditionalism, opposed by an equally strong inclination 'to clean up old images with new paint, fashionable panties and a real wig'. Weismann, *Mexico in Sculpture*, p. 219, notes to plates 162–165. A more abiding difficulty is to know how much Spanish and how much Indian influence went into the images' making. It is for that reason that I prefer to focus on their adornments and accoutrements rather than on the figures themselves.

I would suggest that for long years after the conquest Indian techniques for seeking the sacred – prolonged dance, drink, sacred play, invocation by manipulation of regalias – remained the techniques they had known before the Spaniards came. This is no argument for an unruffled continuity. For the first generations the Indian condition must have been desperate, as they strove to accommodate incalculable losses in all areas of life. Contexts of action, personnel, paraphernalia, social experience, social aspiration, all were changed. Those early colonial drinking performances I have represented as a fast track to the sacred obviously signified very differently when so much around them was transformed: when the pulque was not prepared by local specialists, but had to be purchased, often from Spaniards; when bailiffs stood ready to drag the drinkers to jail; not least when individuals had the option to withdraw from the collective action. Old actions are changed in new contexts, and men innovate as they seek to maintain the familiar.[85] With time religious life came to focus on the local church and its activities, and Indians came to speak and presumably to think of themselves as Christian. But in those relatively uncoerced ritual performances, whether 'secret' and unsanctioned, or exuberantly public and 'Christian'[86], through which Indians caught in the swirl of post-conquest experience pursued the experience of the sacred, the presences they strove to invoke bore slight resemblance to the Spaniards' god.

[85] For a poignant analysis of the jarrings attending the attempted maintenance of traditional notions of legitimate, indeed obligatory fighting in a restructured colonial world, see David McKnight, 'Fighting in an Australian Aboriginal Supercamp', in David Riches (ed.), *The Anthropology of Violence*, Basil Blackwell, Oxford, 1986.

[86] It could be complained here that no generalisation can properly stretch so widely, given the probability of different experiences of different regions of Central Mexico. Yet evolved 'Indian Catholicism' seems remarkably coherent in its characteristics across sedentary Mexico, despite variations in the conditions of initial contact.

5

Landscape and World View

The Survival of Yucatec Maya Culture Under Spanish Conquest

The religions of contemporary Middle American Indian communities fall neatly enough under the descriptive category we call 'syncretic'. Myths and rituals, integrated experiences for the participant believers, betray to the outside observer their Spanish and Indian antecedents. This indicates a methodology of analysing the ongoing flow of religious life into its smallest constituent parts – colours and gestures, sacred objects and sacred locations, the structure and language of invocations – the more precisely to identify the ingredients of the 'mixed' religion we see being lived out. When enquiry moves to the process of imposition and selection by which the mix was initiated, in the early days of Spanish-Indian contact, the same familiar methodology lies ready to hand: Spanish Catholicism, and what is known of the traditional Indian religion, can be analysed into elements, those elements arranged in parallel, and the likely ease of transferance inferred, being judged to be the highest where a match seems good and where evidence from the ethnographic present appears to offer confirmation.

The method has its utility, not least in that it facilitates comparison between cases and allows some estimation of degrees and rates of acculturation. Its defects lie in its assumptions that the Spanish presence was a constant and was identically perceived by all Indian groups, and (more important) in the 'mosaic' models of religion and of culture on which such an analysis rests.

Article originally published as "Landscape and World View: The Survival of Yucatec Maya Culture Under Spanish Conquest," in *Comparative Studies in Society and History*, Vol. 22, No. 3 (July 1980): 374–393. © 1980 Society for Comparative Study of Society and History. Reprinted with permission.

This paper explores another approach. Spanish invasion and colonisation was very differently experienced by different native American groups. The Yucatecan situation presents a distinctive form of the encounter. The military phase of conquest extended over twenty years in Yucatan. In most of the other settled regions of Spanish America (including Central Mexico and Peru), *congregación* and *reducción* – the forced resettlement of Indian communities – was carried out by civil authorities 40 or more years after initial conquest, in response to an already massive population decline; in Yucatan it was implemented by missionary friars a decade after conquest and involved the dislocation and transplantation of still viable native communities. Early in the next decade came a sustained inquisition into 'idolatries'; in this, the friars again displayed their dominance. This sequence of events might well lead us to expect a quite rapid breakdown in traditional patterns of thinking and action among the Maya. What we find instead is a remarkable persistence of old patterns and a highly self-conscious cultural conservatism which persists even into this century.

While generations of scholars have noted the remarkable conservatism of the Maya, few have as yet sought to account for it, and those few have tended to concentrate on the post-Caste War Maya of the Quintana Roo region. The richness of the sixteenth-century documentation permits us to start the enquiry earlier, in the crucial early years of Spanish-Maya contact. How was it that among the traumas of conquest, colonization, and an unusually vigorous, coherent, and ruthless conversion campaign, the Maya were able to maintain a high sense of autonomy and of the legitimacy of their traditional account of the world? The documents permit the identification of those concepts of the old religion consciously and conscientiously preserved by the Maya and the tracing of the processes by which particular Christian elements were selected and incorporated within that familiar frame. It is possible to glimpse the Mayan conceptualisation of the generic features of their landscape through which they were able to recreate their traditional social worlds within the physically restructured villages imposed on them by the friars. Further, we may see how their conceptualisation of time and of their own history permitted them to sustain a sense of autonomy in face of defeat and subjugation by the Spanish conquerors.[1]

---

[1] Work done in Papua New Guinea, where the introduction of Christianity has been sufficiently recent to permit the 'native response' to be traced in some detail, demonstrates the extraordinary flexibility of native cognitive systems, and the various and to us startling

The Franciscan Offensive

The handful of Franciscan missionaries who offered themselves in the mid-1540s for the task of converting the Maya Indians of Yucatan were faced with a discouraging landscape. In Mexico, their brothers had found an obvious focus for missionary action in the great centres of Indian population. In Yucatan, the combination of slash-and-burn agriculture and dependence on natural wells, or cenotes, for reliable water supplies, together with the need for protection from interprovincial raids and the attractive power of a developed collective ritual and social life, had dispersed the Indian population in villages and hamlets distributed fairly evenly over the whole rocky surface of the peninsula. In the vales and hillsides of Mexico, Franciscans had seized the chance to knit the agricultural cycle into the web of Christian ritual, organising masses and processions for rain in direct competition with native agricultural gods. In Yucatan, the milpas or cornplots were littered, apparently haphazardly, through the dry, dense grey forest which hemmed the villages, and the dim paths which led to them blurred easily into bush, at least to European eyes. The friars recognised that the forest could not be controlled: it had masked the preparations for the last desperate uprising of the Maya of the southern and eastern provinces in 1546, when they had destroyed all things Spanish, including the dogs and cats and even the trees of Castile, until their final and bloody suppression, and it was to serve as the last refuge of the most recalcitrant Maya until the end of the colonial period and beyond.[2] After gathering up the sons of the native lords, to be sequestered within the mission schools attached to each monastery until

---

ways in which Christian teachings have been misunderstood. E.g., see Peter Lawrence, *Road Belong Cargo* (Manchester: Manchester University Press, 1964), and Peter Worsley, *The Trumpet Shall Sound* (London: Schocken Books, Inc., 1957). For developments in African studies, see Robert Strayer, 'Mission History in Africa: New Perspectives on an Encounter', *African Studies Review* 19 (1976): 1–15.

[2] The best account of the prolonged conquest of the peninsula and of the Great Maya Revolt, as the Spanish named it, remains that of Robert S. Chamberlain, *The Conquest and Colonization of Yucatan 1517–1550*, Carnegie Institution of Washington Publication no. 582 (Washington, D.C., 1948). For a succinct discussion and useful bibliography on the vexed question of the peninsula's population, and the impact of conquest, see Sherburne F. Cook and Woodrow Borah, *Essays in Population History: Mexico and the Caribbean* (Berkeley: University of California Press, 1974) II, ch. I, esp. pp. 62–65. Cook and Borah estimate the population of the peninsula (excluding Uaymil-Chetumal) in 1543 at 476,200, and in 1549 to have been 233,776. Those six years saw the final 'pacification' of the peninsula. Note also the comment on Uaymil-Chetumal, scene of the bitterest fighting, on pp. 47–48.

they could be transformed into 'Christians' and assistants in the teaching of the faith, the friars turned their attention to the villages. Understanding from their experience within their own order the efficacy of a minutely regulated environment in shaping behaviour into desired forms, they studied the patterns of traditional village life in order to effect their transformation.

In Maya villages, the line between public and private, family and social was vaporous. The long, multiple-family houses, where sons brought their wives after they had worked their years of bride service, denied in their very structure the social proprieties of Christian marriage and Christian parenthood. The private familial area was restricted to the dark sleeping quarters: public space began with the long verandah-like chamber running the length of the house. The houseyard was the women's privileged place. There, many household tasks were performed, as were devotions to the household gods. Through the long hours of the afternoon they could visit together, weaving the slow intricate patterns on their backstrap looms in the fruit trees' shade, free from the restrictions imposed by formal modesty when they left the houseyard to enter the village streets, to visit kin, to barter, or to pursue the endless task of fetching water from the village cenote.

It was while engaged in that task that Maya girls had most opportunity to practice their pretty routines of avoidance of men's glances, for around the wells clustered the spaces and edifices which provided the stages for significant male activity. There stood the temple-crowned pyramid, flanked by the storehouse for the masks, plumes, drums, and flutes required for the great ceremonial performances. In the long warrior house the youths of the village lived from puberty to marriage, learning the chants, dances, and stories which taught them what it was to be a Maya man. The house of the village chief, like those of the lords, was more public building than private residence. In the oratories of the chiefs were preserved the images and the inlaid skulls of specially revered ancestors. Their courtyards and reception chambers were sometimes courts of justice and sometimes the venue for the great feasts which saw the celebration of bonds of mutual dependence, where to meet an obligation was to strengthen rather than to extinguish it. They also provided the setting for major religious performances. Women played little part in those ceremonies – only old women, safely past menopause, were permitted to dance before the gods in the temple – but for the men, the cluster of edifices and framed spaces at the heart of the village provided the setting for the activities we distribute between church, school, court, theatre, and club. This was the focus of their social and religious life. In all the villages, the four ceremonial entrances to the village were linked to this centre by paths wide enough to accommodate the processions which laced them during the elaborate ceremonies ushering in each new year.[3]

This was the world the friars put to the torch. Seizing on the shaky warrant of a series of ordinances issued by the visiting royal judge Tomas Lopez Medel in 1552, a bare six years after the final 'pacification' of the Maya, the Franciscans embarked on an ambitious and ruthlessly implemented programme for the relocation of existing communities, despite bitter protests from Spaniards and Indians alike. At times with no more warning than the unheralded arrival of a solitary friar, Indians were ordered out of their houses, which were then set burning, along with their carefully nurtured fruit trees and their meagre possessions. Then the dazed and weeping Indians were herded off to new sites, which were too often inadequately prepared for them. Some died of hunger and exposure, and others, we are told, from 'the great sadness of their hearts'.[4]

In the villages built to replace those familiar worlds, there were significant spaces, but they spoke very differently of man's relation to man and of man's relation to the gods. The Christian church stood at the centre, but it was not to provide the focus for community action: placed in the charge

---

[3] Most of this information is found in Fray Diego de Landa, *Landa's Relacion de las Cosas de Yucatan. A Translation Edited with Notes by Alfred M. Tozzer*, Harvard University, Peabody Museum of American Archaeology and Ethnology Papers, XVIII (Cambridge, Mass.: Peabody Museum, 1941), esp. pp. 85–106, 124–25, 138–49. Hereafter cited as Landa, *Relatión*, or as Tozzer, *Relación*, when the reference is not to the text but to the editor's notes. For an attractive and reliable secondary account, see Ralph L. Roys, *The Indian Background of Colonial Yucatan* (Norman: University of Oklahoma Press, 1972; first published in 1943).

[4] Relaciones de Yucatan, in *Colección de documentos ineditos relativos al descubrimiento, conquista y organización de las antiguas posesiones españolas de Ultramar*, 2nd series, vols 11, 13 (Madrid: Real Academia de la Historia, 1898–1900), Hereafter *R.Y. 1* and *R.Y. 2*. *R.Y. 2*: 209–210. See also 30–31; 68–69; 187. For the ordinances, see 'Ordenanzas del Lic. Tomas Lopez' in Fr. Diego Lopez (de) Cogolludo, *Historia de Yucatan escrita en el siglo XVII por el reverendo padre Fr. Diego Lopez Cogolludo*, 2 vols, 3rd edition (Merida: Manuel Aldana Rivas, 1867–1868). Lib. V. Caps. XVI–XIX. esp. Cap. XVI. Orders for the gathering of Indians into convenient locations occur from the earliest days of Spanish settlement in the Indies, but the policy of *congregación* or *reducción* was not systematically implemented elsewhere, at least among settled Indian populations (e.g., in Peru and Central Mexico), for forty or more years after conquest, when it was executed by civil authorities in response to massive Indian population loss, and the consequent debilitation of communities.

of the schoolmaster, or another 'reliable' Indian, it was to be kept immac-
ulately clean and, except for brief and specified times, locked, and so safe
from unauthorised use. Close to the church stood the municipal building,
where the chief and his leading nobles still appeared, but now in the guise
of municipal officers in the Spanish system. The whipping post, that elo-
quent symbol of the new regime, spoke of the chief's new role: no longer
custodian of traditional justice, he was permitted to mete out punishment
to his followers for petty infractions of Spanish law. In this shrunken
world, there was to be no stage for communal action; all feasting was forbidden, as were meetings of any kind after nightfall, and with the sounding
of the bell for the souls in purgatory all were to withdraw to the single-
family domestic prisons built to replace the traditional multiple-family
structures. In place of the old complex religious round, from the constant
small gestures of thanks and propitiation offered in the milpas to the great
collective performances before the temple, there was to be solitary prayer,
morning and night, and passive attendance at the church on Sundays and
feast days, and at the occasional special exhortations delivered by visiting
friars.[5]

It is something of a convention among historians of culture contact to
deride the cultural myopia of missionaries, but it will not do to under-
estimate the understanding, the energy, and the psychological astuteness
of the Yucatan friars. They were determined to turn religious energy
inwards, away from collective and existential expression, to the anxious
scrutiny of individual conduct and so to the scrutiny of the individual
soul. They knew much of the complex interactions which structured the
old social system; most of the material in the preceding pages is drawn
from Fray Diego de Landa's great 'Account of the Things of Yucatan',
and some of his fellow missionaries were as fluent in Maya, and as tireless observers, as he. The friars knew what they were doing when they
set the villages to burn and forced the Indians to watch; they knew those
locations were thickly inscribed with the social and sacred meanings of
a way of life and with a view of life they were determined to destroy.
Their energy was formidable: we cannot be certain as to the percentage
of villages and the percentage of Indians actually relocated, but we can
be confident that few villages under Spanish control escaped substantial
reorganisation, at least in external forms. Every village had its church and
school, however modest, and by the end of the century multiple-family

---

[5] For the prescriptions for the structures of the new villages, and the behaviours approved
within those structures, see 'Ordenanzas del Lic. Tomas Lopez', Cogolludo, *Historia.*

houses were rare, being common only where Spanish presence was intermittent.[6]

The friars also understood the effectiveness of more ritualised statements of power. In 1562, after seventeen years of missionary effort, a chance discovery revealed that idolatry was being practised on a massive scale in the province of Mani, home of the Spaniards' most reliable allies the Xiu, site of the first mission to the Indians and heartland of the mission enterprise. The friars responded to this shocking blow with characteristic energy. The chiefs and lords were hastily rounded up, to be kept close in Merida, the Spanish capital, until they could be interrogated at proper length. The commoners, bereft of their traditional leaders, were strung up by the wrists and flogged, until they 'confessed' not only the extent of their own wickedness but also the involvement of their lords. For three long months terror reigned in Mani and the two adjacent provinces of Sotuta and Hocaba Homun, where the enquiry had been extended. Dread spread across the land: at the news of the friars' coming, men fled into the forests or hanged themselves in fear and despair.

Many Indians died under the torture. Others were maimed. One Spaniard recalled that when the penitents were delivered to the whipping post for their prescribed number of lashes, their bodies were already so torn by the tortures inflicted by their interrogators that 'there was no sound part of their bodies where they could be flogged'.[7] But despite the

---

[6] Ralph L. Roys, France V. Scholes, and Eleanor B. Adams, 'Census and Inspection of the Town of Pencuyut, Yucatan in 1583 by Diego Garcia de Palacio, Oidor of the Audiencia of [Mexico]', *Ethnohistory*, 6 (1959): 195–225, esp. 204–05; 'Report and Census of the Indians of Cozumel, 1570', *Contributions to American Anthropology and History*, 6, Carnegie Institution of Washington Publication no. 523 (Washington D.C., 1940), pp. 5–30.

[7] Testimony of Juan de Villalobos, 27 January 1565, in France V. Scholes and Eleanor B. Adams, eds., *Don Diego Quijada, alcalde mayor de Yucatan, 1561–1565*, 2 vols., Documentos sacados de los archivos de España. Biblioteca Histories Mexicana de Obras Ineditas, nos. 14–15 (Mexico City: Antigua Libreria Robredo, 1938), I, p. 66. An official enquiry conducted in 1565 established that 157 Indians had died under torture, and 32 remained crippled. Some 4,549 men and women had been put to the torture, and a further 6,330, who had confessed voluntarily, had been shorn or flogged as penance. Thirteen Indians had committed suicide, and 18 others, who had disappeared, were presumed to have done so. Information collected by Sebastian Vasquez on the abuses committed and tolerated by Dr. Diego Quijada, 25 March 1565, *Don Diego Quijada* II, pp. 213–14. For an account of the trials, see Ralph L. Roys and France V. Scholes, 'Fray Diego de Landa and the Problem of Idolatry in Yucatan', *Co-operation in Research*, Carnegie Institution of Washington Publication no. 501 (Washington D.C., 1938), pp. 586–620. For a revisionist view, see Inga Clendinnen, *Ambivalent Conquests: Maya and Spaniard in Yucatan, 1517–1570*, Cambridge University Press, 1987, 2003.

mounting protests of the local Spaniards and their insistence that the Indians in their anguish were 'confessing' to offences they had not committed, the friars held to their course. It was only the arrival of the new Bishop which brought the Inquisition to an abrupt end.[8] Bishop Toral, although himself a Franciscan, was appalled by his brothers' proceedings. Discounting lurid stories of multiple human sacrifice, with preliminary crucifixion of the victims and other grotesque 'Christian' embellishments, he imposed light penances for idolatry on the imprisoned chiefs and sent them back to their villages and their offices. I have argued elsewhere the difficulties in the way of treating extorted 'confessions' as directly descriptive of reality, but despite the inflations and distortions inseparable from the friars' methods of interrogation, there can be no doubt that the leaders of a number of villages, with the cooperation of the native 'Christian' schoolmasters, had continued to practise their old rituals as well as they were able and, worse, had brought their idols and sacrifices into the Christian church and to the foot of the cross itself.

For the Indians the events of 1562, following so close on a prolonged and bloody conquest and the wrenching relocation of the villages, ought to have been traumatic indeed. The houses of the lords had stood empty, their oratories rifled, while on the patios before the churches great mounds of idols – thousands, eyewitnesses said – slowly burned. The jewelled skulls of the great dead of the ruling lineages were smashed. It had been discovered that Nachi Cocom, territorial chief of Sotuta, redoubtable enemy of the Spaniards, and later friend and informant of the Franciscan Diego de Landa, had been a secret idolator until his death, so his corpse was exhumed and flung on the fire to burn with the idols. Through the strange new rites of judicial torture and *autos de fe*, profound loyalties had been tested, and broken. Landa himself, who had headed the Inquisition, believed it had been effective, and that punishment had brought the Indians to true repentance and a full recognition that the old ways were irretrievably gone.[9] Certainly on the Spanish side there was a fairly rapid decline in the attention given to the conversion programme in the

---

[8] The head of the secular administration in Yucatan, the *Alcalde Mayor* Don Diego Quijada, had taken up his office only in June or July of the previous year. He officially committed himself to the support of the Franciscans in their inquisitional proceedings, but only, it seems, under pressure. Petition of Fray Diego de Landa to Don Diego Quijada, 4 July 1562, *Don Diego Quijada* I, pp. 69–71. For Quijada's early identification of Fray Diego de Landa as a man to be wary of, see Don Diego Quijada to the Crown, 15 April 1562, *Cartas de Indias*, LXVII.

[9] Landa, *Relación*, p. 80.

peninsula, the last decades of the century seeing the development of a comfortable consensus, challenged by very few voices, that the Indians were – for Indians – well enough converted and – for Indians – good enough Christians.

The Maya Response

Historians chronicling the collapse of other native cultures under what sometimes seems no more than the fatal breath of European intrusion grope for metaphors of exquisite fragility; of tender flowers wilting and shrivelling, of shimmering spun-glass vessels shattering at a rude touch. For Maya culture the inelegant image that thrusts itself forward is of a tough, webby, dense sponge, elastic and, given the intricacy and multiplicity of its interconnections, almost impossible to tear. The Maya had suffered savage blows, and some of those blows were intelligently directed, yet a hundred years after the conquest they were reading the world much as they had a hundred years before. To understand the durability of that vision, it is necessary to understand Maya conceptualisations of space and time and how those conceptualisations were figured forth in their experienced world and in their account of their own human past.

The Maya conceived the world as quadrilateral. At each of the cardinal points a Sky-Bearer god sustained, like Atlas, his quarter of the world. Each Direction was identified by its own colour – red for the east, white for the north, black for the west, and yellow for the south – and possessed its own deities of wind and rain. At each corner of the world grew a tree, of the appropriate colour, while at the centre, or the 'Fifth Direction', rose the great green silk-cotton tree, the Tree of Life, whose branches pierced the thirteen layers of the heavens. Below the world lay the nine levels of the Underworld, a chill, bleak, shadowy place where all Maya, save those fortunate few whose manner of death exempted them, were doomed to wander endlessly.[10]

That quadrilateral shape was replicated throughout the seen world in the spaces made by men to frame human activity and in those 'natural' formations of special significance to men. In the Maya language, the classifier AC, which as a noun means turtle or turtle shell, was applied to all things which were recognised as sharing a certain basic shape.

---

[10] Landa, *Relación*, p. 132; J. Eric S. Thompson, *Maya History and Religion*, Civilization of the American Indians Series Vol. 99 (Norman: University of Oklahoma Press, 1970), esp. pp. 194–304.

We would tend to see them as 'hollow objects', but for the Maya they were rather 'enclosed spaces'. The word was used for cenotes, caves, milpas (enclosed by the walls of the forest), villages, which were 'human' spaces in the forest, houses, temples, and (in time), churches.[11] Each of these significant spaces had its four orientations, with their appropriate colours and influences. When a house was to be built, its four corner posts, and the centre post which marked the Fifth Direction, were carefully blessed. In the temples, and in the courtyards of the lords, the shape was repeated. The shape was sketched in the air in the purification ritual preliminary to all religious ceremonial, when four old men held cords stretched tight between them while the priest cleared the space within of dangerous spirits. Each milpa was guarded by its four spirits, very present to the milpero as he worked in the silent forest, which he propitiated again and again in rituals that traced and retraced that significant shape. The village itself was located firmly in the same frame, its four ceremonial entrances aligning it with the great orientations of the universe and marking the boundary between the unsafe, because not ritually controlled, world of the forest and the relative security of the village – a security preserved by the tireless vigilance of the priests. There were few witches in Yucatan villages: significant danger, the Maya knew, lay outside.

Round this four-cornered world moved the endlessly changing procession of deities which for the Maya constituted Time. The smallest unit recognised was the day, probably measured from sunset to sunset. The main sacred calendar, used for divination and prognostication, was based on a cycle of 20 named days, interacting with a numbers cycle from 1 to 13 and so forming a larger 260-day cycle, known as the Sacred Round. (There was also a 'week' of 9 nights, the precise significance of which is lost to us.) The solar year controlled another calendar, which consisted of 18 months of 20 days, along with a nineteenth 'month' comprising 5 unnamed and dangerously unlucky days, the *Uayeb*. Given that structure, only 4 of the 20 named days could begin the 'new year'; they were designated 'Year Bearers', and the influence of the particular Year Bearer was felt throughout his year.

During the *Uayeb* days, the gods were pausing, some slipping off their burdens of time, others readying themselves for the slow onward march. Those days were thus in a sense 'out' of time, and outside the influence of the gods. They were therefore days of peculiar terror for the Maya.

[11] For the classifier 'ac', see Thompson, *ibid.*, XIX.

Men ventured out of their houses only for ritual purposes and out of the village not at all, fearing the assault of uncontrolled forces in the form of wild beasts and serpents.[12]

During those hushed days, lords, priests and commoners together wove an elaborate ceremonial pattern, linking temple, lord's house, and village entrances, until the image of the incoming Year Bearer god was finally installed at his appropriate entrance to serve for the next year as guardian, compass and clock to villagers who passed and repassed, telling them, in the endless spirals of time, and the mindbaffling expanses of land and sky, 'where they stood'.[13]

Longer periods of time the sixteenth century Maya measured by a calendar based on a year or *tun* of 18 months consisting of 20 days each. Twenty *tun* equalled 1 *katun*, or 7200 days, and 13 *katuns* (approximately 256 years) comprised the cycle in terms of which human history was located and understood. Each of the 13 *katuns* was identified by the particular named day and number with which it ended. As the names and numbers identified the gods influencing that particular slice of time, each *katun* was identified with characteristic events, which would reoccur with the return of the 'same' *katun*. Thus 'history' was, simultaneously, prophecy, and prophecy became history again with the next swing of the cycle.[14]

---

[12] Cogolludo, *Historia*, Lib. IV. Cap. V.

[13] Michael Coe has presented an elegant and ingenious model of a complex rotational political system which he claims perhaps operated within Maya communities and replicates the transference of responsibility between deities. His argument is seductive, but I am troubled that Landa, so acute an observer, leaves no account of such a system. M. D. Coe, 'A Model of Ancient Community Structure in the Maya Lowlands', *Southwestern Journal of Anthropology*, 21 (1965): 97–114.

[14] The best discussion of the Maya calendars remains that of J. Eric S. Thompson, *Maya Hieroglyphic Writing: An Introduction*, Carnegie Institution of Washington publication no. 589 (Washington D.C., 1950). For a series of *katun* prophecies, see Ralph L. Roys, *The Book of Chilam Balam of Chumayel*, Carnegie Institution of Washington Publication no. 438 (Washington D.C., 1933), pp. 144–63. The elegance of the interlocking systems is indicated in Father Avendano's 1696 account of the sacred books of prophecy of the Peten Maya. These, he tells us, showed 'not only the count of the said days and months and years, but also the ages (*katuns*) and prophecies which their idols and images announced to them, or, to speak more accurately, the devil by means of the worship which they pay to him in the form of some stones. These ages are thirteen in number; each age has its separate idol and its priest, with a separate prophecy of its events. These thirteen ages are divided into thirteen parts, which divide this kingdom of Yucatan and each age, with its idol, priest and prophecy, rules in one of these thirteen parts of this land, according as they have divided it. Philip Ainsworth Means, *History of the Spanish Conquest of Yucatan and of the Itzas*, Harvard University, Peabody Museum

It was this conviction of the endless repetition of history which enabled the Maya to grasp and to render intelligible, in their own terms, their defeat and subjugation by the Spaniards. At the time of the Spanish intrusion, the Maya knew that the peninsula's political fragmentation and its endemic interprovincial warfare was a decline from an earlier period of harmonious and unified government. That harmony had been the outcome of foreign invasions. Throughout the peninsula, the noble caste based its claim to rule on descent from the lords who had once ruled at Mayapan, the Camelot of the Maya past. The real events are misty indeed, but it seems that sometime towards the end of the tenth century Yucatan was conquered by invaders of Mexican origin led by the Captain Kukulcan, the Feathered Serpent, who established their capital at what was later to be called Chichen Itza. That great city was abandoned in a *Katun* 6 Ahau, which ended in 1224. Then another group of foreigners, the Itza, possibly Mexicanised Chontal-Maya from Tabasco, took over the site, naming it 'the well of the Itza'. Led by a new 'Kukulcan', the Itza transferred their capital to the new city of Mayapan, 'the Banner of the Maya'. Kukulcan continued to rule for a time before his mysterious withdrawal from Yucatan, but Mayapan was remembered in the native histories as a confederation of Maya chiefs ruling together with acculturated Itza. Within the walled city the chiefs and nobles of the peninsula had lived a harmonious round of ritual, feasting, and hunting, activities which expressed the highest human conformity to the great principles which moved the cosmos. In those golden days the peninsula was at peace, the commoners working in their dispersed villages to sustain the exemplary centre. When that world of order collapsed into conflict as, in the Maya view of history, all worlds must, the chiefs and nobles, fleeing in bitterness to their respective provinces, carried with them the esoteric knowledge, inscribed in the sacred books of hieroglyphs which only they could read, which was their warrant and proof of their right to rule.[15]

The Spanish intruders the Maya identified with the Itza. Like the Itza, they were lascivious and unmannerly, but also like the Itza, they had brought new and useful knowledge. Their coming did not abrogate the authority of the native rulers but merely eclipsed it: in time they

---

of American Archaeology and Ethnology Papers, vol. VII (Cambridge, Mass.: Peabody Museum, 1917), p. 141.

[15] Landa, *Relación*, pp. 20–39. See also Tozzer's copious notes on the same pages. The mysteries surrounding the identity of the Itza are engagingly rehearsed and partially clarified by Eric Thompson, 'Putun (Chontal Maya) Expansion' in *Maya History and Religion*, ch. 1.

would either withdraw, as had some of the Itza, or would recognise the legitimacy of the rule of the native lords, as had happened at Mayapan. The failure of the great uprising of 1546 made clear that the Spaniards could not be destroyed and demonstrated to those Maya who had doubted that a period of foreign domination was upon them. That domination they knew they must endure, but they also knew that their authority – enhanced by what they could learn from these intruders – would survive it, and that they would rule again.

Much of what seems puzzling in the glimpses we have of Maya behaviour is rendered intelligible by this reading. Nachi Cocom, the formidable territorial chief of Sotuta and long a mighty fighter against the Spaniards, nevertheless was ready to discuss matters of religion with the young friar Diego de Landa. He was even ready to show Landa one of the sacred hieroglyphic books which were the treasure of his lineage, not in submission, but as part of an exchange between men of special wisdom versed in high matters.[16] The early friars had been as much puzzled as outraged to find that native lords who obstinately persisted in their traditional rituals also readily set up illicit schools and churches where they pretended to teach the Christian doctrine to their followers and to baptise and marry them in fine disregard for the friars' monopoly in that area. Those lords were doing no more than maintaining their traditional role as custodians and administrators of knowledge and authority. The friars also complained of other Indians who, while urging commoners to hide their children to protect them from the dangerous and perhaps fatal rite of baptism, themselves contrived to be baptised time and again. These were clearly sorcerer-priests, 'men of power', who, having recognised on excellent empirical grounds the danger of the rite (did not the

---

[16] 'The successor of the Cocoms, named Don Juan Cocom after [he became] a Christian, was a man of great reputation, learned in their affairs, and of remarkable discernment and well acquainted with native matters. He was very intimate with the author of this book, Fray Diego de Landa, and told him many facts concerning the antiquities. He showed him a book which had belonged to his grandfather.... In this [book] was a painting of a deer, and his grandfather had told him that when large deer of this kind should come to that country (for this is what they call the cows), the worship of the gods would cease; and this was fulfilled since the Spaniards brought large cows with them'. Landa, *Relación*, pp. 43–46. Landa's steady pen is to be admired, given that he had watched the corpse of his old friend burn, along with his treasured idols, in 1562. Landa was later to burn as many of the 'books' as he could lay his hands on, which, he noted, the Indians 'regretted to an amazing degree, and which caused them much affliction', Landa, *Relación*, p. 169.

ailing children and adults the friars, most urgently rushed to baptise usually die?), nevertheless submitted themselves to it again and again, to test and augment their own spiritual force.[17]

The small worlds briefly illuminated in the 1562 trial records reveal chiefs, lords, and priests pursuing their traditional roles as well as the exigencies of their situation permitted, incorporating as they went the new structures of the church, the new prominence given the traditional symbol of the cross, and those elements of the new teaching which illuminated the old.[18]

The new skills introduced by the friars were also called upon by the chiefs to serve traditional ends, as the mission-trained schoolmasters were recalled to traditional loyalties and traditional self-identifications. The chiefs engaged in arranging and sustaining the ceremonies designated illegal by the new regime communicated not by messengers but by letters, written and read by the mission-schooled. Indeed it is possible that the native schoolmasters were not initially fully aware of the friars' requirement that they should choose between the two faiths; as nobles and sons of nobles, it was fitting that they should have been selected to have privileged access to the new knowledge, and control its dispersal among the commoners. One, who while installed as schoolmaster underwent the training to become a priest of the old religion, probably did so to enrich rather than to repudiate his Christian learning.[19]

Scattered reports down through the rest of the century and into the next make clear that chiefs, lords, and schoolmasters remained active idolators, even within the structures of the new order, and actively sustained their old ceremonies.[20] Sanchez de Aguilar, a Yucatan-born secular priest, was sufficiently roused by what he saw as the Maya passion for their old ways

---

[17] 'Ordenanzas del Lic. Tomas Lopez', Cogolludo, *Historia*, lib. V. cap. XVII.

[18] Late in the enquiry, some Indians confessed to having participated in rituals in which victims suffered crucifixion preliminary to sacrifice by the excision of the heart. The identification of the actual events through the double distortion of forced testimony and interrogators' perceptions is too complex a problem to unravel here, but there can be no doubt that, from the array of Christian symbols presented to them in those early days, the Maya recognised the cross as meaningful. Even today the cross is ubiquitous in Yucatan, while the elaborated cult of the saints which flourishes in mainland Mexico is lacking. For the significance of the cross to the Maya before the arrival of the Spaniards, see Merle Green, Robert L. Rands, and John A. Graham, *Maya Sculpture* (Berkeley: Lederer, Street, Zeus, 1972). See also Tozzer, *Relación*, p. 42, n. 211.

[19] Scholes and Adams, *Don Diego Quijada*, I, pp. 104–05, 108–09, 114.

[20] E.g., *R.Y.* 2, pp. 28, 147, 190, 212; Cogolludo, *Historia*; F. V. Scholes, R. L. Roys, E. B. Adams, 'History of the Maya Area', *C.I.W. Yearbook* 43 (July 1943/June 1944);

to write an elaborate account of the 'idol worshippers' of the bishopric in 1613. He was particularly angered by the 'audacity' and 'wickedness' of one Indian who identified himself as Moses and another pair who presented themselves as pope and bishop. What we notice about these chosen identities is that they are all lawgivers.[21]

The clearest evidence of the Maya lords' tranquil and continuing conviction of the legitimacy of their authority comes from the extraordinary compilations of Maya history, ritual, and customs to which scholars have given the generic title of 'the Books of Chilam Balam'. Their beginnings lay in the Maya recognition of the vulnerability of their treasured hieroglyphic books to confiscation and destruction by the friars. Therefore, the books were transcribed into European script and kept jealously hidden. New material was added as the years passed. Through multiple recopying by inadequately informed scribes, the original meanings, deliberately rendered obscure to the uninitiated, have been further obscured, but they remain a rich source of information on the values and ideas of the Maya ruling caste.[22]

Two of the handful of the Books of Chilam Balam which have come to the attention of scholars contain a set of esoteric questions and answers, called 'the Language of Zuyua'. The Language of Zuyua originated in the preconquest period as 'a sort of civil service examination conducted by the *halach uinic* with the object of weeding out from the ranks of legitimate chieftainship the upstarts, pretenders, and those who had obtained office under false pretences'.[23] The test continued to be applied, secretly, during the colonial period, and was held in reserve as one of the main weapons to be used in the purge that would follow the return to power

Eva Alexander Uchmany de De la Pena, 'Cuatro Casos de Idolatria en el Area Maya ante el Tribunal de la Inquisición', *Estudiós de Cultura Maya*, 6 (1967): 267–300.

[21] Pedro Sanchez de Aguilar, 'Informe contra idolorum cultores del obispado de Yucatan', in Francisco del Paso y Troncoso, *Tratado de las idolatrias, supersticiones, dioses, ritos, hechicerias y otras costumbres gentilicas de las razas aborigenes de Mexico*, 2d ed. (Mexico: Ediciones Fuentes Cultural, 1953), Vol. II.

[22] Landa and Tozzer, *Relación*, pp. 27–29; Roys, *The Book of Chilam Balam of Chumayel*; Alfredo Barrera Vasquez and Silvia Rendon, *El Libro de los libros de Chilam Balam* (Mexico City: Fondo de Cultura Economica, 1948). One scholar claims that 'soon [after the conquest] almost every village or town in the northern half of the peninsula had a copy either of these early chronicles . . . or of later ones written by their own native priests . . .' Alfredo Barrera Vasquez in Alfredo Barrera Vasquez and Sylvanus Griswold Morley, 'The Maya Chronicles', *Contributions to American Anthropology and History*, 10, no. 48, Carnegie Institution of Washington Publication no. 585 (Washington, D.C., 1949), p. 10.

[23] Roys, *Book of Chilam Balam*, p. 192.

of the legitimate chiefs, when 'the offspring of the harlot, the two day occupant of the mat [or authority], the rogue of the reign' would be destroyed.[24]

Let us consider the following 'riddle', clearly a postconquest addition to the 'Language'. The candidate is instructed:

> Bring the sun ... bring the sun, my son, bear it on
> the palm of your hand to my plate. A lance is
> planted, a lofty cross, in the middle of its heart.
> A green jaguar is seated over the sun to drink its
> blood.[25]

Resonant symbols indeed. What is actually brought? A 'very large fried egg', over which the sign of the cross has been made, with a green chile pepper sitting beside it. To us, there is something a touch pathetic in those grand images being contained in such lowly domestic objects. But in a society where knowledge was power, the concealment of the highly significant in the apparently mundane must have been intensely gratifying to those who held the key of understanding.

That the Maya lords had not been recruited by the Spaniards is not surprising; they were not asked to become the colleagues of the Spaniards but required to become their servants, and their very status as the defeated protected them from more delicate and seductive techniques of recruitment. They had, therefore, nothing to gain from embracing the Spanish definitions of their roles, as administrators of Spanish policy, or primary teachers of the Faith, especially as the Spaniards operated less by reward for service than punishment for noncompliance. Nor was a learnt desire for Spanish goods liable to erode their authority from within. Of the rather meagre array of Spanish artifacts the impoverished colonists of Yucatan were able to display, only the iron axe (later to evolve into the indispensable machete) seems to have aroused Maya covetousness. But axes were in sadly short supply, and the Maya were reduced to stealing them.[26] The prestige symbols of the Spaniards also appear to have been little coveted. The horse, which for the Spaniards made the difference between a *caballero* and a *peon* and which loomed so large for Bernal Diaz that at 80 he recalled as much about his equine as his human comrades in the great campaign for Mexico, failed to grip the Maya imagination. Some chiefs petitioned and received licenses to ride horses,

[24] *Ibid.*, p. 93.
[25] *Ibid.*, p. 89.
[26] R.Y. *1*, p. 256.

but (as the Spaniards had discovered during the years of war) the beasts slipped and stumbled on the stony paths and keeping them watered was a bothersome problem. The Maya called the horse 'the tapir of Castile', and were content to leave it at that. Their own tapirs remained much more interesting animals, being regarded as such tough quarry that huntsmen considered it 'an act of great bravery to kill them, and the skins, or parts of it, lasted as a memorial down to the great grandsons. . . . '.[27]

A problem remains: why, under the impact of foreign rule and given the real diminution of their power, did the Maya lords continue to command the loyalty of their followers?

We are familiar enough with the phenomenon of men, marginal in their traditional societies, who in a period of alien rule are able to move swiftly to positions of dominance precisely because of their freedom from traditional obligations and restrictions. Yucatan yields few traces of such men. Changes of course there were, and significant ones: there are hints of substantial readjustments in the vulnerable area of sexual relations and in child-bearing patterns, and subjugation sharply reduced the economic distance between lord and commoner.[28] But the traditional social structure, though compressed, survived. In Mexico the Inquisitorial records are studded with cases of Indians opportunistically and voluntarily denouncing their superiors: Landa was persuaded that, among the Yucatec Maya, 'there was not an Indian man or woman who would dare to speak against a lord or a *principal*, even if they were to be burnt alive'.[29] When the lords returned to the villages after the convulsive trials of 1562, no hints of reprisals or readjustments came to Spanish ears: the villages settled their affairs silently.

The peculiar toughness of the bonds between ruling caste and commoners sprang in part from the uncertainties of the agricultural conditions of the peninsula. Rainfall in Yucatan is notoriously unreliable; while the 'average' annual rainfall in Merida is 34.33 inches, records over a 30-year period reveal a variation from 16 to 64 inches, and nothing indicates the pattern was different in the sixteenth century.[30] For the agricultural Maya, the timing of the rains was also crucial. For maximum

---

[27] Landa, *Relación*, p. 203.

[28] With the imposition of monogamy, a number of women with their offspring were cast into a social void. Landa noted a decline in women's chastity and an increase in violence between marriage partners. He also recorded a decline in the age of marriage from twenty to twelve or fourteen with the likely consequence of earlier, more frequent, and less successful pregnancies. Landa, *Relación*, pp. 100, 127.

[29] Reply of Fray Diego de Landa to charges made by Fray Francisco de Guzman, n.d., in *Don Diego Quijada* II, p. 416.

[30] Roys, *The Indian Background of Colonial Yucatan*, p. 10.

'burn', the cleared scrub had to be left to dry as long as possible, but left too long to the coming of the rains, a man's labour and his milpa were lost for that season. Thus time and labour spent in the service of those knowledgeable in the swings of the seasons and the moods of the gods were time and labour sensibly invested. Only the calendar priest could determine the appropriate day for the communal hunt, for the firing of the felled timber on the new milpas, for the bending over of the stalks of the drying corncobs, to save them from unseasonably late rains. For aid in individual misfortune or sickness, the commoner would turn to the local curer or 'doctor', but for those great decisions, and others like them, on which the survival of the group depended, the calendar priest was essential.

Priest and lord were not aloof from the villagers. On those other occasions when calamity threatened the village, it was the priests who led the dances which would climax in the offering of a human life, but the commoners had also fasted, though not so austerely, and had also lacerated ears, tongue and thighs to offer the gods their blood. They knew their small offerings to the lords had helped the lords create the elaborate *mise-enscene*, with the regalia, the sounds, the foods, most likely to please the gods, which consumed so much of their resources. In those experiences, when the life of the whole village was absorbed in the ritual process, men learnt that the differences between priest, lord, and commoner were less important than their shared dependence on the gods and the fragility of their human order. While the man-in-the-village-street could not be privy to the complexities of the Maya pantheon, or the bewildering permutations of the multiple calendars, he was aware that it was the priests' knowledge and the lords' largesse which, by making human action harmonious with the cosmos, were indispensable for the orderly and safe functioning of human life.

When the great Montezuma was prodded and peered at by grinning Spaniards, the highly elaborated mystique that had rendered his person sacred and validated his authority was deeply scarred. The simpler face-to-face communities of Yucatan had evolved more subtle and less vulnerable modes of eliciting and offering deference. In the shared understanding of proper precedence, in the nice calculation of the values of gifts exchanged between superior and inferior, in the throatily-murmured titles, in the very intonations of speech, rank – which is order – was coded and celebrated. Those routines were to prove durable when subjugation had swept the external material signs of rank away.[31]

---

[31] Landa, *Relación*, pp. 62, 97. By the end of the sixteenth century through most of Spanish America those native lords who continued to command deference did so by virtue of their

There were other and more conscious connections, forged by the very experience of conquest. Today, in the remote villages of Quintana Roo, in the southeast of the peninsula, the Maya descendants of the insurgents of the Caste War continue to celebrate their high sense of autonomy in great annual ceremonies at which their shared 'history' is expounded and interpreted in prolonged performances by specially trained and specially respected old men. The anthropologist Allen Burns has brilliantly elucidated the ways in which the histories have been developed into a coherent cultural system, modelling and interpreting the world as experienced by the Maya, and providing modes of evaluating past and future action. Burns also describes the meetings at which the performances take place as 'times of unification and intensification' for the several thousand Maya who attend.[32]

I suspect that tradition of the celebration and affirmation of the community through the celebration of its history has very long roots. The enigmatic surfaces presented by the Books of Chilam Balam are not solely due to the deficiencies of copyists and the uncertainties of translation: they are, deliberately, gnomic. They are texts designed to be elucidated by skilled oral performers. 'Still he who comes of our lineage will know it, one of us who are Maya men. He will know how to explain these things when he reads what is here,' sings the Chilam Balam of Chumayel.[33] A series of Spanish observers tells us of the Maya practice of reading, or rather performing, at secret gatherings, their 'fabulous stories and injurious histories' through the first century after conquest and beyond.[34]

All the Books of Chilam Balam which survive deal with the shared history of the peninsula: of the disruptive but fructifying invasions of

position within the Spanish system. Charles Gibson tells us that in the valley of Mexico Indian lords retained *Tecuhtli* titles within their own communities into the sixteenth and even into the seventeenth centuries, but that by late colonial times cacique status of its own was no longer of any significance. Charles Gibson, *The Aztecs Under Spanish Rule* (Stanford: Stanford University Press, 1964), pp. 156, 163–65. In Yucatan the *almehenob*, members of traditional ruling lineages, even although otherwise indistinguishable from commoners, were accorded their titles by those commoners into the nineteenth century. Roys also notes that in the Chan Kom area territorial boundaries which had received no official validation since the sixteenth century were still known and acknowledged by the native inhabitants as late as the 1930s. Ralph L. Roys, *The Titles of Ebtun*, Carnegie Institution of Washington Publication no. 505 (Washington, D.C., 1939), pp. 47,62.

[32] Allen F. Burns, 'The Caste War in the 1970's: Present Day Accounts from Village Quintana Roo', *Anthropology and History in Yucatan*, ed. Grant D. Jones, Texas Pan American Series (Austin and London: University of Texas Press, 1977), p. 261.

[33] Roys, *Book of Chilam Balam*, p. 78.

[34] 'Ordenanzas del Lic. Tomas Lopez', in Cogolludo, *Historia*, lib. V, cap. XVI; Sanchez de Aguilar, *Informe . . .*, 325; Cogolludo, *Historia*, lib. IV, cap. VI.

the legendary Kukulcan and the mysterious Itza; of the great exemplary centres of Chichen Itza and Mayapan; of the diaspora which followed their collapse; and all these events are set within, and so explained by, the great cycles of the *katuns*. Each book also contains a local history. In the Chumayel, for example, we follow a wandering group which names water-holes and resting places, conferring significance on previously undifferentiated locations, so that, memorialised in place names, the group history was inscribed upon the landscape.[35] My guess is that the meetings Burns describes found their origins in the immediate postconquest period, when the pressures of the conquest situation led to a democratization of participation in what had perhaps previously been a more exclusive celebration of the lords. The history of the dominant lineage was transformed into a statement and account of the identity of the local community, while the story of the Itza rendered intelligible and unthreatening the presence and behaviour of the Spanish overlords.[36]

Maya knowledge was demonstrated to be adequate to explain the intrusion of previously unknown foreigners and their dominance. Even more powerfully, the landscape itself attested the truth of the traditional account of the world. Like all agriculturalists, the Maya lived according to the rhythm of the yearly agricultural cycle and the lesser growing cycles it contained. The seasons were strongly marked: during April, the sun burned hotter and more cruelly day after day, until, at last, the flying ants began to swarm, signalling the crashing thunder which announced the coming of the Chacs, with their life-giving rain. But that yearly cycle was embedded in larger cycles. As a milpa could be planted for only two or three seasons before the yields grew too light and the scrubby forest regrowth too stubborn, each man tended milpas at different stages of their cycles, marking out a careful space in the forest at one place, and beginning the hard labour of felling the larger trees, gathering what he knew to be his last crop in another. All around him were the signs of this endless process: the blackened square of a milpa being created; the dim shapes of milpas in the course of reclamation by the forest. Even the tallest forest, he knew, had been milpa once, and would be milpa

---

[35] E.g., Roys, *Book of Chilam Balam*, pp. 72–77.
[36] E.g., Roys, *Book of Chilam Balam*, p. 79. 'Then with the true God, the true *Dios*, came the beginning of our misery. It was the beginning of tribute, the beginning of church dues . . . the beginning of forced debts, the beginning of debts enforced by false testimony . . . But it shall still come to pass that tears shall come to the eyes of our Lord God. The justice of our Lord God shall descend on every part of the world . . . '

again. Those cycles within cycles the priests could discern in the majestic wheelings of the stars could also be read by the commoner, for they were inscribed upon the land.

Human settlement told the same story. Where population growth in the mother village enforced the dispersal of the milpas beyond the tolerance even of Maya legs, a few families moved to 'hive off' to form a temporary hamlet for a few years until that area of the forest had been exploited. All around were the traces of those brief habitations, in the slowly collapsing wattle and daub huts or in the slight elevations which marked the house mounds on which the huts had once stood. And, of course, there were the great stone structures, thrusting up through the forest, testifying to the much larger and more permanent habitations of the past. Some of the ruins were of cities the Maya knew from their myths, like Mayapan, Chichen Itza, and Uxmal, and recalled past conflicts, past invasions, past harmony. Regarding others the myths were either silent or confused. But as Indians, under Spanish orders, dragged the shaped carved stones from the ruins of Tihoo to build the city the Spaniards called Merida, or destroyed a pyramid to build a monastery, it is likely that the lesson they drew was not of the dominance of the new regime but of the transciency of all such human devisings.

In 1545, Nachi Cocom had carried out a prudent survey of the borders of his province. Although he and most of his entourage were still unbaptised, he readily utilised crosses as his boundary markers.[37] In later land maps of the sixteenth century, within the distinctive Maya circular form with the significant direction of the east to the top of the page, crosses identify boundaries, and churches identify villages. Through the landscape itself, crosses proliferated, in private houses, in front of churches, at village entrances, along the roads, at the corners of milpas. There is nothing to indicate the Maya were responsive to the specific resonances of the cross as Christian symbol: rather the cross was taken over – 'encapsulated', in Vogt's useful word – to mark out, as idols and images had once done, significant locations and boundaries in the Maya map of the experienced world, just as it had been utilized, under Spanish direction, to designate locations and boundaries in the painted map of that world.[38] In the Books of Chilam Balam, the coming rule of the Lord Jesus Christ and of the Lord God is celebrated and welcomed, but the two lords of the

---

[37] 'Docuraentos de Tierra de Sotuta', appendix in Roys, *The Titles of Ebtun*, pp. 421–33.
[38] Even Z. Vogt, *Zinacantan: A Maya Community in the Highlands of Chiapas* (Cambridge, Mass.: Belknap Press of Harvard University Press, 1969), p. 582.

new cycle take delight not in Christian offerings but in the jade, the precious green plumes, and the mead-like balche which delight the gods of the Maya. The 'Christian' deities are neatly inserted into a Maya scheme of things: the world they inhabit is the four-directional world of the traditional cosmology, and it is the Maya sacred numbers of four, nine and thirteen which reverberate through their ceremonies. For the Maya there was no tension between their repudiation of the Spanish claim to rule and assertion of a monopolistic control of Christian truth, and their acceptance of the Christian gods as deities whose time had come: when the Lord Jesus Christ entered at last upon his rule, it was the Maya lords who would rule under him.[39]

The world as the Maya experienced it, even in the relocated villages, remained the traditional world. For the women, rising in the grey light of dawn to pursue their round of women's tasks, grinding the sacred corn, weaving and spinning, nurturing their children and tending their animals, it was the familiar Maya goddess of fertility, sexuality, and things domestic whose protection they solicited, whatever name the friars gave her. House and houseyard, church and patio, echoed the four-sided shape of the world, and the new village, like the old, protected itself from the forest by guardian crosses at its four entrances. For the men too, making their swift offerings as they passed the crosses marking the traditionally dangerous and sacred places along the paths between milpa arid village, the continuity of the old order was constantly pledged by the rhythms and shapes of daily experience.

To the Spaniards, colonists and friar alike, the only locations of significance in Yucatan's grey monotony of forest were the human concentrations of the villages. The idols they found in caves, cenotes and milpas, the secret meetings they stumbled upon in the forests, they saw as evidence of Maya inventiveness in deceit, for those areas the Spaniards had defined as mere terrain. The Maya read their landscape very differently. The small cleared spaces of village and milpa, linked by the narrow and perilous paths, still spoke at once of the mutability of human endeavour and of its glory, evoking as they did in their shape and orientations the great exemplary centres of Mayapan and Chichen Itza. Only the forests, the water-holes and the gods of the World Directions were constant. The friars of Yucatan had enjoyed in those first days after conquest an unusual freedom of action, but despite the intelligence and the ruthlessness of their assault on the imaginative universe of the Maya, they had crucially

---

[39] E.g., Roys, *Book of Chilam Balam*, pp. 98–107; 120–25.

miscalculated. An account of the world which dismissed the forests as mere nature, and which postulated the progressive nature of time and the primary value of the individual human life, could not, in the ironic context of the Yucatan landscape, compel belief.[40]

[40] The conscientious conservatism of the Maya persists. In parts of modern day Yucatan where plantation henequen production has long dominated the milpas, many towns must import the *h-men* (Maya priest) from other areas for the annual Maya *cha chaac* ceremony. In some areas, where government redistribution of former plantation land has permitted the restoration of the milpas after a long hiatus, the milpa ritual has also been revived. Irwin Press, *Tradition and Adaptation: Life in a Modern Yucatan Maya Village* (Westport, Conn.: Green-wood Press, 1975), p. 34.

6

Breaking the Mirror

From the Aztec Spring Festival to Organ Transplantation

By a process of development against which it would have been useless to struggle, the word 'psycho-analysis' has itself become ambiguous. While it was originally the name of a particular therapeutic method, it has now become the name of a science – the science of unconscious mental processes.
                                             Sigmund Freud, 1925.

Freud's literary allure provides part of an argument for understanding psychoanalysis as an interpretative activity comparable to literary criticism – a humanistic endeavour, in other words, rather than a scientific discipline.
                                             Daniel Mendelsohn, 2000.

I think I was originally invited to present this paper at a conference on narcissism[1] primarily as a talking document, a case study for the collective: a once-intact and complacent body which illness first magically transformed and then had radically carved up. It is difficult for the amateur to probe any distance into Freud's writings, not least because of the problem of translation (does 'The Ego' really mean only 'the I', and 'the Id' 'the It'?[2]) Nonetheless, I have my own agenda. I want to know

---

[1] I take the definition for the term 'narcissism' from my usefully bad dictionary to mean 'an excessive admiration for and interest in oneself', and more particularly, given the theme of this conference and my interest in the Aztecs of Mexico, a 'morbid love for one's own body.'

[2] 'The Standard Edition of Freud's work ... (Strachey's translation, Hogarth Press 1953–74) has ... often been thought to misrepresent the tone of Freud's original precisely

Article originally published as "Breaking the Mirror: From the Aztec Spring Festival to Organ Transplantation," in *Australasian Journal of Psychotherapy*, Vol. 21, No. 2 (2002). © Inga Clendinnen. Reprinted with permission.

where Freudianism stands now: as 'the science of unconscious mental processes' or as an 'interpretative activity comparable to literary criticism,' and whether the two are incompatible. I want to know whether classic Freudianism and modern psychoanalytic practice are, unlike physiological medicine, necessarily culture-bound, and therefore inapplicable to, for example, sixteenth-century Aztecs, or 21st century Aztecs, for that matter. I also want to learn when and why I might need the concept of the unconscious. My natural sympathy here is with James Joyce when he says: 'Why all this fuss and bother about the mystery of the unconscious? What about the mystery of the conscious? What do they know about that?'[3]

My scepticism is grounded partly in my (inadequate) reading in psychoanalytic literature, more solidly in my effort to understand something of Aztec thinking and doings, most in personal experiences of illness and organ transplantation, coupled with the effort to comprehend those experiences sufficiently well to write about them.

Finally, I will have a brief and bitter word to say about the impropriety of psychiatric evaluation without consent.

Aztecs

The Aztecs were a warrior people who established a tribute empire in Central Mexico in the latter part of the fifteenth century. Their power was obliterated in 1521 in a war engineered by Hernán Cortés, but effected by the military strength of oppressed Mexican tribes. In their brief heyday the Aztecs had embellished their own and other human bodies in flamboyant public display, and then proceeded to the carnal analyses of those bodies we call human sacrifice, and then to the redistribution and re-use of some of the body parts in processes we call cannibalism, and others in uses unfamiliar to us.

The Aztecs have had a very bad press (Ted Hughes famously labelled them 'squat disembowellers'). My aim in *Aztecs*, the book I wrote about them, was to make them humanly intelligible: to penetrate the barrier

---

because it makes formidably 'scientific' certain terms and locutions that, in the original, have an accessible, quotidian flavour, The most famous example of this is Strachey's rendering of Freud's *das ich* and *das Es* – 'the I' and 'the It' – as the Latin pronouns 'Ego' and 'Id': what in German is perfectly ordinary diction becomes, in the translation, rarefied and specialized.' Daniel Mendelsohn reviewing Israel Rosenfield's *Freud's Megalomania* in the New York Review of Books, 2 November 2000, 26–29, p. 26.

[3] James Joyce, 1918 quoted Richard Ellman, *James Joyce* Oxford University Press, Oxford, (1981) 1965, p. 450.

of what seems to be inexplicable behaviour. I wanted to penetrate their painful docility in face of religious obligation: their self-torture, the brutalities routinely inflicted on themselves and each other, and the even more extreme brutalities inflicted on outsiders in the ritualised killing of men, women, children, infants. I wanted to understand their devotion to the glamour of male physical combat, despite the most intimate daily acquaintance with its messiness and pain. And I wanted to bring other people to comprehend them too.

Of course there were aspects of their behaviour for which I will give explanations unacceptable or unintelligible to the Aztecs themselves, but that problem attends all our attempts to understand and explain our fellow humans, including intimates. Do we always acquiesce in our spouse's or parents' or children's explanations of our character and motives, especially if they have taken Psych. 1? But my main aim has been to understand what they did as they understood it, and I will therefore give a close-up account of one particularly intense and publicly absorbing ceremony.

Aztecs romanticised the young male body even more than they did the female, representing it as shining, smooth, as full and subtle as a ripe fruit. Remember this is Mexico: the land of the sleek squash, the swelling tomato, the smooth-skinned avocado. The most important vegetable fruit, the maize cob, was symbolised first as a young girl in tender youth, with her silky plume of hair, and then, as the cob swelled and hardened, as a young warrior in the glory of his manhood. Vegetable metaphors dominate representations of humankind in Aztec formal, daily and playful speech.

On grand occasions the high priests at their high altars slaughtered droves of helpless victims from enemy tribes, so that the victim, walking or being dragged up the steps of the pyramid, met a slow tide of blood descending. But it was not these mass performances which most gripped the Aztec imagination, but what we call the 'gladiatorial stone' sacrifice in the month of the spring planting celebrating the deity called 'The Young Warrior,' or 'the Flayed Lord,' Xipe Totec. Warrior captives were secured in one-to-one combats in a pre-arranged period of war in which top warriors from among Aztec allies as well as enemies took part. As strangers died on the Aztec killing stone, so Aztec captives were dying on the festival stone of other cities.

The star captive was prepared like a fighting cock and paraded about the city for a period by his equally gorgeous captor in a variety of magnificent regalias which dramatised their male beauty. Then on the appointed day both captor and captive were stripped of their warrior regalias and painted with the white body paint of the sacrifical victim. The captor led his captive through the cheering streets to an elevated stone probably about a metre high, and slightly wider. The captor then withdrew to one side to observe the performance of his mirrored self, and the captive, tethered by the foot to a central ring to restrict his movements, was handed a heavy club. A feathered club. Feathers replaced the usual razor-sharp obsidian or flint blades. Then the first of four high-prestige Aztec warriors came against him to give an exemplary display of warrior skills. Their clubs were the regulation blade-studded kind, and their aim was to exercise such skill as to slit the victim's skin delicately in a multitude of places, but perforce largely about the legs, given their relative positions, so that the blood would flow. In 'real' battles a warrior's aim was to exhaust, disable and capture, not to kill the enemy, so they had cultivated these particular skills. Sometimes the captive would prevail for a time. He had to be a quick learner and go for a killing blow to the head, which had been no part of his training, but he did have the advantage of height, and the club was heavy. There are stories of one or two legendary foreign warriors triumphing against all four Aztec warriors in sequence, and being applauded and offered high places in the Aztec warrior hierarchy. But usually the victim would be brought down, often through loss of blood, by the first or the second warrior, and then the priests would move in and cut out his heart as he lay fainting on the stone and offer it to the sun, first in gesture, then by fire.

End of Act 1. Then the deep action started. The opened body was flayed by expert old men, the skin being split down the back and peeled carefully off like a chicken skin, with the sex intact and the feet and hands left dangling. For the next several days the captor wore the skin like a soggy union suit over his naked body as he ran through the streets of the city. He was an image of the god through this time, an emblem of the sacred, and therefore he was offered gifts and devotions. Wearing his skin he carried a gourd of blood between the different temples to anoint the mouths of specified images of deities (most of them female) and then to distribute parts of the body for ritual consumption: a thigh to Moctezuma, the other thigh to a specified goddess, and so on. I won't go into all of the details of the distribution. His immediate household ate a formal meal of a piece of the captive's flesh roasted over a fire and served with dried maize stew – food in its simplest form, which I think is an abbreviated way of telling us and reminding them that for Aztecs all flesh is maize. For this domestic feast the captor again put aside his captor's regalia, and wore the white paint and feathers of the dedicated sacrifical victim. He did not eat the flesh because it had become his own, and his kin wept and lamented as they ate for the predestined fate of their own young warrior.

Meanwhile the flayed skin rotted and dried, tightened and finally crackled and shredded. We are told that throughout the days of skin-wearing the captors 'stank like dead dogs', and this in a society which valued cleanliness highly. At last at the appointed time the brittle skins were set aside and buried, there was a great ritual cleansing, and the captor warriors, released from their sacred state, were returned to society in a round of feasting and general celebration.

So what was going on? A number of things, but what impresses me in view of our topic is the intensity of that induced identification between captor and captive which extended to the experience of every stage of the skin's decay on the captor's own body. The Aztecs got a lot of excitement, prestige and addictive emotions out of all these paradings and performances, but I think it is that last phase of ambiguous reward which raises most questions for our theme of narcissism.

First, what did they think had happened to the non-carnal elements involved? At what we might call, I think mistakenly, the theological level: a man who died on the killing stone or on the field of battle died a privileged death in that he did not immediately dissolve into nothingness, or rather everythingness, which was the common fate. Instead, for four years and four years only, he became a member of the warrior escort of the sun during its daily progress across the heavens. During this period of posthumous celebration there was shouting and leaping and the pleasures of display, but no sex, no violence and no alcohol. Instead there was feasting of a rather odd kind: the warrior spirits were supplied with plentiful chocolatl, a frothy mixture of cacao and honey prized in the highest circles rather as we might prize single malt whisky.

And that was the end. After those four years there was no individual survival save in the memory of family and comrades. The warrior had dissolved into the general lifeforce, the same force which was believed to animate butterflies and hummingbirds, creatures which seemed summoned into existence by the sun. (Again we see that close observation of the natural as it is scrutinised for transcendental import.) And note the renewed emphasis on the pleasure of sweet fluids in the mouth. Butterflies and hummingbirds are represented as endlessly displaying their beauty, dancing in the sun, and sipping the sweet nectar of flowers.

The ubiquity of vegetable metaphors for human growth locates the human world into full dependence on the processes of the 'natural' sacred powers, and derives ultimately from Mexican notions of plant physiology and human reproduction. Indeed they seem to go beyond the 'metaphoric,' to be directly descriptive of what Aztecs thought they saw happening all around them. The joy of the period of suckling finds its focus here. In Aztec poems and chants and homilies free access to the flowing female breast is evoked again and again as marking a time of bliss. We see those baby pleasures of the mouth celebrated not only for suckling babes, who are explicitly envied, but in the imagining of the Aztec warrior paradise. My reading of all this is that only the milk of the lactating mother comes free. With the first mouthful of vegetable food (weaning was regarded as a perilous time) the individual was locked into the terrible cycle of obligation to the impersonal consuming sacred powers of earth, rain, and growth effected by the Sun. The mother's breast is the only free lunch. With weaning innocence is lost, and humankind enters upon its servitude.

In my view these are the understandings which sustained the vision of the sacred encounter enacted in rituals at all different levels, at different levels of intensity, from the domestic household to the Central Temple Precinct. That shared cultural vision locked the world of the everyday into what we choose to define as 'high' metaphysical matters.

If the captive died to sustain the sun's heat with his heart, and to feed the gods with his blood, what was happening to the captor? Ideally, I think the process of combat, capture and offering initiates a moral transformation, so he will fully embrace his warrior fate, which is to die on the stone, or on the field of battle. That acquiescence will allow him to become like a pure jade, jade being the Aztecs' most valued jewel: clear to the depths. He will have achieved metaphysical understanding. And if in combat he feels himself failing, that his moment has come, he will step forward to embrace his fate. It's a strange aesthetic and metaphysics in which moral grace is achieved by the systematic violation of the body.

Wives and Mothers

I used the sort of simplified Freudianism now integral to our understanding of human nature when I discussed the roles of Aztec women (see the chapters called 'Mothers' and The Female Revealed'). Aztecs take us a long way from debased commonsense notions of the inescapable role of women in a warrior society as mere breeders and feeders. They were notably relaxed about sexual matters, with the vagina's pet name being 'the place of joy'. (Female breasts aroused a more complex, more infantile eroticism.) Candid pleasure in sexual activity was assumed in women as in men, and wives had a right to be sexually satisfied by their spouses. It is also true that some women were understood to be sexually insatiable, and therefore dangerous. The favoured metaphor is of a gaping cavern which can never be filled by the men's 'honey'. Such witch-women could prepare a drink for men they want to destroy which caused them to exhaust themselves in sexual activity: one night of wild excess, and they would die.

There is also a deal of excitement surrounding women's mouths and teeth. Prostitutes, who were to be avoided because as insatiable women they would dry men up and transform them into dribbling wretches, were described as going about the marketplace not swinging their hips or jiggling their bosoms but with rouged lips and clacking their chicle, their chewing gum, like castanets. This was apparently unbearably exciting to the Aztec male.

That fascination with the ambivalence of the masticating female mouth and teeth connects with the blinding transformation which took place should a woman die in childbirth. In that moment she would be changed from a cherished girl to devouring monster, because she had died when 'possessed' by the sacred power of the Earth Mother, who was a sort of Kali figure, creating life out of the destruction of life. Human blood was named 'most precious water.' There is a thick mist of stories and propitiatory gestures against the power of the Sacred Female: for example, offerings were made at crossroad shrines to these Celestial Princesses, the dead mothers returning as monsters intent on destroying children.

There is to my mind a marvellously explicit coherence here, which does not require the underpinning of an unconscious.

Personal Experience and how I have made sense of it.

Just as I was finishing the Aztec book came one of life's charming ironies. I fell ill with an auto-immune liver disease and four years later, instead of Aztec public excisions of living hearts from warrior bodies, I became the star of a drama involving the removal of a living organ from a stranger's dying body and its installation inside me. The Aztecs would have been affronted by the sheer perversity of such an enterprise.

Before and after the transplant I was naturally under significant physical and mental stress, combined with a heavy drug regime which brought lurid dreams melting into sustained and surprisingly coherent hallucinations. Where did they come from? Throughout my personal and intellectual life I have been impressed by the mysteriousness of human consciousness, but, as the Joyce quote indicates, I have never felt the need to locate that sense of mystery in something called the unconscious. (I note that Freud himself saw hypnosis as 'widening the field of the patient's consciousness and putting within his reach knowledge he did not possess in his waking life'.[4])

This was my opportunity to explore the boundaries of consciousness. During this time of assault on the physical and the mental self, my way of preserving my sense of self was to put what I was experiencing into words, and then, when I was able, to write those words down so that I could analyse them and reflect on them. For me all writing is highly conscious, a radical translation out of less formulated consciousness.[5] From the analysis of those writings, which recorded, among other things, the fruits of long periods of introspection, I made what I thought were interesting discoveries about, for example, the ways in which memory can be activated, and how it manifests itself: how it is made, how it is modified, how it is stored, how it is transformed, how it is released. For me it was released by and large as Marcel Proust had said: a tiny tuck of sensation is teased free, pulled – and a magician's rope of silk handkerchiefs unfurls, releasing scents and colours and moods as it comes, along with a couple of doves.

All the material thrown up by the hallucinations was unexpected, but none of it was new. (Most of it is laid out in my book *Tiger's Eye*.) I take the hallucinatory material to have emanated from the fringe of consciousness as yet another manifestation of stimulated memory and reflection. The dominant images pivoted around the social facts of war: that societies send young men out to kill and to maim, and expect them to come back unblemished – or, in the Aztec case, to be tamed and exorcised by orchestrated ritual experience into renewed sociability. I 'remembered' that these were facts which had impressed themselves bitterly upon me when I was about seven, when some young marines who were friends of the household were sent to Guadalcanal, and were killed or ruined there. The hallucinations revealed to me a deeper story organising my life choices than I had 'consciously' known.

Physical transformations; social and psychological consequences.

I fell ill precipitously and rapidly became a full-time invalid, exiled from my old activities and relationships. I was also alarming to those who

---

4 Freud, *An Autobiographical Study*.
5 James Wood (*London Review of Books*, June 2000, p. 36) claims that Shakespeare's characters 'manage to sustain the paradox of feeling real to themselves without necessarily knowing themselves, which is the very paradox of consciousness, since I have no way of knowing that I do not know myself.'

loved me because I went through a series of startling physical transformations. For a few weeks after an episode of liver failure I was a
recumbent skeleton except for a remarkable inflating belly, unable to sit
up or to feed myself, my voice diminished to a whisper. Then a diet of
prednisolone transformed me into a bulging kewpie. I minded all this
much less than I thought I would because the changes were so dramatic.
When my mind began to be affected by encephalopathy, 'inflamed brain
sickness,' I minded much more, but I clung to my lifeline of words to catch
even these experiences, and so had an illusion of remaining in control.

I think I have been relatively unchanged by the experience – tougher,
more impatient, more reckless, more responsive to nature in its multiple
forms, firmer in my belief that there is only the here and that life is
short. For me throughout, whatever was happening to my body, what
quite consciously mattered was keeping my mind in and under control by
noting, analysing, understanding what was being done to me and how I
was responding. It is writing which continues to hold my life together.

Other people's responses and notions of the body.

One question is solemnly asked of all potential liver transplant candidates:
'What relationship do you think you will have with your new liver?'

The question struck me as comic. At that stage I was still making a very
clear distinction between mind and body, and to me the liver was simply
a bit of apparatus. I said I expected to have much the same relationship I
had with my old one: a distant affability. (That turned out not to be true;
I'm actively fond of this one.) I was casual about it, but by asking around
I found that quite a few friends viewed with great distaste the notion of
yielding up a bit of themselves, and even more the notion of taking in a
bit of someone else. These weren't people who were especially protective
of their bodies – some had led quite adventurous sex lives, for example –
but they could not stomach the idea of this kind of carnal invasion.

The disgust can be more generalised, and more paralysing. A small
story to illustrate: a fellow transplantee had gone back to his farm after
his transplant, still with the e-tube to the bile duct coiled and packed
away under a wad of dressings, but otherwise looking pretty normal. A
friend called in to help him with some chore. He had brought a lad with
him, introduced him, and told him Graham had had a liver transplant.
The boy was duly impressed. Then after a bit of chat about the operation
he asked Graham how the donor was doing. Graham was naturally taken
aback, but explained as well as he could: the donor was dead, he'd been

dying when they took the liver; they'd installed that liver inside him. The boy said 'Do you mean you've got a dead man's liver inside of you?' And backed away, staring at Graham with horror. He had to be taken home.

The boy's reaction to my friend Graham was, I suppose, visceral, but I suspect it might have had an additional source. Three years ago *Time/CNN* published a poll in the USA which claimed that 64 percent of Americans believe that creatures from elsewhere in the universe have recently been in personal contact with human beings. The 64 percent are the kind of the people who think *The X-Files* are documentaries. The allure of this stuff is fed by film and television, and powerfully reinforced by the moral, intellectual and historical vacuum which is the Internet. But it is terribly real to believers. They believe that aliens are already among us, tampering with our minds and tampering with our bodies, too, even recruiting a chosen few into involuntary highly secret breeding programmes. The psychoanalytically aware will recognise what a dangerous cocktail of beliefs this is. It can bring terrible suffering to afflicted individuals. Men have killed their families to save them from the aliens. But even more potentially destructive of social peace is the belief that this race of hybrids is being bred to take over the world – hybrids who look like humans, but who are not.[6]

Beliefs in alien abductions became prevalent in the '80s, just when false repressed memories of childhood sexual abuse became a flood. 'Memories' were adduced by the application of psychodynamic theory to the images unearthed by hypnosis, dream analysis and assorted techniques for stimulating and guiding fantasy. The sex-abuse specialists saw recollections of alien abduction as screen memories for incest. The abductionists take the opposite view.

I don't know whether any of this comes under the rubric of 'narcissism', but what interests me is the alienation, the pervasiveness of a sense of physical vulnerability, implied by such beliefs. Why, at the end of a century of extraordinary scientific achievement, should a majority of the American population have so little confidence in their capacity to understand the world in which they live that they retreat into a kind of collective paranoia – 'we are good but powerless, others are evil and strong? Given my training and my turn of mind, I naturally favour socio-cultural explanations. I think this numbing sense of helplessness must have to do with

---

[6] For an overview see Frederick Crews, 'The Mind-snatchers' *New York Review of Books*, 25 June 1998, 14–19.

an alienation from one's actual human neighbours, and from a loss of confidence in the continuity between one's own and one's parents' past. What the delusion most clearly indicates is an impoverishment of imagination, an inability to imagine 'otherness' with any specificity at all, and therefore to decide that 'otherness' can only equal danger and terror.

The application of psychiatric evaluation without consent.

Before a potential liver-transplantee is accepted on to the waiting list you have what's called a 'work-up'. You spend a fortnight in hospital undergoing a great array of tests to expose the secrets of your particular body – hepatic arteries and so on. They also need to know the condition of your other organs before they go in. It's moderately gruelling, you are handled a great deal by nearly everybody, and it would be possible to find it destructive and some did. I didn't. Rather I was impressed at how very hard it was to know what was going on in my darkest interior without opening me up and taking a look. I felt the essential mysteriousness to be preserved. I felt the same way after the transplant. Even after I had been opened up and unpacked and repacked the Liver-Unit team would come trundling in and puzzle over the information the great array of figures and blood tests and machines were giving them: the body reduced to a numbers game. That group puzzling was ego-restoring for me. These people had literally turned me inside out, but I was still an enigma to them.

I felt very differently about the psychiatric assessment which came as part of the work-up. I knew that very few of the many people referred to the Transplant Unit were promoted to the waiting list. It took me about a year of frightening deterioration to do so. Livers were a very scarce resource. If there was an emergency – if a previously well person suddenly collapsed with liver failure – they had a good chance of getting a liver if one turned up, but most people on the waiting list die waiting. Officially it was denied, but of course there was a queue. A competition. That meant that you were pleased if your tests went well – if your heart and lungs and the rest of the things that mattered were in good shape, because if they weren't you would not be a good transplant risk. But there was nothing you could do about it. It wasn't your fault, so you could live with it – or, if necessary, die with it.

The compulsory psychiatric test was different. You had no notion what was required of you, yet you knew your own words might condemn you. This polite stranger would decide your rating without discussion. Perhaps it didn't always happen like this, but my psychiatric test came at the very end of the physical testing, and that is how it felt. Because of the grotesque power imbalance I found the experience seriously humiliating. My life was at stake, so I co-operated; I tried to do well in this absurd, mysterious test. But I resented it. And I could not see its utility: a 30 minute interview when other people to do with the Liver Transplant Unit had been seeing me daily for ten days under conditions of stress. Surely they could assess my stability? I did and I do see it as offensive.

To end with the long leap from narcissism to altruism. Transplant patients are a motley lot: different classes, levels of education, religions, ethnicities. Most of them are the sorts of people I would never meet in my daily life. Now we feel a special tenderness for each other. We have been and are in the same boat. We are all bound to the people of the Liver Transplant Unit because we owe them our lives. I have never been of a docile temperament, but I do what the LTU people tell me, because I am their creation.[7]

There is another more astonishing bond. I was at the Adelaide Writers' Festival, waiting for a panel I was on to begin. That's always scary. You feel very much on your own. Then I noticed a woman rather younger than me sitting in the very front row and beaming at me. She came to the edge of the platform, I went over to her and she pointed to her lapel pin: a tiny golden rose. The donor family sign. Without thinking we kissed and hugged each other. Her only daughter had died two years before. 'Seven recipients', she said proudly, tears on her face. Then we went back to our places, the session started, and she watched me lovingly throughout.

It looks as if there might be rather more to life than narcissism.

---

[7] Here is the insight of a distinguished literary journalist, who has herself been through analysis, on the relationship (or a relationship) between psychoanalytic writings and literary art, along with another brisk definition of the unconscious:

'Real people...are so much more complex, ambiguous, unpredictable, and particular than people in novels. The therapy of psychoanalysis attempts to restore to the neurotic patient the freedom to be uninteresting that he lost somewhere along the way. It proposes to undermine the novelistic structures on which he constructed his existence, and destroy the web of elaborate, artful patterns in which he is caught. There are people (psychoanalysts among them) who think that the action of psychoanalysis is, as it were, to transfer the patient from one novel to another – from a gothic romance, say, to a domestic comedy – but most analysts and most people who have undergone the therapy know that this is not so, and that the Freudian programme is a far more radical one. Patients in analysis sometimes say they feel they are being driven crazy by the treatment. It is the denovelisation of their lives, and their glimpse into the abyss of unmediated individuality and idiosyncracy that is the Freudian unconscious, which causes them to feel this way.'

Janet Malcolm, *The Journalist and the Murderer*, pp. 122–3.

7

Reading Mr Robinson

I grew up in a once-upon-a-time land when milk and loaves appeared at the door to the jingle of bells and the clopping of hooves, when housewives were Cinderellas in sacking aprons and hair permanently rollered for the ball, when men wore hats, and lifted them to the funerals of strangers passing in the street. That time – the forties, the early fifties – has been mythologised into a Camelot of Anglo-Celtic virtue, or a dark age of tribalism and British cooking. In my recollection, of course, it was neither, but simply the way things were. It is disconcerting to find one's private past, one's collection of ordinary memories, become a matter of ideological dispute, and to discover, after peaceful decades spent reading historical documents, that you have become a historical document yourself.

The elevation is the more disconcerting because I know almost nothing of the history of which I have now become an artefact, having abandoned Australian history in my heart (the formalities took a little longer) in the fifth grade of primary school. To that point 'Australian History' comprised a doleful catalogue of self-styled 'explorers' who wandered in what large Mrs O'Loughlin used to call 'dretful desarts' glumly littering names about – Mount Disappointment, Mount Despair, Mount Hopeless – until, thankfully, they 'perished'. (Even in those benighted days I noticed that during their wanderings they would occasionally totter past little bands of people they called 'Aborigines', and I would think 'at least somebody knows how to manage out there'.) I would look at the wavery little tracks the feckless white fellows had left on the school-reader map,

Article originally published as "Reading Mr. Robinson," in *Australian Book Review*, No. 170 (1995). © Australian Book Review. Reprinted with permission.

and know I wanted nothing to do with them, or any who came after
them.

For over thirty years as a professional historian living and working
in this country I avoided our history. I know the Australia of the past
as I know Chekhov's or Tolstoy's or Nabokov's Russia: from novels.
Like my Russia, my Australia floats somewhere beyond historical time
and geographical actuality. It is a bleached valley, a cluster of tall rooms
embraced by a verandah; a suburb; a style, a set of possibilities.

Or so it was. After my liver transplant, returned to precarious health,
for no reason I can fathom, but perhaps a desire for a wider, more stable
context, I wanted to learn more. Another round of novels? Biographies,
perhaps? No: I wanted direct access. I would do what historians always
do; I would go to the sources. Or, rather, to one source. This was to be
a Sunday stroll, not a major expedition with elephants and guns. And I
wanted at least the illusion of serendipity: I wanted my source somehow
to come to me, to appear like a note in a bottle, a message from another
time tossed to land at my feet.

And so it happened. Pursuing a quite different matter, I came upon a
couple of paragraphs written by a Mr G. A. Robinson. I already knew
something of Robinson: that he had been Protector of the Aborigines in
Tasmania in the early days, that he had been somehow mixed up with
Truganinni, the 'last of the Tasmanian Aborigines', that he had brought
her to Victoria. That he affected a strange cap, like a pastry-cook gone
to sea. That he was a foolish and arrogant man, or was I mixing him up
with someone else?

I asked an Australianist busy consulting me as a historical document
if he had any of Robinson's writings. He had: Robinson's journal of a
five-month-long horseback journey made during the winter of 1841 from
Melbourne to Portland and back, with a swing through the Grampians
on the home leg. In 1839, after Tasmania, he had been appointed Chief
Protector of the Aborigines for Port Phillip District. He was to make over
twenty similar expeditions through his new territories, keeping journals
throughout. Did I want more? Did I want a full bibliography?

I did not. The transplant had murdered patience. I had my note in
a bottle. I would uncork the bottle, and release the Mr Robinson held
inside. I would get to know him; he would be my guide into one slice of
our past. Of course there were other Mr Robinsons: in the memories of
those who had known him, lurking in libraries in the pages of novels and
histories. There were the Mr Robinsons of all those other journals: men
of the same name and much the same body, but differently freighted by

experience and expectation. It was the Mr Robinson revealed between 20 March and 15 August 1841 that I was after.

For a historian it is luxurious indulgence to settle to a single, circumscribed text. Private journals can be expansive, unbuttoned affairs, and if kept regularly hold the promise of revealing not only 'character', but the natural movement of the writer's mind. A couple of hours reading, and I knew I was in luck. Mr Robinson was a most devoted journal-keeper.

Almost every night, whatever the hardships of the day, and after he has talked with any 'sable friends', as he called Aborignes, who happend to be about, he secludes himself to write. The white men traveling with him are convicts or servants: he neither desires nor brooks intimacy with them. He has his journal for company. His tone slides easily from the practical to something very like the conjugal. He might begin with the weather and an analytic account of terrain traversed. There might be some household accounting to do: out-goings of potatoes, blankets, shirts; incomings of natives contacted. He jots down words to add to his lists of places seen and persons met with, of plants, animals, tools. He relaxes, remembering beguiling things – a flight of blue parrots, a genial dog, geese thick as waterlilies on a reedy lake. (He notices animals, and is tender towards them.) And he rehearses the events of the day: confides conversations and encounters, shapes them into narratives, sets them down. His journal will serve as a source for official reports, but it is very much more than that: it is a reviewing, a refreshment, a re-creation of his most private self. He and his journal, in whatever frail light, on those wintry nights, in those comfortless camps.

And we, you and I, reading over his shoulder. Against the odds, the Chief Protector is a natural writer. Occasionally he strikes a conventional attitude or a too-laconic note stares mutely back at us, but typically he is as direct and crisp as his weather reports: 'Severe frost during the night, ice this morning near thick as a dollar. Fine sunny day, tranquil light air.' He wastes little ink on men's appearances – it is character he cares about – but he can toss off the memorable vignette, as of his deplorable convict servant Myatt, negligently negotiating 'the van' through a pass, 'chanting over a doleful ditty peculiar to his class . . . his hat over his eyes as he generally wore it . . . occasionally run[ning] against stumps and then damning the horses for not taking care'. Arrived at Portland town, Robinson is dined, with metropolitan formality, by Commissioner Tyers. The rest of the company is 'a Mr Primrose, who fills a plurality of offices here as clerk to the bench, sub-collector of customs, and post master. He wears moustaches, and rings on each finger, is tall with a morose countenance', and there stands Mr Primrose the rusticated dandy, waiting for Chekhov. Robinson's drawings speckling his text are equally vivid: they are as awkward, serious and expressive as a child's. Every cross-hatch of a net, every rail of a fence, is firmly inked in. An Aboriginal girl peacocking in a European frock vibrates with delight; an Aboriginal dancer massively hooded with grass explodes from spindly legs.

Mr Robinson proves his worth as a guide. He links me back to places long known, but known in the flat, two-dimensional way of places called into being by one's arrival and dissolving on departure: places with no known past. On a still autumn day near Port Campbell many years ago I watched my young sons dive for sea treasure. Crusts of blue pottery glinted in their hands. More sea treasure: in April of 1841 'a large quantity of wax candles' drifts ashore on a nearby beach. Local blacks tie the candles in their hair; local whites trade in them. The price rockets: Mr Robinson is gratified to be given 'three or four'. For years I have felt a subliminal twitch of irritation when I cross a bridge on the way to our Anglesea beach house, thirty kilometres and half a lifetime away from my childhood beach house further down the coast. 'Merrijig Creek,' the sign says, all too sweetly. But Mr Robinson tells me *Merrijig* means 'good' or 'fine' in the local tongue: 'They asked me if I was pleased, saying Merrigic Elengermat, Merrigic Warr Nerbul, of course I say merrigic, and they were pleased.' Now I hear a babble of soft voices when I pass. Trivial things, but they render time transparent. A small new fact, and a landscape dulled by familiarity is suddenly sharp and clear; the details disaggregate, rearrange themselves, perspectives steady – and open like flowers. The past is present again: contingent, heavy with promise.

Or with shame. Elsewhere Robinson encounters a wandering family: a man, his wife, an infant, two very young girls. They are Wol-lore-rer, or what is left of them; the tribe, they say, is 'plenty all gone', 'plenty shoot him white man'. Robinson suspects that the little family is allowed to survive because the girls are kept at the 'nefarious disposal of white men.' His suspicions are confirmed when he hears them saying over their few words of English: 'Well done fuckumoll, go it fuckmoll, good night fuckmoll.'

'Wol-lore-rer.' A flinch of recognition: I know a place called Willaura, a small town between Ararat and Hamilton. I spent a few school holidays close by an even smaller place called Stavely. There were no people around then; just the scatter of big sheds and the little weatherboard house, with the Harbells' place somewhere across the railroad track and over the rise. Nobody else. Just sheep, a few crows, the usual rabbits. Now there will always be people there: a man, his wife, a baby, and two little girls telling over the white man's litany: 'Well done fuckmoll. Go it fuckmoll. Good night fuckmoll.' And behind them, others. How many others?

Mr Robinson is a fine guide, to things unknown, or unacknowledged. He is also, it must be admitted, a rather foolish man. He lacks political sense, inflaming resentment in men on whom he must depend: he bullies and badgers subordinates, bores and irritates superiors. Easily flattered, he is even more easily offended. He is impatient: he is always 'going on ahead' and getting lost, and when he does he blames somebody else. He is humourless, priggish, jealous and vain.

He is also brave, independent and tough. He is making this journey, like most of his journeys, by choice. As Chief Protector he could have left the 'fieldwork' – the noting of past traces and present signs of Aboriginal presence, the listing of Aboriginal names of persons and places, the 'protection' of Aboriginal survivors – to his four assistants, who would have much preferred him to stay at home. But off he jogs in 1841 in his fifty-first year, a portly, high-coloured person. He rides with a leaf between his lips to protect them from sunburn, ranging up to fifty kilometres a day with the van dawdling along somewhere behind, subsisting largely on flour and tea and mutton – when he can get it, when Myatt hasn't lent the tinder box to a crony or forgotten to make the damper, when he hasn't got himself lost and has to spend the night hungry and huddled under a tree.

Physically tough, his moral toughness is almost excessive: he advances on homesteads where he knows he will be less than welcome, where he must depend on the settler's hospitality; we tremble; in he stalks stiff-necked, looking for trouble. These are desperate times. Violence among blacks is increasing, between and within tribes, even within families, but it is violence between blacks and whites that he dreads. Rumours run ahead like marsh-fire: they must be tracked down and scotched, or many blacks might die. He can seem absurdly partisan: whatever the fall of the evidence, he always favours the natives. If sheep are missing, wild dogs did it, or the shepherds let them stray, or exchanged them for access to a black woman. A shepherd speared through the walls of his hut as he sleeps must have provoked the attack. He believes such men, 'the sweepings of New South Wales and Van Diemen's Land', to be capable of anything. While their gentlemen employers might have little stomach for casual killings, they know the value of sheep hauled stiff and seasick from the bowels of ships or walked overland from Sydney. They are too valuable to fetch up filling a native's shrunken belly. It is difficult to identify the shadows fleeing from the sheepfolds, difficult to identify them among the stringy figures down at the river camp. Best be rid of the lot: clear them off and keep them off, and if you have to use a few bullets to do it – well, so be it.

Robinson can see, in the silence of deserted habitations, in the faces of the frightened survivors, how close the settlers are to success. The signs are everywhere. At one of the few stations where blacks are still tolerated, a large swivel gun stands mounted at the homestead. Travelling through a specially tense region he makes only one entry for the day, but that is enough: 'All the shepherds I saw today have double barrel guns. The natives say, "by and by no good".'

The facts of white violence are easily discovered: the natives tell him. Their stories have the surreal authenticity of a silent film. At a camp near the Wannon in the Western District the people are weeping. A man and two women have been shot. 'The men had told them to come and they would give them damper. When they went, they shot them.' The little figures run, jerk, throw up their hands, fall. Who are the killers? 'Purbrick's men.' Their names? 'Jem, Barry and Bill or Paddy Jem and Bill or Bob and Larry . . . ' The names are fluid as water. Robinson perseveres. He tracks the accused men down and takes their statements. But he knows that nothing can come of it: with native testimony inadmissible in the courts, 'the whole matter falls to the ground, and the white ruffian may with impunity deny his black victim.'

Even when the killings are admitted, there is no redress. Pyrenees natives give him the names of seven blacks shot by a leaseholder called Francis. Robinson records the names. Some days later he visits Francis at his homestead. The settler tells his story: he was riding down by the creek, natives attacked him, he shot four. He also caught a black at his fold, and shot him, too. He had reported the incidents to the government. That, he assumes, will be the end of the matter.

As it proves. Robinson steps aside. 'I told [Francis] I did not intend to enquire, it was in [Assistant Protector] Parker's hands and was his duty.' Then he seems to forget the whole miserable business. Later that night he is deep in his domestic war with Myatt: the dolt has failed to shield the van against the weather, failed to make up his bed; he has had to do it himself; the rain beats in on him all night. But the killings are not forgotten. Francis had offered him a bed – a warm, dry bed, with 'clean sheets and pillowcases.' He had been insistent. He had even promised to play his fiddle – Francis is a lonely man. Robinson refuses: he will not be beholden to such a man. For the first time we hear what will become a little refrain: 'He acknowledged to five. The natives say seven.' Robinson goes back to his camp and his rain-wet bed, and writes it all down. Even if the law – the law whose agent he is – averts its face, he will keep the record. 'He acknowledged to five. The natives say seven.'

The evidence for some black crimes cannot be talked away. Robinson meets Governor La Trobe in Portland. La Trobe warns him not to take a newly contacted band of 'wild' natives too near the town. There has been a 'horrible murder' by Glenelg natives of a Mr Morton, a 'kind and humane gentleman', and his man Larry. The servant had been stretched on his back with spears driven through the palms of his hands, and 'they had cut the flesh off his bone when alive and eaten it'. They had also eaten of Morton's dead flesh. Robinson is shaken: he typically dismisses tales of cannibalism as hysterical fantasy ('all fudge!'), but he cannot impeach this source.

Later the same morning he is shepherding his 'shy and savage' flock to a more secure camping ground when they are hallooed after by a mob of predatory whalers, promising blankets, tomahawks, handkerchiefs in exchange for Aboriginal women. He chivvies his people along, gets them settled. At midday Mr Blair, police magistrate at Portland, and Mr Henty, its leading citizen, seek him out at the camp. He records the ensuing conversation energetically, and at length. (They were too mistrustful of the blacks to dismount, so he must have had to look up at them throughout the exchange, which cannot have helped his temper.) They show him the letter giving the gruesome details of the Morton killings. The two men 'were under great excitement – thought the natives of this [Glenelg] tribe should be exterminated'. Robinson admits his own dejection of spirit, but pleads the necessity of more knowledge, and more understanding. The discussion becomes warm. 'Mr Blair said he knew what he would do if he was Governor. He would send down soldiers and if they did not deliver up the murderer he would shoot the whole tribe. I said it would not perhaps be so easy. Mr Henty said there would be no difficulty on the Glenelg as they had only the river to fly to and they could soon flush them out from among the rocks.'

And so, heatedly, on. Two days earlier Robinson had been desperate for these gentlemen's approbation, but when they finally turn their horses' heads for town he is heartily glad to be rid of them. It is a taxing night. Both his own and the 'wild' people are in an excitable state; in a squabble over a piece of bread one of his men hurls a spear, which whizzes close by his head. More blacks arrive, strangers, 'the most turbulent and noisy natives' he has ever encountered. They settle themselves close by his tent. Sleep is impossible. Nonetheless, the old energy is back, and he is himself again. Alienated from his own people, surrounded by unknown, possibly dangerous natives, he is where he chooses to be.

It is that steady preference which makes him remarkable. Irascible with whites, he is preternaturally patient with Aborigines. He is, in fact, a most earnest anthropologist. On Saturday 17 April he writes from Assistant Protector Sievwright's camp: '8 a.m. Heavy rain and a westerly wind . . . Busy collecting vocabulary. My tent, as usual, since day dawn thronged with natives.' This could be an extract from the great Malinowski's diary – except that Malinowski would never tolerate 'savages' in his tent. Robinson aims to record the name, land and family affiliations of every Aborigine he encounters. They yield their whitefellow names readily enough, but are reticent about their own. He coaxes them, carefully recording the strings of unfamiliar syllables. The driving, eye-baffling hand slows to careful legibility here. Talking with one group, he suspects a connection with a tribe to the east. He begins to pronounce the easterners' names. No response. He perseveres.

'Ning.cal.ler.bel.' The natives begin to sing. It is a long song, and 'at the end of each stanza Ning.caller.bel was mentioned by name.' Bravo, Mr Robinson!

Yet he has the wit and grace to acknowledge that even hard-won 'knowledge' can be wrong, and tirelessly checks his information. He is alert to the rhetorical element in native violence. When a melée erupts at Sievwright's camp – the men 'in single combat and then all together clubbing and wrestling', the women 'vociferating at the top of their breath' – all is ferocity and pandemonium. Yet, he notes there are interesting intermissions: 'at intervals the fighting would cease and the combatants would stop and taunt. A boomerang or spear would be thrown to provoke the combat and the battle renewed.' 'It reminded me,' Robinson writes, with uncharacteristic dryness, 'of a Hibernian fracas.'

He accepts close physical contact, and its penalties. 'Wild' Aborigines 'paw . . . me about', one in particular 'rubbing his hand about me . . . feeling my limbs and soliciting my clothes.' Vigorous investigation of his person escalates to what looks like a collective attempt at a shakedown: hands tug at his clothes, pull at his reins, slap at his horse; he retains his physical and moral poise. And when he contracts a painful and obstinate 'pustulence [sic] irruption' (scabies?) from those patting, poking hands he continues to offer up his person, saying: 'I could not rightfully be cross or unkind to these people. It was their custom and, as the old saying is, when in Rome do as Rome does.'

There is vanity in this. He enjoys the accoutrements of office: travelling heroically light, he nevertheless carts his Chief Protector's uniform with him, and wears it on grand occasions. And he loves being recognised. Riding ahead of his party, he comes upon women and children gathering yams. Normally they would scatter at the sight of a white man. 'When they saw me they ran to where I was standing. Joy was in their countenances.' He is even more delighted when a recognition scene is witnessed. Proceeding with his natives, a convict, and, by most happy chance, a local settler, Mr Adams, they see a long file of 'wild' natives, most of them armed, advancing towards them. 'The spears . . . were newly sharpened,' he says with relish, and we wonder how he knows.

Undaunted and alone, Robinson goes forward to meet them. 'I held up my hands.' They halt. Working his way down the line, 'I shook each of them by the hand and patted them on the head.' Their submission is immediate, total, glorious: 'They repeated every word I spoke to them . . . I distributed to each a medal which I suspended to their neck . . . ' Gifts cascade from his hands: headbands, handkerchiefs, necklaces to the children. Then comes the punchline: 'Mr Adams said he never saw natives so obedient to anyone as those natives were to me.'

Mr Robinson's cup runneth over. That night he has a sack of (Mr Adams's) potatoes sent to the natives, and throws in a piece of pork for VDL Jack, his trusted Tasmanian assistant, and the reprobate Myatt. On the evening before a planned rendezvous with all the blacks of the Port Fairy region he is blissful: 'My mind is now at ease and I feel satisfied. Providence has crowned my endeavours with success.' The next day he crows, 'Such a meeting has never been held with these people, either within or out of their district . . . What has been done in 7 weeks!'

There are equally rapturous accounts of the trust he inspires in individuals. One example:

I started from Synnott's with the Barcondeet native to give me information but as it was raining hard I cantered on at a brisk pace and my Aboriginal friend ran and kept pace with me. He was armed with spears. He kept chatting about his country and calling out the names of different locations and said his country was good country. I answered in the affirmation [sic] which afforded him satisfaction. I am certain the poor fellow would have run the whole way, 12 miles, had I not stopped him and desired him to wait for the van and come with it.'

It is an affecting picture: the young black rendered immune to rain and natural fatigue by affection, chattering freely in the benign presence of his Protector. Who, taking thought for his charge, gently puts an end to this enchanted run at the stirrup. We splutter and choke; Robinson glows. On the day of triumph near Port Fairy he had gone to the assembly point early, and had addressed no more than a few words to the nervous crowd when his entourage (van, Myatt etcetera) rolled in. Immediately, one old man 'thrust his arm in mine as if apprehensive of danger . . . and walked with me whilst I gave the necessary directions to my people'. Later, distributing gifts, 'I became most popular with the juveniles, even the little children came and clung onto my knees like children do a papa.'

Mr Robinson is getting a lot in return for those potatoes and headbands and handerkerchiefs. Can a balance be drawn? To begin at the material level: it is painfully clear that the natives are hungry; that food is a most urgent necessity. Robinson keeps an anxious watch on the depletion of native game, but the vestigial groups he and we encounter are too reduced to hunt effectively anyway, and their vegetable foods were being ravaged by imported flocks. He does what he can, coaxing and bullying flour or sugar or the occasional sheep out of grudging settlers, but it is never enough. Even the feeding of his immediate entourage reads like a continuous loaves-and-fishes miracle. Knowing the bitter cold of southern nights, he hands out blankets when he has them, but blankets are in chronically short supply. For the rest, he might barter a knife for a spear, or reward a special courtesy with a tomahawk, but what he mainly gives are small, cheap, easily transportable things: caps, beads, medals, and lots of cards, or 'letters', as he sometimes calls them, magnificently inscribed with his own or the Governor's name.

At a casual glance this looks to be the familiar swindle: the European trash deployed in a thousand shameful encounters to bamboozle and diddle the locals. Certainly Robinson seems blind to the gulf in utility between the objects he offers and those he covets for his 'collection': a yellow cap for a cherished spear or a woman's indispensable bark bucket is no exchange. Perhaps there can be no equitable exchange between a people with an abundance of mass-produced items, some of them purely decorative, and another whose economy is so dour that bodies are rendered sacred by the application of clays. The one-way flow of small, gaudy objects has more to do with power than trade. To Mr Robinson, they signify personal authority. To other whites they offer reassurance: a warrior sporting a cap and clutching the Governor's card seems no longer a warrior. There is, however, another effect. A native in a cap holding out his card or his medal can be less easily classified as an undesirable infestation of the land. He is marked, however feebly, as human, and so potentially within the protection of the law.

There is a kind of reciprocity here, if a skewed and fragile one, and the limits are firmly drawn. Coming upon some native shelters Robinson and his party prowl about, and pry into the baskets they find hidden in a couple of hollow trees. Robinson acknowledges some feelings of delicacy – he looks, he says, only because 'the customs and manners of these people were new to me' – but he looks nonetheless. He finds a jumble of objects: bone awls; bits of broken glass, of lava, of scoria; lumps of ochre and pipeclay and iron; a stick for stripping bark; an amulet; a few items of European dress.

It is a poignant collection, this survival kit for difficult times, and we can only guess at its meaning. Robinson takes two of the awls, leaving 'a new cotton handkerchief' in return. He takes something else, and for this he leaves no payment: 'I found a lead pencil whole in their basket and as I needed it, I took it away.' He does not wonder how they got the pencil, or why they treasure it. The instruments of literacy belong to him.

On the emotional plane the scales tilt differently. Robinson is a good anthropologist because he is attentive to his subjects' behaviour, and he is attentive because they charm him. For a time I was puzzled by his inattention towards his most familiar black companion, 'VDL Jack'. He had brought Jack with him from Tasmania, along with Trugannini and fourteen others, as 'personal attendants', but he also called them his family. (The Governor felt himself duped, and complained at the expense.)

Jack – alias Tunerminnerwait or Napoleon – and four more of Robinson's Tasmanians, three of them women, one of them Truganinni, were to become suddenly, shockingly famous as black insurrectionists late in 1841, when they carried out a series of raids and robberies around Point Nepean – robberies in which two whalers were killed. Desperation had a lot to do with it, their rations having been stopped by frugal Governor La Trobe. Jack would be hanged for murder in January 1842. At this stage, half a year before, he is indispensable: he guards the camp, finds lost wagons and horses, and informs on black and white alike, and when Robinson wearies of the all-too-carnal investigations of curious 'friends', he hands Jack over to them like an amiable long-limbed doll. Yet Robinson's references to him are few and coolly instrumental. I suspect it is Jack's sophistication, his learnt amenability, which has rendered him uninteresting in his master's eyes. Robinson is quickly wearied by excessively 'wild' natives, with whom he can have no 'intelligent conversation.' He is bored by docile ones, save as stock figures for the tableaux-vivant of his private theatre of vanity. What he likes are people sufficiently knowledgeable of white men's ways to be attentive, yet who retain their exuberance and spontaneity.

Consider his attitude to Eurodap, alias 'big' Tom Brown, who makes his entry into the journal on 6 April 1841. Initially he is allocated three characteristics: 'This was an intelligent man,' 'he had on a jacket and trousers,' '[he] was quite delighted to see me.' Thenceforth Eurodap slips constantly in and out of the pages. He is useful: he knows the country, he supplies names for places and things, and when strange natives are sighted it is Eurodap who is sent out to fetch them in. But Eurodap is primarily valued not for his usefulness, but for his personality: his vivacity, his expressivity, his gaiety. When new groups must be entertained with song, Eurodap excels. He also takes joyful liberties. Robinson detests obscenities, especially in native mouths: 'Fudge!' is his own most violent epithet. So Eurodap plays Grandmother's Steps with irascible Robinson: 'Eurodap said white shepherd too much no good talk to black fellow and then gave me a specimen of his proficiency etc. g – d d – m, you bl – y lyer; you old bug–ger; be off; d – mn you, etc., etc.. He was going on with these blasphemous epithets when I told him to desist and that they were very bad.'

Then comes the journal entry for 25 June. It comprises two sentences: 'Tom Brown killed. Went from McRae's to Winter's.' The entry immediately following briefly describes Eurodap's death: he has been speared in some fracas, seemingly while trying to mediate. And the journal's sturdy march through the days collapses. It is impossible to establish clear detail or sequence: there are seven separate entries, all of them confusingly dated, for the four days following the death. Only on 29 June does the steady progression re-assert itself.

Am I making too much of this break in what seems to be a pattern? Perhaps. Were this fiction, I would know that all things said and left unsaid, all disruptions, were intended to signify. But this is not fiction, and I cannot be sure. I do know that Robinson, among whites a stiff, awkward fellow, and tensely competitive, is with Eurodap and others like him relaxed and genial because he need fear no challenge. With them he believes he finds the security of uncontested because uncontestable inequality. In their company, and possibly only in their company, can his human affections be fully liberated.

This is, perhaps, 'condescension' in the old sense, of affability towards one's putative inferiors. But it is also something very like love. While most whites view the exuberance of black sociability with distaste shading into revulsion, Robinson basks in it. Blacks swarm in and out of his tent without let or hindrance. Information sessions are informal to unruliness: he grumpily complains of the impossibility of getting everything down on paper when two or three people are simultaneously roaring out the names of creatures they have collected for him. He attends corroborees eagerly, and stays to the end. When the going is hard he walks so that blacks may ride – 'to encourage them,' he says. He persuades nervous novices to climb on his horse, and laughs at the result. And he responds with expeditious tenderness to individual distress. An old chief he had talked with through a long evening is embroiled in what becomes 'a general fight with clubs and mulgas' at Sievwright's camp, a fight which Robinson implies he quells: 'I went among them.' The old man, wounded, excited, urges the whites to get their guns and shoot the opposition. Robinson coaxes him into the assistant protector's hut, soothes him with tea and damper. Later he orders a general feast of 'mutton, potatoes and tea' for all combatants. I have become very fond of Mr Robinson.

Robinson also actively enjoys physical contact with bodies other whites see as diseased, verminous, loathsome. 'Pustulent irritations' notwith-standing, if he is hugged, he hugs back. On no direct evidence whatsoever I am confident that he shares his blanket from time to time with one of the 'fine, sprightly girls' he admires so frankly. He accepts other gifts freely offered, he is susceptible to women, so why not? ('When in Rome . . . ') It is the brutal sexual politics of most black/white couplings which appals him, not the act.

Of course he does not really 'do as in Rome'. The assumption of spe-cial status is always there. He records the native protocols governing encounters between strangers – the period of silent watchfulness, iden-tification through the painting of faces and bodies, the formal exchange first of words, then of song and dance – but he does not follow them. On the contrary, 'when natives appear I break through all Aboriginal cere-mony . . . and go forth and meet them'. Once again we hear that biblical reverberation. But I doubt his physical tolerance and ready emotional inti-macy find their ground in some bloated messianic fantasy. His relaxation and warmth of spirit before Aboriginal otherness is a private, secular grace.

The traffic is not entirely one way. A recurrent anguish in the study of cross-cultural communications is to watch questions being asked from one side which can make no sense at all to the other. Across the gulfs of time we hear the silence of perfect incomprehension. But Mr Robinson asks the right questions. This is an accident: his purpose is, above all to collect the names of individuals, clans, places, and he is eager to get the affiliations right. Fortuitously, the blacks take him to be mapping the Aboriginal world of meanings and imagination.

That makes him a man worth talking to – a man to whom it is possible to talk, who will understand. Just west of Mount Cole he falls in with several families. 'I repeated a string of names of tribes and localities all of which they knew, and were astonished at the extent of my information.' He so impresses another woman with his knowledge of 'tribes and persons and localities' that she is persuaded that he must have been a native of those parts come back as a white, and grills him until she has constructed a plausible genealogy. An old woman, wandering with the remnants of her family over their usurped land, responds to his questions after they have lit a fire, and sat down around it. She 'enacts a variety of events connected with the history of her country', and then, 'in a dejected and altered tone', laments its loss.

Robinson interprets all such eagerness to talk with him as naive tributes to his personal charisma. He does not ask why the magic works best on blacks who have already experienced white depredations. But we must remember that Robinson presents himself as a man of authority, claiming connection with distant white powers. He also enquires into serious matters, and then he writes those matters down (remember the pencil). I suspect it is this rather than his personal allure which makes Aborigines ready, even desperate, to talk with him.

He is also a man capable of astonishing, painful opacities. A few days before the end of his journey, when he draws nearer to Melbourne, a handful of natives, survivors from two tribes, attach themselves to him. He notes that they are 'very communicative'. They are also painfully eager for connection: they give him a new name, 'meaning in their own tongue "great" or "big" chief', and beg his protection against whites who 'drove them away and said be off'. 'Too much "be off" all about,' they say.

Robinson tells them he might help them later, but that he has no time now. They weep. Then they ask him for a 'letter'; when he leaves, their leader pursues him to offer a last-minute gift of a particularly fine emu-feather belt. Surely they are desperate for his intervention? Surely he can smell their fear? We can: the pages reek with it.

It seems, however, that he cannot. He remarks on the intelligence of one of the young men ('a promising youth if attended to') as if we were still at the dawn of the world. Then, charmed with his new name, delighted with his gift – flattered by the tears – he rides cheerfully on. He finds the day 'beautiful', the country 'uncommonly good and pleasant'. He concludes the entry with a casual observation: 'These plains must ultimately be made use of for sheep grazing. The government must lease them.'

Sir Thomas More summed up the human agony attending the great land-grabs of sixteenth-century England in a masterly image: 'Your sheep, that were wont to be so meek and tame, and so small eaters, now . . . be become so great devourers, and so wild . . . that they eat up and swallow down the very men themselves.' Three centuries later, we watch that perversion in nature being re-enacted in an English colony. Two peoples whose interests are perfectly inimical are in contention for the land. The Aboriginals are the weaker; they will go to the wall. Astonishingly, no provision is made for them: they are cast out of their territories to die. That much is cruelly apparent from Robinson's own writings. So how to explain that casual, shocking comment? What is wrong with this man? Is he a fool, a hypocrite, a moral imbecile; another thick-skinned imperialist playing bumpo with a wincing world?

I think he is none of those things. Rather, he, like so many others, has contrived ways to live with the appalling, immutable fact of Aboriginal death. Initially his brisk tone, his lack of introspection, his radiant vanity, led me to think him a straightforward sort of chap. That was, as it always is, hubris: 'simplicity' in humans is a reflex of distance. How many of us dare to pretend to understand those to whom we stand closest, and how great the punishment of those who do.

I have come to think that Robinson lives in the stretch of a terrible contradiction, the tension of the stretch being betrayed in persistent patterns of conduct – for example, that compulsive 'going on ahead' – and equally persistently, if more subtly, in certain oddities of style. As I read, I was more and more struck by disjunctions not adequately explained by appeal to the 'journal format': too-abrupt transitions between subjects, irritable returns to matters done with, radical switches of mood. An unmoored sentence recalls some past contretemps. The affair bites at him still. He rails for a sentence or a paragraph against 'the condition of the original inhabitants of this land' – then pivots abruptly back into busywork.

These disjunctions thicken at times of tension. It is as if his mind suddenly lurches and swerves from an unseen impediment. I have come to think that these judderings, along with his irritable, urgent energy, are indicators of what we used to call 'cognitive dissonance': an uncomfortable condition in which a mind veers and twists as it strives to navigate between essential but mutually incompatible beliefs. Time and again he approaches overt acknowledgment of the incorrigibility of black/white relations; time and again he pulls back into the refuge of the trivial and merely vexing.

He 'believes' in his work: that is transparently clear. But he also knows, at some level, if only intermittently, that his naggings about the law and his handing out of blankets and letters are futile; that he can do nothing to slow the avalanche. His treasured authority gives him power to coerce only the victims, not their oppressors: 'I sent for this native but the man said he would not come. I said he was under my protection and I would soon make him.' The equations are bleak. The law is the blacks' only protection: the law grants away their lands, and fails to protect them from wanton, most deliberate murder. The 'Chief Protector', for all his posturings and protestations, can effect nothing. The Chief Protector is a sham.

These are unendurable truths. So he keeps himself busy: he quibbles and quarrels and shifts the blame, lectures stiff-faced settlers, pats the patting black hands, hands out his blankets and his cards. He is hopelessly divided: scanning the land for kangaroos, he is simultaneously assessing its potential as pasture. He indulges in the fantasy of missionaries everywhere: somehow, the natives must be quarantined from the contagion of evil. 'White men of respectable character', men like himself, should 'attach themselves to the native tribes and control their movements'. But even if that were to happen (he knows it will never happen) where could they go? He strives to gather up his wandering people like some Old Testament prophet in flight from catastrophe. But the catastrophe is all around him, and there is no Promised Land.

So on he rides, watching for signs: a curl of smoke, boughs bent to shelter shivering bodies. He is searching for ghosts and the shadows of ghosts. He sees crumbling mounds of shells or the long depressions which mark communal ovens, and hears the silent hubbub of a vanished encampment. He gathers up the survivors, distributes his little gifts, lights his illusory flares of hope. He counts his flock; he records their names. Absurdly, he gives them new ones, but these are not real names. Real names differentiate and connect; they have social meaning. These names, like his medals and his letters and his blankets, are tokens merely: amulets against death. These people are ghosts already, they have no substance. At a station one day, begging flour, they are gone the next. They can be made to vanish at a word: 'He said he would have none of them about his station.' 'Be off!' These Joes and Jacks and Mollys have entered the numbered anonymity of death: 'He acknowledged to five. The natives say seven.'

Every night this burdened, driven man steals time from sleep to assemble his information, to fix the flux of experience, to construct his self-protective, self-exposing account of things. He is an addicted writer. Some entries – those triumphalist narratives and tableaux, with their preposterous Biblical resonances – must have been long in the writing. He has taken pleasure in their crafting. And occasionally, just occasionally, especially when he has been forced to stare for a moment into the abyss between rhetoric and action, he stumbles upon an image of haunting power.

From the first days of his journey he makes frequent reference to a place called Boloke. There is a lake there, and an abundance of fish and fowl which still draws natives from all over the region. So rich is the abundance that Boloke is a traditional meeting-place for the ceremonial resolution of conflict, a place of feasting and of celebration. Through the slow drudge of days Boloke shimmers on the edge of awareness as a vision of peace and plenty. Then he goes there – to find desolation. The lake waters have been sucked up by drought. There are signs of many natives: 'a vast number' of old shelters, abandoned tools, and everywhere on the beach their tracks 'thick as sheep tracks'. But there are no people. Instead he sees dead eels, on the sand, on the banks, strewn along the beach. At the deserted camps 'dead eels lay in mounds; thousands of dead eels, and very large ones too'. Crows are feasting upon them. There are also 'numerous tracks of cattle, sheep and horses'.

Robinson lingers: he looks, wonders, notes down what he sees. Then he moves on to more practical matters – but not before he has fixed an image which murmurs awareness of that other, invisible, more terrible destruction. Later, visiting the Francis homestead, he flounders, making his only protest against the settler's self-admitted slaughter of blacks by refusing a bed for the night. Even when an Aboriginal eyewitness confirms his suspicion that Francis and his men had killed the people down at the river camp without provocation, Robinson keeps his miserable peace.

Then, as he mounts his horse to leave the following day, he sees a human skull. He has seen skulls on display often enough, nailed to doors and posts in particularly troubled areas, but this one is lying on open ground, a few metres from the woolshed and hard by the road, 'on a small bare hill where sheep had been folded.' Robinson realises that it must be the skull of the man Francis had shot at the sheepfold; that he has ordered the body be left to lie where it fell. 'I showed it to the natives and they said "Mr Francis killed him, Mr Francis shot plenty blackfellows, all gone black fellows." "What had happened to the rest of the body?" "Taken away by the dogs".

Robinson picks up the skull, puts it in his van. And then he continues with his travels and his general observations: 'Francis is fencing in a paddock; he has a woolshed and several huts. The soil in this part of the country is of an inferior quality, red sandy loam from 2 to 3 inches deep...'

From horror to banality in a breath. Nonetheless, the horror is preserved, and now it is there in the record, for any of us to read.

Across a landscape transformed by our meeting I look back to Mr Robinson. He is riding through a cold rain. A figure runs beside him, running easily over the land. He is young, and strong, but he is already a ghost. Perhaps he knows that, because as he runs he names the places of this his country. Measuring his breath to his stride, he sings its names and its beauty. It is possible that this white man will hear, and hearing, write. It is possible that someone, some day, will read, and remember.

Index

Aborigines (Australia), 3–5, 191–208
Acosta, José, 135n37
Adams, Eleanor B., 101n23
aesthetic, and Aztec view of war, 23
afterlife, Aztec concept of, 42–3. *See also* Underworld
agriculture: Aztec society and *chinampa* form of, 7, 36–7, 42; slash-and-burn and water sources in Yucatán, 158, 172–3, 175–6
Aguilar, Sanchez de, 169–70
alcohol consumption, 146–8, 155. *See also* pulque
Aldana, Juan de, 97n15
alienation, and contemporary popular culture, 188–9
altruism, and organ transplantation, 190
Anales de Tlatelolco, 81
Anderson, Arthur J. O., 118n4
animals, and Mexican lexicon of battle, 73. *See also* eagle; horses; jaguar
archaeology, and interpretations of Aztec rituals, 28
Auerbach, Ellen, 151n76
Augustinians, and missionaries in New Spain, 106
Australia: journals of G. A. Robinson and history of, 191–208; and relevance of Mexican experience for understanding of inner history of Aborigines, 3–5
authority: Franciscan ideology and missionaries in sixteenth-century Yucatán, 104–7, 110, 111, 113–15;

Robinson's journals and Aborigine/white interactions in Australia, 204; and survival of Maya culture in post-Conquest period, 170
autonomy, and Maya culture in post-Conquest period, 157, 174
Avendano, Father, 166n14
Azcapotzalco (Valley of Mexico), 7, 8
Aztecs: inaccuracy of European view of "empire" in context of, 68; interpretations and explanations of behavior, 180–4; and song-poems, 6, 39, 81; use of term, 6n2, 116n2; warrior ideology in society of, 6–48. *See also* Mexico; Nahuatl language; ritual performances; Tenochtitlan

ball-game, and pre-Conquest ritual performances, 137
Barrera Vasquez, Alfredo, 170n22
battle: Aztec warriors and reconstruction of, 19–27; and Mexican views of war, 66, 68–9
Beidelman, T. O., 91
belief analysis approach, to religion, 123–4, 151–2
Berdan, Frances, 9n8, 118n4
Bienvenida, Fray Lorenzo de, 101, 115
Bierhorst, John, 81n72, 137n41
blood: and Aztec ritual performances, 37–8, 41; and Christian self-flagellation, 144n59; and Tlaxcalan dance performances, 134

body, personal experience of chronic illness and notions of, 187–9

Bohorqués, Bartolomé de, 98n16

Books of Chilam Balam, 170–1, 174–5, 176–7

Borah, Woodrow, 158n2

Borges, Fray Pedro, 96, 114n52, 116n1

Bossy, John, 122n12

Broda de Casas, Johanna, 9n8, 29n39

Brooke, Rosalind B., 103

Brotherston, Gordon, 7n4, 81n72

Brumfiel, Elizabeth M., 8

Bruner, Edward M., 125n17

Bundle of Years (*Xiumolpilli*), 14, 76

Burns, Allen F., 175

Calderón de la Barca, Fanny, 145n60

calendar: and Aztec seasonal rituals, 36, 126–8; and Maya concept of time as cyclic, 165–6, 173. *See also* time

Calnek, Edward A., 7n3, 9n8

calpulli (lineage group), 7, 8

Campeche (Yucatán), 98

cannibalism, ritual forms of in Aztec warrior culture, 30, 32, 69n40, 180

captives, and Aztec view of war, 10, 21, 23, 68, 70. *See also* ritual performance

Carrasco, Pedro, 9n8

Caribbean, brutality of Spanish toward indigenes of, 82

Carrithers, Michael, 125n17

Catholic Church: and evolution of "Indian Catholicism," 155n86; and fasting, 136; and Indians' care and use of religious images, 149–55. *See also* Augustinians; Dominicans; Franciscans; Inquisition; missionaries; religion

Cempoalla (city), 60–1

Chamberlain, Robert S., 158n2

Chartier, Roger, 151

Chavez, Angelico, 144n57

Chichen Itza (city), 167, 175, 176, 177

Chichimeca (northern steppes of Mexico), 69n38

Chichimecatecle (Tlaxcalan chief), 82–3n73

children: childbirth and warrior ideology in Aztec society, 17–18, 185; and festival of Izcalli, 126–8; image of "Indian as child" and Franciscan paternalism, 107–13

chinampa agriculture, 7, 36–7, 42

"Cholula massacre," 62

Christian, William, 122n12, 123n14

Cihuacoatl (aspect of Earth Mother), 42

Cinteotl (Young Lord Maize Cob), 39

Cjikszentimhalyi, Mihali, 45

class, and role of warrior in Aztec society, 8, 9, 12–13, 35–6, 47

Clendinnen, Inga, 123n13, 138n42, 144n55, 162n7

Codex Borbonicus, 28, 40

Codex Mendoza, 117

Coe, Michael D., 166n13

cognitive dissonance, and Aborigine/white relations in Australia, 205–6

Collins, Steven, 125n17

communication: Robinson's journals and cross-cultural in Australia, 203–4; and Spanish-Indian misunderstandings during Conquest, 57–9, 89–90

congregación and *reducción*, and Spanish colonial policy, 157, 160n4

consciousness, and personal experience of chronic illness, 186

conservatism, of Maya culture, 157, 178n40

context model, and pre-Conquest ritual performances, 137

conversion, Franciscan ideology of in post-Conquest period, 92, 97–8

Cook, Sherburne F., 158n2

Cortés, Hernando: and consequences of Conquest, 82–7; and initial phase of Conquest, 49–65; and second phase of Conquest, 65–82; and Spanish accounts of Aztec battle, 20n23

cosmology, "Christian" deities in Mayan traditional, 177

Council of Four (Aztec), 12

creation myths (Aztec), 37–8

Crews, Frederick, 188n6

crosses and crucifixes, and religious symbolism in sixteenth-century Mexico, 152–4, 169n18, 176

Culhuacan (Speaker), 7

culture: aliens and alienation in contemporary popular, 188–9; and historians on religion and context of emotions, 126; and views of war during Conquest, 65–82, 89–90; warfare as expression of, 21

dances and dancing, and pre-Conquest
ritual performances, 132–3, 135, 137–8
Dancing with Strangers (Clendinnen 2003), 4
"day signs," 76–7n58. *See also* signs
death, and god-representations in ritual
performances, 142–3. *See also* captives
Delumeau, Jean, 129n23
Demause, Lloyd, 112n46
Díaz del Castillo, Bernal, 20n23, 24n27,
53, 61, 65, 66–7, 73, 74, 75n54, 77,
79n66, 87n84, 171
Dibble, Charles, 29n38
difference, and second phase of Spanish
Conquest of Mexico, 74–5
dominance, and Aztec ritual performances,
15–16
Dominicans, and missionaries in New
Spain, 106
Dorn, Ed, 81n72
dreams, and religion in post-Conquest
Mexico, 145–6
Durán, Diego, 9n9, 11n11, 28, 56, 64,
68n37, 120–1, 122, 123, 144–5n59,
145, 147n68

eagle, and Aztec lexicon of battle, 24, 73
Elliott, John H., 8n7, 54, 63n28, 83n74,
85n81
Europe: and concept of "empire" in Aztec
context, 68; and imperialism in
historiography, 58; and use of living
images in religious performance,
129–30, 154. *See also* Spain
Exponi nobis (papal bull), 98
extraterrestrials, and alienation in
contemporary popular culture, 188

fasting, Indian versus Spanish concepts of
in sixteenth-century Mexico, 133–6
fate, and structure of Indian and Spanish
accounts of final battles of Conquest,
75–82
Feast of the Flaying of Men (warrior
festival), 25, 26, 29, 37
festivals, and Aztec calendar, 36, 126–8.
See also Feast of the Flaying of Men;
Izcalli; Panquetzaliztli; processions;
Quecholli
Florentine Codex, 10n10, 11n11, 20n23,
28–9, 41, 47n58, 55, 57n15, 66n34,
69n40, 72, 76–7n58, 78n63, 82,

147n67. *See also* Sahagún, Fray
Bernardino de
"Flowery Wars" (Aztec), 13–14, 23
Foster, George M., 130n24
Francis, St., 103, 104
Franciscans: ideology of and missionary
violence in sixteenth-century Yucatán,
91–115; and survival of Maya culture in
Yucatán of post-Conquest period,
158–64
Freud, Sigmund, 179–80, 185–6
Fuentes, Patricia, 20–1n23
Furst, Jill Leslie, 41n50
Furst, Peter, 143n54
Fussell, Paul, 16

García de Icazbalceta, Joaquín, 131n26,
139n47
Geertz, Clifford, 3, 14, 63, 102, 124n15,
126n18, 141
Gibson, Charles, 2, 118n5, 130–1n25,
151n76, 174n31
Gingerich, Willard, 41n50
Graham, John A., 169n18
Great Maya Revolt (1546), 158, 168
Great Speaker (Aztec): Moctezuma's role
as, 64; Quauhtemoc and collapse of
empire, 79. *See also* tlatoani
Great Temple (Tenochtitlán), 16
Green, Merle, 169n18
Greenleaf, Richard E., 95n8, 9–100n20,
119n8, 133n30
Guzmán, Nuño de, 108

hallucinogenic drugs, and religious
performances, 143, 148n72
Hassig, Ross, 67n35
Herrera, Juan de, 101–2n25
hieroglyphic books (Maya), 168, 170
history and historiography: and analysis of
ritual, 27; on consequences of Conquest,
82–90; on Cortés and initial phase of
Conquest, 49–65; on Cortés and second
phase of Conquest, 65–72; on cultural
myopia of missionaries, 161; and current
status of scholarship on Mexico, 2;
journals of G. A. Robinson and
Australian, 191–208; Maya view of,
166–7, 174; and Nahuatl texts in
post-Conquest period, 118; on religion
and cultural context of emotions, 126

Honduras, and Cortés expedition, 89n89
horses: and Maya in post-Conquest period, 171–2; and second phase of Conquest, 73–4
"House of Youth" (Aztec), 9
Huitzilopochtli (god), 7, 15, 16, 19, 44–5, 77–8
Hymes, Dell, 123n14

ideology: and battlefield in Aztec rhetoric, 33–4; of Franciscans and missionary violence in sixteenth-century Yucatán, 97–115
Indians, use of term, 116n2. *See also* Aztec; Chichimeca; Maya; Mexico; Tlaxcala and Tlaxcalans
imperialism, in European-and-native historiography, 58
Inquisition, in sixteenth-century Mexico, 99, 101, 114, 117, 131, 163
Itza (Maya history), 167–8, 175
Itzcoatl (Great Speaker), 8, 15
ixiptlas (god-representations), 142–3, 149–55
Izcalli, festival of, 41, 126–8, 147

jaguar, and Aztec lexicon of battle, 24, 73
Joyce, James, 180, 185

Kagan, Richard, 109
Kapferer, Bruce, 124n15
katun (Maya calendar), 166, 175
Kartunen, Frances, 118n6, 142n52
Keegan, John, 16, 78–9, 85
Klor de Alva, J. Jorge, 118n5, 119
Knowles, David, 104n29
Kukulcan (Maya), 167, 175
Kurath, Gertrude Prokosch, 135n37

Landa, Fray Diego de, 99, 100, 101, 111, 112, 113, 115, 160n3, 161, 163, 168, 172
landscape: religious processions and sacred, 138–9; and survival of Maya culture after Conquest, 156–78
Language of Zuyua, 170–1
Lawrence, Peter, 158n1
Leon-Portilla, Miguel, 47n58, 81n72, 152n77
Levin, David, 50n5
Lienzo de Tlaxcala, 24n27, 87n84

Llaguno, Jose A., 131n26
Lockhart, James, 65n33, 118n4, 118n6
López Austin, Alfredo, 29n38–9, 41–2n50–1
Lopez Cogolludo, Fray Diego, 160n4
Lopez Medel, Tomas, 160
Lorenz, Konrad Z., 21, 79n65
Lorenzana, Francisco Antonio, 100n21, 131n26
Lukes, Steven, 125n17

maize: role of in Aztec ritual, 39, 48, 182; and vegetable metaphors in Aztec rhetoric, 182, 183–4
Malcolm, Janet, 190n7
Mañé, Rubio, 111n42
Maní (Yucatán), 98
Marina, Doña, 57
Martí, Samuel, 135n37
Martín de Valencia, Fray, 93, 103–4, 105, 115, 144
Maya: and bloodletting rituals, 134n33; Franciscan ideology and missionary violence in sixteenth-century Yucatán, 97–115; landscape and world view in survival of culture after Conquest, 156–78. *See also* Great Maya Revolt
Mayahuel (goddess), 152
Mayapan (city), 167, 168, 175, 176, 177
McAndrew, John, 125
McKnight, David, 155n85
Mendelsohn, Daniel, 180n2
Mendieta, Geronimo de, 106, 109, 113, 115
Mérida (Yucatán), 98
Mexico: and consequences of Conquest, 82–90; Cortés and initial phase of Conquest, 49–65; Cortés and second phase of Conquest, 65–82; current status of scholarship on history of, 2; reconstruction of religion in sixteenth-century, 116–55; and understanding of experience of indigenous Australians, 3–5; and use of terms "Mexica" and "Aztec," 6n2, 116n2. *See also* Aztec; Maya; Yucatán
Michoacán (city), 153n81
Miller, Mary Ellen, 134n33
missionaries: Franciscan ideology and violence in sixteenth-century Yucatán, 91–115; Franciscans and survival of

Maya culture in Yucatán, 158–64; and Robinson's journal on Aborigine/white interactions in Australia, 206

Moctezuma: and interpretations of Cortés and Conquest, 50, 51, 52, 54, 55–6, 57, 58–9, 62, 63–4, 82; and ritual performances, 38; and Tlaxcalans, 88

Moctezuma, Eduardo Matos, 15n17

Moctezuma the Elder, 8, 13

Molina, Alonso de, 39n48

Montejo, Francisco de, 111

Moore, Sally Falk, 140n48

More, Sir Thomas, 205

Morley, Sylvanus Griswold, 170n22

Motolinía, Fray Toribio de, 50n3, 108–9, 117, 119, 120, 123, 131, 132–3, 135, 137n40, 144, 145n62, 146, 152, 153n80–1

Mottahedeh, Roy, 124n15, 145n60

Muñoz Camargo, Diego, 127n20

Myerhoff, Barbara, 140n48

mysticism, and religion in post-Conquest Mexico, 144–5

mystification program, of Cortés during second phase of Conquest, 65–82

Nachi Cocom (Maya chief), 163, 168, 176

Nahuatl language: and Aztec empire, 88; and Indian texts in post-Conquest period, 117–18. *See also* Codex Borbonicus; Codex Mendoza

narcissism: and altruism in organ transplantation, 190; and Freudianism, 179; and explanations of Aztec ritual performances, 183

narrative, of ritual experience, 139–40. *See also* story-making

Narváez, Pánfilo, 52

Nemontemi (end of yearly calendar), 128

neuro-physiology, and religious performances, 140–1

New Fire Ceremony, 14

Nicholson, H. B., 15n17, 28n36, 29n38, 59n19

"Noche Triste" (June 1520), 52, 77

Ocelotl (Martin Ucelo), 119, 148n72

One Rabbit year (1454), 13

oral performance, and Maya culture, 174

organ transplantation, and personal experience of chronic illness, 185–90

Otomi (Aztec warrior), 47

Otumba, battle of, 77, 78

Padden, R. C., 59n18

Pagden, Anthony, 49n1, 11, 71n43, 85n81, 116n1

Panquetzaliztli, festival of, 138n44

Papua New Guinea, and native response to introduction of Christianity, 157–8n2

Parsons, Jeffrey R., 8n7

Pasztory, Esther, 15n17, 59n19

paternalism, Franciscans missionaries and image of "Indian as child," 107–13

Pazos, Manuel, 96, 114n52

performance. *See* oral performance; ritual performances

personal experience, of chronic illness and organ transplantation, 185–90

Peru, and model of Mexican Conquest, 65n33

Phelan, John Leddy, 50n3, 107n35, 116n1

Piho, Virve, 11n11

poetry, Aztec lyric, 46–7. *See also* song-poems

politics: of competitive spectacle in late fifteenth- and sixteenth-century Mexico, 14–16; and confusion in post-Conquest Mexico, 83; and Franciscan rhetoric of autonomous control over Indians, 111–12; and Nahua-speaking cities and provinces of Aztec empire, 88; and smallpox epidemic, 89n87

Ponce, Pedro, 122n12

population: estimates of in pre-contact Valley of Mexico, 14n14; estimates of for pre- and post-Conquest Yucatán, 158n2

Porter, Eliot, 151n76

Powell, Philip Wayne, 69n38

Prell-Foldes, Riv-Ellen, 125n16

Prescott, W. H., 50, 53

Press, Irwin, 178n40

priests: and Maya calendar, 173; and ritual performances, 142–3

processions: and sacred landscape, 138–9; and structure of Maya villages, 160

Proust, Marcel, 186

psychiatric evaluation, and personal experience of chronic illness, 189–90

psychoanalytic literature, and understanding of Aztecs, 180

pulque: and festival of Izcalli, 127–8, 147; identification of Virgin with in eighteenth-century Mexico, 152. *See also* alcohol

Quauhtemoc (Great Speaker), 79, 80, 81, 85
Quecholli, festival of, 41, 141n51
Quetzalcoatl (god), 37, 42, 55, 82, 143
Quetzal Owl (Aztec warrior), 80
Quijada, Diego, 111, 162n7, 163n8
Quiñones Keber, Eloise, 15n17, 28n36, 59n19
Quintana Roo (Yucatán), 174

Rands, Robert L., 169n18
Ranger, Terence, 116n2
Ravicz, Marilyn Ekdahl, 125, 137n41, 138n45, 139n47
reading, Maya practice of, 174
reducción. See congregación and *reducción*
religion: Cortés and initial phase of Conquest, 60–2; reconstruction of in sixteenth-century Mexico, 116–55; Spanish writing on Aztec ritual and, 28, 43–4; syncretism and interpretations of in post-Conquest Mexico, 123, 156. *See also* Catholic Church; priests; ritual performances; sacred
Rendon, Silvia, 170n22
resistance, and consequences of Conquest, 83–5, 87
"returning god-ruler" theory, 55, 82
Ricard, Robert, 95, 118
ritual performances: and Maya culture, 173; and theatrical approaches to religion in post-Conquest period, 124–55; and warrior ideology in Aztec society, 16, 25, 26–48, 141, 142, 181–3, 184
Robertson, Donald, 117n3
Robinson, George Augustus, 3, 192–208
Rock, Paul, 29n39
Rosaldo, Michele, 126n18
Rounds, J., 11n11
Roys, Ralph L., 98–9n16, 160n3, 162n7, 166n14, 174n31, 175n36
Ruiz de Alarcón, 146n64, 147n68, 148n72

sacred, and continuity in Indian practices in sixteenth-century Mexico, 155

Sahagún, Fray Bernardino de, 9n9, 20n23, 28–9, 50, 55, 64n30, 67, 78, 94n5, 120, 121, 123, 126, 149n73. *See also Florentine Codex*
Salas, Alberto Mario, 71n43
Sanders, William T., 8n7
Santayana, George, 97
Santley, Robert S., 8n7
Schechner, Richard, 126, 140n49
Schele, Linda, 134n35
Schmitt, T. J., 129n23
Scholes, France V., 98–9n16, 111n42, 162n7
Schwartz, Stuart B., 65n33
sculpture, Aztec forms of as abstract commentaries, 44
Sebastian, St., 129, 154
Sepúlveda, Juan Ginés, 49–50
shamans. *See* sorcerer-magicians
Shergold, N. D., 139n46
Sherman, William, 143n55
signs, and final battles of Conquest, 79, 80–1. *See also* "day signs"
Simeón, Remi, 39n48
Sisson, Edward B., 28n36
smallpox epidemic, 66, 89n87
society and social order: Franciscan ideology and missionaries in sixteenth-century Yucatán, 110; role of warriors in Aztec, 6–48; and survival of Maya culture in post-Conquest period, 172, 173
Solomon, Robert, 126
song-poems (Aztec), 6, 39, 81. *See also* poetry
sorcerer-magicians, as native religious specialists in sixteenth-century Mexico, 119, 148n72
space, Maya concepts of time and, 164–78. *See also* landscape
Spain: and consequences of Conquest, 82–90; Cortés and initial phase of Conquest, 49–65; Cortés and second phase of Conquest, 65–82; and folk religiosity, 130; Franciscans in sixteenth-century, 103; and religious dramas, 138–9, 149; and texts on Aztec ritual and religion, 28, 43–4; and texts on religion in Mexico in post-Conquest period, 119–23; and urban-imperial image of Tenochtitlán, 36; use of living images during religious performances in, 129. *See also* Europe

Index

215

story-making, and Spanish sources on
Conquest, 53–4, 59. *See also* narrative
Strayer, Robert, 158n1
syncretism, and interpretations of religion
in post-Conquest Mexico, 123, 156

Tápia, Andrés de, 88n86
Tasmania, and Aborigines, 192, 201
Taylor, William B., 2, 118–19n7, 146n66,
147, 148n70–1, 152n77, 152n79
Tedlock, Barbara, 135n37
Tenochtitlan: attack on pyramid of
Huitzilopochtli, 77–8; Cortés on, 83–7;
last stages of battle for, 69, 80–1, 87–9;
and Franciscan missionaries, 94; Spanish
"difference" and siege of, 74–5. *See also*
Aztecs
Teotihuacán (city), 15
tequitl (vocation or offerings), 44
Texcoco, Lake, 74
Tezcatlipoca (god), 66n34, 37, 43, 44, 46,
47–8, 143
Thompson, J. Eric S., 166n14, 167n15
time: and Aztec concept of cycles, 14, 48;
Maya concept of and survival of culture
in post-Conquest period, 164–78;
Nemontemi and yearly cycle of, 128; and
structure of Indian and Spanish accounts
of final battles of Conquest, 75–82. *See
also* calendar
Tlacaelel (Aztec general), 13, 28n37
Tlaloc (god), 42
Tlatelolco (city), 68n37, 44
Tlaltecuhtli (Earth Lord), 47
tlatoani ("Speaker"), 7, 8. *See also* Great
Speaker
Tlaxcala and Tlaxcalans: Cortés and initial
phase of Conquest, 57n15, 62; Cortés
and second phase of Conquest, 73; as
co-venturers with Spanish in siege of
Tenochtitlan, 87–9; and fasting, 133–4;
and Franciscan monastery, 92–3
Tlazolteotl (god), 40
Todorov, Tzvetan, 51, 76–7n58, 89,
123n13
tonacayotl ("things of the sun's warmth"),
39
Toral, Fray Francisco de, 100–1, 115, 163
Townshend, Richard, 15n17
trade, and Aztec society, 9
Tree of Life (Maya), 164
Trexler, Richard, 129–30, 137

tribute: and Aztec view of war, 20, 68; and
final battles of Conquest, 79;
miscommunications and use of term, 57
Triple Alliance (Tenochtitlán, Texcoco and
Tlacopan), 8
Truganinni (Tasmanian Aborigine), 192,
201
Tula (city), 7, 15
Turner, Victor, 27, 45, 125, 140n48

Uayeb days (Maya calendar), 165–6
Underworld, and Maya concepts of space
and time, 164. *See also* afterlife
Uxmal (city), 176

Vasco de Quiroga, 95
Vasquez, Sebastian, 161n7
vassals: references to by Cortés, 80n68;
Spanish-Indian miscommunications and
use of term, 57
Veyne, Paul, 52–3, 55
villages, structure of traditional Maya,
159–60, 161, 163, 165, 177
violence: and description of Tlaxcalans by
Cortés, 89; Franciscan ideology and
missionaries in sixteenth-century
Yucatán, 91–115, 162–3; toleration of in
Aztec society, 25, 26, 48
Virgin Mary, religion in sixteenth-century
Mexico and "belief in action" analysis,
151–2
Vogt, Even Z., 176

war, and implications of cultural views of
during Conquest, 65–82, 89–90. *See also*
battle; captives; warriors; weapons
Warman, Arturo, 137n40–1
warriors: and courage in Aztec society,
6–48; and cultural meaning of individual
challenge, 68–9, 71; and dances,
135n35; and final siege of Tenochtitlan,
75, 80. *See also* battle; war
Wauchope, Robert, 53n8
weapons: analysis of Aztec armoury, 22,
23–4; and final siege of Tenochtitlan, 84,
86; in Spanish versus Indian accounts of
Conquest, 71n43, 72
Weismann, Elizabeth, 150, 151, 153,
154n84
women, Freudianism and roles of in Aztec
society, 184–5. *See also* children
Wood, James, 186

world view, and survival of Maya culture after Conquest, 156–78
Worsley, Peter, 158n1

Xipe Totec (god), 29, 31, 35, 39, 153n82, 181
Xiumolpilli ("Bundle of Years"), 76
Xocotluetzi, festival of, 141n51

Year Bearer (Maya), 165, 166
Yucatán: Franciscan ideology and missionary violence in sixteenth-century, 91–115; landscape and world view in Maya culture after Conquest, 156–78

Zumárraga, Bishop, 94, 99